Think Like A Tycoon

How to Make a Million in Three Years or Less

The Wealth Building Classic
Written By Dr William G Hill

Published by
Fleet Street Publications Ltd

© Copyright Dr W G Hill and Scope International Ltd 1993, 1994, 1996

9th Edition published by Fleet Street Publications Ltd.

Fleet Street Publications Ltd.
11th Floor, Centre Point Tower,
103 New Oxford Street
London WC1A 1QQ

For questions and further information, contact the author care of the publisher.

British Library Cataloguing in Publication Data. A catalogue record for this book is available from the British Library.

ISBN 0 906619 27 0

Typeset by Fleet Street Publications Ltd.
Printed in Great Britain by The Cromwell Press, Trowbridge, Wiltshire

CONTENTS

The Buck Starts Here 1

The Tycoon Mentality 6

Fuzzy-Thinking Leftists 11

Acquiring Financial Independence 14

The Stock Market – A Game For Fools? 21

How To Profit From The Recession 24

You And Your Banker 43

Preparing For Your First Investment 53

Buying Distress Property 65

Buying Property Without Money 79

Finding Super-Deals 107

Get Yourself Organised 123

Negotiating Tips And Ploys 147

The Magic Question 151

Managing Property And Problem Tenants 157

Partnerships Can Make You Rich 163

Inflation Can Make You Rich 171

Extra Hints and Tips For Property Tycoons 177

New Directions 185

Chapter 1

THE BUCK STARTS HERE

Getting rich is fun. More fun than being rich. That's why we'll start with a game.

Sit down in a comfortable place.
Pretend that someone you know and love is giving you some money as a gift. Start with a day's wages. Then in your imagination add two zeros, then two more zeros.

What will you do with it?
How will you enjoy it?
There is no right answer.
Just close your eyes. Take a while.
Do not turn the page until you have mentally spent that money.

Drift off… daydream…
Spend that money…

Have fun!

Is this what you did with 200 pounds or dollars?

Get drunk?

New camera, new watch,
weekend vacation?

Night on the town?

Get high?

Next, try it with 20,000.

Would you spend it on a terrific car and a trip round the world?

Now suppose that someone gave you

2,000,000

Yes, TWO MILLION

What would you do with it?
Think about it.

On the next page is the answer most of my students gave…

"Give it to the bank to manage!"

But if a bank manager is so good at investing,
how come he's a wage-slave?

Probably you were a dummy!

There are *right* answers!
All the answers you saw were wrong!
Daydreaming about how you will spend the money will
ensure that you stay on the
wage-slave treadmill all your life.

If you are not financially independent now, part of
the reason is that you squander seed money –
on trips, presents, consumer goods, trinkets and junk
you don't need.

The first barrier between you and a net worth of
a million or more is the 'consumer mentality'.

In the real world you can get $200 ahead with ease.
But if your first thought was how to 'consume' your
first $200 you'll never be worth $20,000 or $2,000,000.*

Nevermore think of what you are going to spend money on!
Small sums are the seeds that grow into great fortunes.

Concentrate on:

What useful goods can you produce?
What services can you provide?
What needs can you fill?

These thoughts will help make you a millionaire.

* Obviously, our non-dollar thinkers will want to convert to their own currency.

Chapter 2

THE TYCOON MENTALITY

If you sincerely want to become a tycoon, you must think like a tycoon. You can learn to think like a tycoon by reading this chapter very carefully. Though I will be talking much about property, the principles covered here apply to all forms of managing your money. Living a good life or being exceptionally successful in business requires more than a can of beer, a TV set and wishing for a winning lottery ticket.

Tycoon is a Japanese word meaning *ty* – great and *coon* – shogun; a military leader. A tycoon is someone with ambition and drive who has placed himself in a position of importance. In the case of a great general like Patton, or a great politician like Winston Churchill – or anyone great – one characteristic is universal:

Great people thoroughly enjoy what they do. To be great at what you do, you must believe that what you do is fun.

An episode of the '*Peanuts*' cartoon strip once showed Charlie Brown playing with half a yo-yo. It was broken. But he was having a good time dangling it, bouncing it up and down the wall and playing 'fetch' with his dog Snoopy. Suddenly Charlie Brown's girlfriend Lucy comes along. "You stupid dummy," she says, "you can't have a good time with half a yo-yo. Everybody knows that." Poor, dejected Charlie Brown throws his toy on the ground. "I'm sorry," replies the little boy. "I didn't know I couldn't enjoy myself with a broken yo-yo."

This story has a moral for prospective tycoons. Fuzzy-thinking leftists and other depressing types like Lucy have convinced many people that doing something that makes a lot of money is abnormal, immoral or, at best, dull. They would like to make us capitalists feel guilty for becoming rich and – shudder – actually having fun making it. Albert Einstein, the great scientist, when asked on his last birthday what he'd do to benefit the world if he could live his life over again said, "I'd like to go into business and make some serious money."

So ignore the socialist do-gooders. They don't produce products or services. All they want to do is make us feel guilty. Fuzzy-thinking leftists fail to realise that capitalists don't just rake in money and count it – bank clerks do that. A tycoon is involved in something creative and beautiful. He (or she) must invariably bring forth upon the world a product or service that people want. A 'something' that people willingly part with their earnings or savings for. He's not ashamed to take their money because (unlike forcibly extracted tax money, which pays for dubious social services or more tax collectors that nobody wants) a capitalist exists for the people. He works for the people. He serves them only so long as his products and services meet their needs. A tycoon needs the people as much as they need him. However, being creative – like an artist, musician, or new mother – a tycoon has far more fun at living than the wage slave at his routine job. Tycoons enjoy doing what they can be great at, providing an abundance of goods and services that people want and can afford. Every tycoon has an invisible directive flashing like a neon sign in his brain:

FIND A NEED AND FILL IT

A tycoon doesn't count his money every day to measure his success. Dollars or pounds are just evidence of votes from the previous day; votes of confidence in the particular goods or services that the tycoon is providing. A tycoon gets his confidence from within himself, not through these monetary votes. Any businessman who wants to keep on being successful, however, must continue to deliver needed goods and services or the people will vote their money for a new tycoon.

Some individuals, of course, can never become tycoons. They thwart themselves right from the beginning. They make excuses: "I'm not smart enough." "I don't have enough money to start." "I have no business sense." These are all cop-outs. With the right attitude, anyone, including you, can become a tycoon. If you think you're dumb – relax. Most tycoons have average IQs. The straight-A students are too busy getting PhDs and looking for teaching jobs to make it in business. You can begin with little or no money and become a multi-millionaire. Most of today's industrialists were poor a few years ago. So not having any money to start with, the second excuse, doesn't wash either. As for having no business sense – well, you're reading this report. That's pretty sensible. Whatever acumen you lacked before today, you'll have by tomorrow.

Other individuals wait until they are ready to become tycoons before they thwart themselves. All people should learn from their own mistakes, but you can benefit more cheaply from other people's mistakes. It helps to look at what some successful tycoons who failed have in common. Businessmen who have made it big once and then went downhill have frequently over-expanded. They got careless and didn't attend to emergencies or details. They didn't have time anymore. In contrast, a successful tycoon leaves nothing to chance. He makes time to watch over his investments or hires competent help to do it for him. It's much easier to be extremely successful on a small scale when you're starting out in familiar territory than it is when you have the riches of Howard Hughes. Does that surprise you? Allow me to illustrate.

Once a business deal was proposed to me in Reno, Nevada. The big selling point was that one of the richest men in the world, Donald Trump (who made his fortune in real estate), had taken 25 per cent interest in it. Therefore (I was told) I should be willing to take 10 per cent (10 'points' in tycoon-talk), because Trump was pretty smart and wouldn't have had a 25 per cent interest in a deal if it wasn't any good. The deal went sour shortly after that. I should have known it would! Now when I hear that extremely rich people have an interest in a project, I run the other way.

A 'red ribbon' deal usually won't make money for anyone but the promoters. Super-rich people seldom have time to investigate new ventures; they are too busy keeping what they have to be effective in fields outside their immediate area of expertise. I am sure that if Trump had a good deal that he investigated and put together personally, he would have taken all of it for himself and not sold any point to outside investors. But the fact that Trump, a super-rich New Yorker, was investing in a Nevada property deal, probably meant that he relied on someone else's judgement. That 'someone else' would not have sought me out as an investor if it had been a super deal.

Tycoons who have been very successful often make bad investments. They don't attend to the details of investigating a situation as thoroughly as they would have done when they were starting out. The best deals are the deals that you go out and find yourself. They are not prepackaged 'no work, no worry' deals all wrapped up with a red ribbon, where all you do is write a cheque. The red ribbon deal will only tie you in financial knots.

The Red Ribbon Rule:

If a deal sounds too good to be true,
it *is* too good to be true!

Another common characteristic of a tycoon destined to go downhill is that he feels 'too important' to attend to humble work. He passes by one of his properties, for example. In the old days he would have taken time to pick up junk spilled by the rubbish collectors and put it in proper cans. At the very least he'd have given the janitor or the tenants a gentle reminder to clean up their act. But now, looking at the mess, he doesn't notice. He's too busy whizzing off to negotiate a pie-in-the-sky deal or fighting with his wife in a divorce case. A lack of pride in ownership means the start of decline – the beginning of the end. When you're no longer concerned with detail (and willing to see to it yourself), you're heading for trouble. If an owner doesn't care anymore, his business goes to pot.

Another characteristic of ageing tycoons is a sudden fear of competition. When new at the game, competition is a challenge. The embryo tycoon steals his competitors' best ideas and avoids their mistakes. Determined to beat the competition one way or another, the upstart comes up with innovative methods. He works at it all day and Christmas too. However, once on top, some tycoons start to worry about all the young upstarts moving into 'their' backyards – as if it were an exclusive preserve. In the case of manufacturers it is 'cheap foreign goods.' 'Why,' they worry, "are those Sayonara Sleeping Pills becoming more popular than my Yankee Doodle Doze?"

Instead of trying to produce a new or better product, some old tycoons retreat into deep leather chairs at the Old Fogey Club. Old, has-been tycoons never die, they just become ineffectual aristocrats. At worst, a formerly successful tycoon these days becomes a 'gold bug'. A 'gold bug' is someone who buries or stashes most of his assets in a Swiss bank in gold. Of course, in a nation run by irresponsible politicians who print and spend money like toilet paper, building one's personal gold reserves, to a reasonable level, is only prudent. But when you start concentrating on reducing the size of your business operations and finding ways of becoming 100 per cent liquid, then you can produce no products, no progress and no profits. The entire French nation nearly collapsed economically in the pre-de Gaulle era because a large number of French people (perhaps for good reasons) chose to take their wealth, convert it into gold coins and bury them in their gardens. Buried gold coins (while providing some degree of safety and security in times of political turmoil or revolution) will not make you rich. A business operation is like a vine. Once it stops growing, it dies.

What are the characteristics that help a tycoon succeed? A tycoon on the way up is always able to motivate his staff, partners and the people who work for him. When he makes it big, an enthusiastic, loyal staff will be needed more than ever. But sometimes a tycoon forgets his staff. Don't forget – when you become valuable in terms of dollars, your staff becomes equally so in terms of support. Some employees respond best to praise and titles, others, to money. Imaginative gifts or bonuses can score you more points than money! How about a round-trip ticket to Hawaii for your secretary or property manager? The successful tycoon always keeps thinking of ways to put a smile on the faces of his team.

Some tycoons believe that inspiring fear in their associates is an effective method of getting them to work. I strongly disagree. Fear is good only for incompetents, because only incompetents are afraid of getting fired. If an employee or business associate is good enough, he can always find work with the tycoon down the road. Thus, if you can't make the work situation pleasant for those who contribute to your success, something is wrong. You can never get the best out of employees through fear. Remember: motivation is better accomplished by carrots than the stick.

On the home front, the same rule applies. Keep the peace. Give recognition and daily compliments to the people around you – your children, your spouse, your friends. Make the people you know feel good about themselves. Act like a loving, concerned human being – even if you really are a selfish slob. Donald Trump took his wife for granted and is said to have ordered her to "go and fetch" things like a dog. His inconsiderate behaviour cost him half his fortune – besides breaking up his once happy family. If your staff and family feel good about themselves, they'll work harder and feel better about you. If you're giving a compliment, don't make the mistake of taking it back. I've heard people say things like, "Gee, you look younger. Are you dyeing your hair?" Say it and *mean* it. If you personally get a compliment, don't argue. Accept it graciously, a simple "thank you" will do. Make the people in your family or organisation feel secure. If you feel like it, say, "I love you." Give praise and recognition generously! Tell them, "I really like being with you." Or, "I like working with you." Give the reasons. Your own life will be better if those you live and work with know that you like them. If you have to be critical, try to be positive in your criticism. When the toast is served burned to a crisp, say, "I really enjoyed the breakfast, honey, but next time around could you set the toaster a bit lighter?" For business associates, just substitute different words. Try it – it works.

Read this chapter once a week for a year. When you start thinking and acting like a tycoon, then you will be one!

Chapter 3

FUZZY-THINKING LEFTISTS

The first fuzzy-thinking leftist I recall in my life was Mr Stanley, a very brilliant high school social studies teacher. He had reputedly inherited a small fortune from his 'old money' family, and he imbued us all with the desire to make the world a better place in which to live. At the time this meant wearing a green feather to symbolise opposition to the military-industrial-corporate conspiracy and solidarity with oppressed blacks in South Africa.

Mr Stanley's parents had placed his inheritance with the trust department of a major bank. This gave him a monthly cheque. He had the disdain for private property that seems to come only with a regular welfare or trust-fund cheque. His parents were wise because Mr Stanley, the impractical idealist, would have given his money away to worthy causes – had he been able to.

He mobilised many generations of privileged upper-middle-class kids to support all the favourite leftist-liberal causes, from the women's movement to gay rights and ecology. As far as we were concerned, Mr Stanley was as right as anyone could be. He was clearly a good man: a Quaker, a pacifist, a vegetarian and a man who got behind all benevolent causes – sometimes latching on even before they became fashionable.

I remember him telling us in class, "There's nothing more stupid than nations going to war over how to distribute God's bounty – that's the only argument between the capitalist and communist world." Of course he was very wrong, but kids liked his simplistic world-view.

He influenced us all. No one in the class considered going into business as a career. We all hoped to go into teaching, government service or the professions. We were determined to 'help people'. It never occurred to us that the production of goods and services for profit might be more help to the world than becoming a political scientist or social worker.

Our Mr Stanley was multiplied by 50 when I got to college. I never received an hour's positive exposure to Libertarian thought. Laissez-faire was presented all right, but as a long-dead, no longer applicable 19th century philosophy. On our first day of orientation one of the many fuzzy-thinking academics I was to come into contact with there announced the purpose of our education. "We are going to turn you into good administrators, so that when the coming socialist revolution is over, they'll still need you to run the business, whether or not you control the stock."

Not all fuzzy-thinking leftists look like this.
They just think the same.

In the 1950s when I was a student, there was a lot of talk about 'people's capitalism' and how our form of government was becoming more Sovietised, just as the communists were discovering the 'profit motive' and becoming more westernised. It was predicted that within a decade or two we'd truly become 'one world'. At the time, none of the academics mourned the predicted passing of the free enterprise system. I didn't know there was a choice or that there was any wave of the future outside of socialism.

It took me another 20 years of dealing with the real world and real people to see things differently. I still feel that the Mr Stanleys had okay moral positions in matters of individual liberties, civil rights and such – but they were dead wrong in their anti-business attitude. The fuzzy-thinking leftists made us all believe there was something wrong with owning property and producing goods and services for profit. They made us feel that to be rich was almost criminal because if one person got rich, it meant that many had to be deprived. As a result, government was allowed to erode the economic freedom of the individual with progressive confiscatory taxes and incredible regulatory burdens. The result was a 35-year shift of interest and employment away from the private sector into 'public service'. Today in the western world more than two out of every four people are, directly or indirectly, government employees. Of the remaining two, one spends their whole time coping with red tape and tax planning required by the public sector. That leaves one person to support three drones and their dependents.

Thus has the fuzzy-thinking leftist vision of utopia been fully implemented by total government control over almost all segments of the economy. Property is the last bastion of capitalism and free enterprise. That's why westerners are the best-housed people in the world. Yet, despite the great job a free market of private property owners are doing, it could be the next to go. Trouble is, socialism doesn't work. As a result of the 'welfare state' there is now far less individual freedom in the West than there has been (in any peaceful era) since the end of the Middle Ages. How to regain freedom and outwit bureaucrats is the subject of my best report, written in 1990, *PT* 1 or Prior-Taxpayer, Perpetual Traveller, etc. See the back of this report for details. But before you become a PT you'll need either capital or enough skill to earn a living outside of your home country. So let's start you off on your path to financial freedom. We will talk in terms of property, but the basic principles apply to any business asset be they gemstones or a chain of beauty shops.

Chapter 4

ACQUIRING FINANCIAL INDEPENDENCE

What is financial independence? To me it's the wonderful feeling of getting up in the morning without having to go to a job I hate. It's living where I want to live – not worrying about what I can afford. It's living with people I love – not enduring someone I am stuck with because they are supporting me. Financial independence is never worrying about rent money, grocery money or doctor bills. It's going out and having steak or lobster any time you feel like it. It's having basic needs and even a few luxuries, without being a wage slave or doing work that makes you feel like a prostitute. It is, in a word, freedom!

Some would equate financial independence with servants, a summer home in Monte Carlo and a Rolls Royce. But to me that is show – not freedom. Financial independence will buy freedom from a boring job. It will buy time to pursue your own interests: freedom to travel, to read, to write, to create, to play, or to do your life work, whatever it may be. It's not necessary to be fashionable, chic or jet set. A mansion, poodles, servants and a temperamental Rolls Royce only tie you down. I know. I've tried that lifestyle.

The political freedom we have (to a limited extent) is nice. It's wonderful to be able to write to your local politician. You can even climb on a soapbox and call the national leader a few choice names. You can complain. I wouldn't want to take away that sort of freedom. But what value is freedom to exercise your vocal chords or pen if you are stuck in a daily inescapable rut of earning a subsistence living? The only worthwhile freedom we, as individuals, can hope to achieve is financial independence and the mobility that goes with it.

In this report I am going to tell you how to get this freedom in less than three years. It will take all your spare time and energy. I will show you how to use your energies to effectively accumulate wealth. I'll show you how to work for maximum results. With a hell of a lot of effort you can make your first good deal within ten days. And one good deal can make you more than you could save on your job in 10 years. In a few months you may be able to do that (make a deal) once or twice a week. If you are willing to work very hard you could be a millionaire in a year. Using my methods you should be able to make *your* millions in less than three years.

After you have your first million, whether it's dollars, pounds or marks, you have freedom. It won't be exactly what you imagined, because a million isn't what it used to be. Being a millionaire today is about the same as being worth 10 per cent of that right after World War II. But a million still spells financial freedom for a small family.

With a million you should have no trouble investing for a return (pre-tax) of around 10 per cent a year. Only about half of that will be left after taxes. If you plan to spend a quarter of that on rent in a major city, you'll note the rent you can afford hardly buys the sort of apartment that one associates with millionaire status. Rent alone can take more than half a millionaire's income. Only a pittance is left for food, entertainment, bills and supporting the family. Since a first-class maid and butler team commands a salary of your entire after-tax income, obviously there are going to be no servants, Rolls Royces or summer houses in Monaco even if you have a million.

Obviously, without an extra income from working, you can't manage such a luxurious and unnecessary lifestyle on the after-tax income from a million invested in risk-free securities.

If you've got a million, you have freedom. You don't need an expensive apartment, and you don't need to put on a show for anyone else. You can afford to live where (in whatever climate or country) you want. Not regally, perhaps, but comfortably. I think I will convince you, if you are not already convinced, that the steady buying of property, primarily investment (or rental) property, is a policy of minimum risk, maximum return. Looking for good deals in property – real estate – is one of the best things you can do with your time and small amounts of money. It can make you a million dollars in less than three years. Particularly in a slow or depressed market where most people are dead in the water. You can never hope to save anywhere near a million (in today's money) working for someone else.

Most of my disciples start out being what I call wage-slaves. They work at a nine to five job. If you are a wage-slave, maybe you don't understand why it seems impossible to save and why it becomes harder and harder to get by on what you earn. Each year, though you may work harder and even get decent raises, your standard of living seems to be going down. Fact is, it doesn't only seem that way. It is that way.

The wage-slave mentality

The western standard of living is dropping! At the same time, the real standard of living in a few inflation-free countries, like Switzerland, seems to be rising steadily. In the US, after 50 years of having the highest per capita income in the world, the American standard of living has now dropped to a miserable fourteenth place. The average Chinese worker in Taiwan or Japanese in Osaka is able to afford more goods and services than most Westerners! Right now, workers in Switzerland, Arabia, Japan, as well as in Sweden, Denmark and Norway do better than the Americans, British, Australians and New Zealanders. Why? Inflation-eroded, highly-taxed earnings simply buy fewer and fewer good things than they used to.

Let's assume you are lucky enough to make 20,000 pounds, dollars or marks a year. In most countries, the tax bite on 20,000 is roughly 34 per cent for a single tax payer, meaning roughly 6,800. That leaves you with 13,200 to spend.

Now, let's assume in the following year that you don't get a raise. You still make 20,000 a year, but inflation has pushed up the prices of normal things you buy at an average of five per cent a year. (Although current rates of inflation are slightly lower than five per cent, I am using this figure as an average because inflation rates have been much higher in the past 10 years and undoubtedly will return to higher figures.) This means that the cost of rent, coffee, sugar, bread and just about everything else are all pushed up. Since prices are going up a minimum of five per cent a year, in year two you end up with the same 13,200, but with five per cent inflation you are left with only 12,540 in actual purchasing power. So, if you made 20,000 last year, you had 13,200 in purchasing power. But if you made the same amount of money this year, your purchasing power dropped by over 500. This little mathematical exercise explains why your real standard of living is dropping drastically every year.

Now, suppose for a second example that you are lucky enough to have received a five per cent cost of living raise. Next year, your salary will be 21,000. But guess what? Most governments will also raise your tax bracket slightly, say from 34 to 36 per cent. Remember, every time you get a raise, your tax bracket gets a little higher. So therefore, when you deduct the new higher taxes from your 21,000 salary, you are left with a net of 13,440, because your tax is now 7,560. Taking the five per cent inflation rate into consideration, you take off 670 to arrive at your real purchasing power, a net of 12,770.

Remember, in year one you earned 20,000 and your net purchasing power after taxes was 13,200. But with 1,000 raise in year two, your purchasing power is down to 12,700. So you have taken a loss of almost 500 in your purchasing power even with a 1,000 wage increase.

Why is that? Because your tax bracket went up at the same time as your country's currency went down in value. This is not even taking into consideration increases in other taxes such as social security, state, local or council taxes. Nor do we consider the effect of hidden taxes, such as sales, VAT or fuel taxes. These are a very sneaky way that governments manage to pull the lining from your pocket almost without you being aware of it. VAT, which is customarily included in the asking price of goods in most stores in Europe, is a staggering 17.5 per cent in the United Kingdom. Watch out for increases in these taxes as they are a particular favourite of politicians.

In view of this situation, many people want to find a scapegoat. Some say (with a degree of accuracy) it's the 'politicians' that are just taxing us to death. Therefore, the answer of some irate citizens is to become tax resisters. Break the law! Don't pay any taxes! Go to jail! I don't like this 'solution', because if you go to jail, the government will just raise the taxes of the rest of us to keep you in prison.

Some others would say (with accuracy) that most western countries have irresponsible socialistic governments. What we ought to do is emigrate to a real free, well-managed country like Switzerland where they don't have such a big, bad government and so much inflation. Well, unfortunately, at least until we are independently wealthy, we are stuck. Why? Because 'real good countries' like Switzerland generally don't want us. We have to make the best of a bad situation right where we are. What to do in the meantime to benefit from the government's irresponsible printing of money to cause inflation?

From my point of view, one of the best things you can do is find and invest in well-selected, income-producing property. Done right, a properly geared or leveraged property investment programme will make you a millionaire in a few years. With property, a government's inflationary and unfair tax policies will actually help you become very rich. Since many politicians pay little in the way of taxes, partly because of their property holdings, there are tax laws or loopholes favouring property and home owners. The 'responsible freeholder' is, after all, the strong backbone of democracy. Besides, too many burdens on property owners would hurt most politicians too much. They themselves are usually major investors in land and buildings.

If property investment is so sure fire, why isn't everyone into it? Virtually all rich people *are* into it. But what about the non-rich? Let's look at how the great unwashed masses spend their time and view their future.

Most people, and that may be you, have a nine to five job. You may feel pretty secure while you are in the job. It's not too bad a job. And after a day at the salt mines, you sit down to dinner, watch a bit of TV and that's about all you have energy for. The weekend with the spouse (and more TV?) goes by so fast you don't have time to think about any financial plan, much less have time to do anything constructive. The average Joe feels reasonably secure in his rut of a wage-slave job. He feels secure for up to 20 or 30 years. Right? Until the day the redundancy slip comes and he's fired. Joe Lunchbucket may feel secure, but it's a false security. The vast majority of retired or laid-off older workers are destitute.

It's not uncommon to see people fired after 30 years. And when they look into the pension plan that was going to take care of them in their old age, there's a loophole. If fired before retirement, they may not get anything or inflation has reduced the value of what once seemed like generous retirement benefits. Don't you be misled into feeling that there is any security in a job working for someone else. Even with a union, the plant may fold and you can be laid-off at any time. Even if you're the one who owns the company you'd better have a nest egg that is purely within your control – preferably outside of your home country's jurisdiction. And as far as pensions and public social benefits are concerned, I'd call most people's retirement plans *social insecurity*.

Though governments, with their taxes and your pension fund contributions, take more and more out of your income, they give you back less and less. You get back inflation-eroded money when the time comes to retire. Social Security insurance or pensions won't give you enough to live on with style and dignity. Worst of all, if you wait until you're legally entitled to retire with full benefits, statistically you'll very likely be dead within two years anyway. In my view, two years of doddering retirement when you're too old and worn out to enjoy many things (especially sex) is no decent reward for 45 years of work.

Let's suppose that you want to provide for your own 'golden years'. You hope to live in a reasonably comfortable manner. The most common choice is a savings account. Banks and savings and loan associations are paying a certain amount of interest. But after inflation and taxes you are not really earning a penny. The sad truth is that in terms of purchasing power (on home, for instance) you are probably *losing* 15 per cent a year on money left in savings accounts. Property values do not increase (or decrease) with predictable precision. But they do tend to rise (in good locations) at an average rate slightly above that of inflation.

The doubters amongst you are probably thinking that, with current inflation rates of two to three per cent, this outlook is simply no longer true. However, one must consider that many economists predict that inflation will once again return to higher rates in the next few years. Although this author doesn't have a perfect crystal ball for predicting the future, he

Inflation chews up your lunch money

can observe. History has shown time and time again that no sooner do governments succeed in lowering inflation rates than the economy takes a beating. Hence, the recession.

As governments considered high inflation the number one economic enemy in the mid to late 80s, so the recession has become the number one economic enemy of the early nineties. What does this mean? Inflation will no longer be a major concern, and the money printing presses will start rolling once again to combat the recession. The fact of the matter is that politicians simply can't resist running those presses. Keeping money in cash, even in the current economic climate, has to be nothing less than economic imbecility.

Buying insurance is the absolute worst thing you can do with your money. Insurance gives you about a two per cent after-tax return on the 'pure investment' feature. That translates into something roughly between breaking even and a one per cent annual capital loss after inflation. So, unless you need some term insurance to take care of youngsters who are unable to support themselves in case you die in the next few years, stay away from insurance entirely. If you need insurance to provide for dependents, stick with term life insurance. This has no 'investment' feature, but it will pay back substantial sums if you die unexpectedly at an early age.

Then there are 'tax shelter' schemes. These are package investment deals that stockbrokers, building societies, property agents and promoters put out. They are only for the unwary. Wrapped in a red ribbon, complete with printed brochure and smooth salesmen, they stink! My own personal survey of widely promoted tax shelter deals indicates that only one or two per cent of these deals ever return an investment after inflation, much less any true profits.

There are, of course, a few worthwhile promoters, stockbrokers, unit trusts and deal-makers who have good long-term records. Almost everything they touch makes a good profit for their investors. But what someone else can make on your money will be peanuts compared with what you can do yourself. An ordinary property deal that you can make today should return over 300 per cent a year tax-free on your investment. The best salesmen won't be advertising it or going to look for you with a smooth sales pitch. They won't be advertising this deal because they have their own money and don't need or want your business for anything except the garbage deals. There is a lot of money around, but no red ribbon deals. Good deals exist only if you know how to create them. Right now, you don't. You can only buy turkeys – the rejects of the professionals.

Yet the deals are there. The best deals can be created when not too many buyers are out shopping the market. A quiet, dormant market equals opportunity. Over the long term (any 10 year period or cycle) what has done very well? What has always been a good deal? What has happened to prices and rents in all major cities for the past 300 years? I'll tell you what: home and moderate to low-rent income property where rents pay off the loans. Even during the most inflationary times in Argentina, Brazil and Germany, when money was worthless and rent controls went into effect, most property ownership worked out well for people who owned a private home and turned part of it into a rooming house. Equally good was a two or (less good) three-unit, low-rent apartment building with short-term, non-rent controlled tenants.

By the end of this report, I am sure you will have a good understanding of how to make money out of property. For now, let me show you how to buy your first investment property. Every journey starts with a first step. But before you take your first steps to financial independence, let us look at one detour you shouldn't take – the stock market.

Chapter 5

THE STOCK MARKET –
A GAME FOR FOOLS

Many people feel that the stock market is a bad bet just because they lost their shirt in it. Others hope they will be 'lucky'. The truth is that more than 50 per cent of all individuals who trade regularly, lose all their chips within a few years. Money put into an average portfolio of European, American, South American or South African stocks ten, 20 or 30 years ago is worth, in terms of purchasing power, slightly less than if it had been kept in cash at interest. That means that (after adjusting for inflation) an investor who put 10,000 dollars, marks or pounds into reasonably good stocks 10 years ago has purchasing power of about the same as what he started out with.

Of course the Tokyo stock market, for a long time, was the big exception. For a while, virtually all Japanese stocks went up over 20 per cent a year even after adjusting for inflation. However, the Japanese market went on to lose nearly 50 per cent of its value from 1989 to 92. Hence, to make a judgement about the future only from looking at the past can be a shallow and misleading analysis, like driving a car while looking only out the back window. When 'most people' feel that a particular investment is good and shows great promise, that is usually the signal for the astute, for the tycoons, to sell out. When everyone is depressed and articles in the media bear pessimistic titles like my chapter heading, smart money can move in and pick up the bargains.

With that said, you might expect me to reverse the thought of the title and tell you that when any stock market is depressed, it is time to take the plunge. In one sense, if you already have a million or more and don't want the hassle of managing an active business, you can probably make 15 to 20 per cent a year by seeking out bargain stocks in depressed markets – or you could let one of our tried and tested portfolio managers do it for you. But generally, we don't like stocks and bonds because you have no control over security prices. It's a mug's game. Using investments in the stock market to go from peanuts to millionaire status is as unlikely as putting your money on the line in a gambling casino and winning 10 times in a row.

Remember, before a single ordinary Joe makes money out of the New York Stock Exchange, all of the men in suits wandering around Wall Street have to get paid. (And they will!) The same goes for all of the lads in the City before a single pence comes out of the London Stock Exchange.

Still, here's a general rule. This could be your guide when property prices are booming and abnormally high, and stock market prices are depressed and have gone so low that switching from property into stocks seems to be a good bet.

My strategy would be:

1. Never sell property to purchase stocks – rather borrow against property to invest in stocks. Keep your stock ownership a secret by making your purchases in a different country, preferably with an alternate identity.

2. The signal to begin shifting assets from property cash into stocks will come only when: (a) Common stock dividends earn you a greater net return, cash on cash, than real estate rents give you. (b) You can borrow money at a long fixed rate of interest that is less than the return you can realise on property earnings. In down-to-earth terms, if your cash investment in a property, after paying all expenses inclusive of loan amortisation, yields 1,000 per year, you would be wiser to invest in a company stock only if it were paying a secure dividend of over 2,000 per year.

On a pure numbers investment basis, one would shift from property into stocks if there were a ratio of only one to two, on post-tax earnings. The greater regulation of companies, the greater possibilities of lawsuits, labour disputes, higher business taxes and the general outlook for most private enterprises cause me to look at stock only if it earns at least double what I'd earn in my own property deals.

These recommendations apply only in places where property retains a favoured status, being both relatively unregulated and effectively tax exempt. If rent controls or tinkering with existing tax incentives becomes a possibility, I would borrow heavily against my property, invest in other assets like gold, silver, stocks, bonds, antiques or art works and make plans to abandon properties. This was the only path open to thousands of residential property owners in New York City, Paris and London when rent controls inflicted terminal cancer on the property markets there after World War II. Only the removal of such controls makes real estate a viable medium for accumulating wealth. Once any business becomes 'government-regulated' it is time to move on.

Chapter 6

HOW TO PROFIT FROM THE RECESSION

At this point, you may well be thinking something along the lines of, "Who the hell does this Hill guy think he is, telling me I can make a million in three years through property of all things. Hasn't he heard of the recession, hasn't he heard that property prices are falling?" Well, to answer your questions, yes.

As you have probably noticed, much of the world is currently entrenched in the worst recession that has been seen in 50 years. Property prices have fallen, unemployment has risen and, overall, the doomsday predictors are, well, predicting doom. You may know (or perhaps even be) one of the hundreds of thousands of people caught in the so-called negative equity trap, where a house bought at an inflated 80s price is no longer even worth the mortgage secured against it. Times are tough; the perfect setting for the budding tycoon.

However, before taking into consideration the effects of the recession, let's take a look out at how one generally goes about making money out of property. Suppose you had US $500,000 ten years ago. Instead of investing in the stock market or a savings account, you might have bought for 'all cash' four ordinary, three-bedroom, two-bath homes in any desirable high-growth city of California. In those days a nice, above-average tract house cost $100,000. Now, 10 years later, that same home would be worth a minimum of $500,000. You could have bought five homes then, but today, with the same money, you could only get one.

The same story exists if you speak of apartments or homes in Paris, London or Sydney.

So, fine, if you had started buying up property 10 years ago, before the boom of the late 80s, you could have made a fortune. Who doesn't know that? You were just barely out of school then, so, of course, your property buying activities were limited or non-existent before the late 80s. That's why you're reading this report. 10 years ago doesn't matter fiddly sticks. What about now? What about the recession and falling property prices?

Let's take a look at what happened during the worst depression the United States has ever seen, 1929 to 1935. In those days, a low-rent apartment went for about $10 a month. During the course of the depression, these rents went up $14 a month. Why? Because people moved out of their expensive $40 apartments and doubled up in cheaper places. Low-rent housing did very well as an investment during the Great Depression of the late 20s.

Of course some people in those days, like in the late 80s, bought expensive, high-rent properties with negative cash flows. They went bankrupt. Some people do lose money in property, but not if they go about it intelligently. The intelligent property deal involves arrangements that make it impossible (well almost impossible) for you to lose. By buying property well below market value, or without putting any of your own money down, you are assured a good deal. I will shortly talk at length about buying repossessed property and the no-money-down deal. It should be obvious that if you can snatch up a super-bargain, there isn't much to lose.

Okay, so you can now see that by buying low-rent flats or apartments, you will be assured a stable rental income. The next obvious question is: but what about the actual price of the property? Isn't that the thing that is breaking all records and constantly plummeting through the floor? Yes, property prices are falling now, which makes this the perfect time to start buying, before prices start to go back up yet again.

What makes me so certain that property prices will start to rise once again? Well, first of all, by following my techniques you can make money even if property never increases in value again. By buying a house, apartment or flat well below market value, you can make money just by selling it at the accepted market price. No overall increase in the market is needed.

Secondly, even the most casual glance at history will show you that property prices, although subject to temporary dips, have steadily risen over the last 300 years. Stretching even further back, remember the Middle Ages from history class? Who were the wealthy people back then? The landowners, of course. Who were the peasants and serfs? Those who were forced to farm the land for them because they didn't own any of their own land from which to generate an independent income. The game has changed only slightly since. We all need a place to sleep, and those who own the places make money from those who don't.

After all, when you come right down to it, what else is there on this planet, except for it, the planet, property. Since the beginning of recorded history, people who have had, or have made, money have owned bits of the planet. For now, we're stuck with it. Perhaps some day in the year 2130, some tycoons will be making a fortune from their Lunar Lofts or Martian Maisonettes, but for now, we're better off buying property in areas with a booming rental market, namely most major or developing cities on little ole' planet Earth.

Thus, it is the goal of the tycoon to acquire as much income property and productive assets as possible. Needless to say, there will be occasional disappointments. How can you deal with them effectively? If a deal you've been negotiating falls through, there is a game or mental trick that you can play on yourself to feel better. Say this: "Had the deal closed, it would have made me at least 20,000. But if ten of my offers are rejected, I know that at least one out of 20 deals I try to negotiate will eventually work out. Thus, every failure, every deal that falls through, amounts to a 1,000 dollar, pound or mark experience. And that's pretty good going for one morning's work." If you can think positively about what others might consider failures, the next failed deal will only encourage you to get on with it. Not dwelling on what you did wrong, but thinking about what you did right, will soon have you scanning the classified ads again.

There's an old Scottish proverb, 'No man ever died from overwork.' But people do die and certainly get sick from emotional problems such as anxiety or worry. These lead to ulcers and other diseases. So one of the best habits a tycoon can develop is to laugh at problems. Many times things will go wrong, but if you can manage to grow a funny bone, your body will never develop ulcers or high blood pressure. Take life easy. Remember, money should be thought of as gambling chips and life as only a game.

Look back at the big tragedies of you, pre-teenage life. Not winning the best position in the football team – it was so important then. But does it matter now? You can laugh about it. When you were a teenager and got stood up by a sweetheart or were rejected as a member of the team, you were miserable, right? But now it's funny. If you can cultivate the ability to laugh at your predicaments at the time they occur, you will be way ahead of other people who spend their time worrying, dwelling on their failures and feeling sorry for themselves. Laugh a lot. Don't take yourself, your deals or your money too seriously!

My father knew an Italian agent named Joe Garibaldi (a fictitious name but a real person). Joe had come to the US as an orphan and worked at a Chicago news stand when he was only 11 years old. In 20 years he had bought that first stand, and it had grown into a chain. Joe, finding himself wealthy and lusty at the age of 31, sent for a mail-order bride from his home town. She duly arrived and enjoyed living in America, being the wealthiest lady in her neighbourhood. By 1929, Joe Garibaldi, like other newspaper dealers, tailors and barbers of the era, fancied himself an expert in the stock market. He took profits from his newspaper stands and everything else that he could borrow and invested in stocks.

We all know what happened in 1929. Joe Garibaldi went through the wringer and by 1931 was back selling newspapers at good old news stand number one. He took his losses like a tycoon, realising that it would be only a matter of time before he could repeat the wealth-building process and recoup his fortune. Yet all around him people were jumping out of windows. They didn't realise that they should have thought of money only as gambling chips. If they lost their chips, the game wasn't over. Joe Garibaldi knew how to think like a tycoon. To him, losing a hand meant accumulating more chips by selling papers again. He'd find another game to play someday. Not poor Mrs Garibaldi. Joe's bride was unable to face the neighbours after having to sell the Cadillac and take in boarders. She went looney and was put away. To this day, she has never recovered from the fact that Joe lost their fortune in 1929. She didn't know how to think like a tycoon.

Joe adjusted quickly. He merely reduced his expenses, got back to work and, within half the amount of time it took him first time around, he was once again prosperous. Like all tycoons, Joe knew it's easier to make a million the second or third time around.

The Million-A-Year Difference

Tycoons always have goals. Some weeks it's possible to make great progress towards these goals. At other times, due to circumstances beyond your control, everything goes wrong. Tycoons stay on course. Having no goals is like starting in the middle of nowhere without a road map. It's impossible to know where you are or where you're going. Goals must be selected and a plan established to give your life some positive direction. Any goal is preferable to just drifting. Selecting financial independence as a goal and thinking like a tycoon will get you there. The first step of the tycoon plan, then, is to decide that you want to be independently wealthy and that you'll do what it takes to achieve that goal. Once that first decision is made, with proper follow – through, you will be independently wealthy in one to three years.

Let me tell you about Clara, a girl who sold soup wholesale to grocery stores. She did well in her job and was very effective at pushing clam chowder. At 23 years of age she made 50,000 a year. A great start! At the same time there was a boy we'll call Gunslinger. He got very enthusiastic about using tycoon techniques in property dealing. He had no job, was a school drop-out and had no real direction in life until he took my advice.

Clara was less enthusiastic about becoming a tycoon. She continued to do well pushing fish stew, but she didn't do much about property. In a year, Clara looked at a total of three condominiums and eventually bought a pleasant middle-class condo apartment costing one year's salary. She moved into it. Period. Of course, the girl was better off than had she done nothing. But two years have now gone by. Clara still owns the one condominium she bought on a '20 per cent down' standard deal. She now makes soup commissions of 62,000 per year and saves little or nothing. She has a small unrealized profit on the condo. In other words, if she sold it she would get back her down payment plus an equal amount. Nothing wrong with that, but it's hardly spectacular.

Gunslinger, on the other hand, followed my advice like a fanatic. Property seemed to become his reason for living. He looked at hundreds of properties and, once he knew the market, began making ridiculously low or no-money-down offers on every deal he saw. Today he owns approximately eight different buildings. One year into the game, Gunslinger was a bona-fide 22 year-old multi-millionaire. One year it took him! Is that the American Dream or not?

Two people had the same information, the same level of intelligence. (Actually, Clara was a bit brighter.) The one you'd have expected to be more successful, a girl already earning substantial commissions each year, now owns one property and as a result, will soon have a net worth of her annual gross earnings. The boy, who had no job and no assets, became independently wealthy in 12 months. What accounts for the difference between them?

Gunslinger got off his backside, looked at many deals and made lots of offers. He had motivation! Big but realistic plans! Gunslinger's goal was to be worth a king's ransom by the age of 30. He acquired large amounts of property for little or no money down. A day did not go by in which he didn't make three or four offers on properties. Clara, in contrast, already considered herself successful and didn't want to change her life drastically. She made only one offer in an entire year, and only one deal. On that one investment she did create more of a net worth than most people have. On her one little carefully-selected property deal she made more than she'll save from her job in 10 years. She's very proud of her one property deal. But compared to Gunslinger, she's hardly a tycoon.

If there's any moral to be drawn, it's that reading books like this and taking get-rich courses by itself isn't going to make you a dime. But self-motivation, setting goals and doing what has to be done to make it happen can result in a difference worth a million. How much money you will earn is soley up to you. What about luck? Luck is simply having people who like you and steer you into good deals. Cultivate successful, honest people and luck will follow you around! When should you start this programme of achieving the goals you set for yourself? I'll tell you when. Today! Every day is a new beginning. Once you have written goals, life has a purpose. Every day will be a pleasure and a challenge.

Do It Today!

As I said before, most people's problems come from over-worry, not over-work. They agonise about what happened in the past. But the past is over! It's finished. Forget about it. Concentrate on what's happening now.

Other people worry about the future. Equally unproductive! Get on with it. If worry can't be eliminated, try channelling it in constructive directions. Estimate what percentage chance there is that what you are worrying about will actually occur. For example, people used to say, "Don't buy California property because of the next earthquake." What is the percentage chance that there will be a major earthquake in California? My research showed that there has been a major earthquake about every 60 years. Therefore, viewing the situation optimistically, the possibility that it will happen the year after a big one is about one in 60. If these odds are precarious enough to make you feel you should acquire earthquake insurance, or should avoid brick properties likely to tumble down in an earthquake, then take appropriate action. Get insurance. Buy wooden houses. Taking sensible precautions in view of a reasonable estimation of risk makes sense. Worrying about something uselessly is a waste of energy! Worry and fear easily translate into paralysis and no action at all.

Don't Worry About It. Do Something! No business deal is perfect or totally risk free; all you can do is use common sense and forge ahead.

Along with worry, another thing that will get in the way of success is fear of change. Change or innovation is always uncomfortable. Even going on vacation in some foreign country is a lot less comfortable than staying in your home town. But if you want to grow intellectually and if you want your fortune to grow, you have not only to accept change, but to seek it out. Sure, the results are not definite. When you're a tycoon there's no steady paycheck waiting for you at the end of each week. Tycoons must not be plagued with feelings of insecurity. If you feel secure only in a steady job that offers nothing in 50 years but a pension and a gold timex, you are not thinking like a tycoon. A tycoon thrives on insecurity. He or she can achieve financial success and security in a few years which is far beyond what a wage-slave can expect in a lifetime.

Security is more feeling than reality, anyway. It's a state of mind. Don't forget, company pensions alone won't usually support a decent standard of living at the time they become payable. If you live that long, social insurance or social security is even worse. That's why I call it *social insecurity*. Subsistence isn't living nor worth living for. Retirement payments provide, more often than not, only a poverty-level existence. The tycoon who acquires large amounts of income property or businesses will have the real thing – an income to keep pace with inflation. As with love or happiness, security is a state of mind that nobody else can give you. It's a feeling that only you can give yourself. Go out! Get a piece of the action going on all around you!

The feeling of being in a comfortable rut is not what a tycoon wants. Naturally, there is always the problem of conflicting goals. A fat man might say, "I want a beautiful and healthy body, but I'm not going to give up eating bons-bons and ice cream. And I am not willing to exercise or diet." Obviously, if you're not going to do what is necessary to achieve a goal, you're not going to get it. It's that simple. If you can't give up a nice secure rut or hobby that makes you feel good for a chance of making 10 million, then you will never get the 10 million. You can't say, "I'd like to be very rich, while keeping my present job and still spend all my evenings and weekends sailing." If you're going to become independently wealthy within one to three years, your time must be allocated ruthlessly. You should expect to spend virtually all your spare hours on achieving financial independence.

Can you go halfway? Sure! It will just take longer. If, for instance, you decide to spend only Saturdays looking at deals, it may 10 ten or 15 years to get rich instead of one or two years. To my way of thinking, if a million can be made in one or two years, it's worth spending all your spare time and energies on achieving that goal. The time to start your entrepreneurial activities is now. But don't quit your income-producing job until your other income is big enough to replace it.

A tycoon always prepares written plans. He or she will schedule time, establish priorities and will stick to those objectives both long and short-term. A tycoon should have both a life plan and a series of five-year goals. The first five-year plan should outline what he hopes to achieve in half a decade, and how he is going to do it. It should then break down into more detailed periods for the first year, namely, a monthly plan, a weekly plan and a daily plan.

One man-with-a-plan was Frank Harris, who lived in the 19th century. One day, at the age of 15, he sat down and mapped out his life-time goals. He made a list of 500 ridiculous things he wanted to do before he died. He set up his goal list in order of priority, and, as the years passed, he proceeded to work on them one by one. Sometimes they were prosaic goals like learning German. But other times they were glamourous or exciting things most people only dream about: visiting every country in the world, seducing 5000 of the world's most beautiful women, becoming an American cowboy. At a ripe old age, Frank Harris died, having accomplished 90 per cent of his 500 objectives. His story is told in a spicy Victorian classic called *My Life, My Loves*. Good reading even though Harris never was, nor wanted to be, a business success.

But Frank Harris was undoubtedly a success at knowing how to get the most out of life. How did he cram the adventures of 500 men into one lifetime? By setting goals. By planning ahead! By plotting and working steadily to achieve those goals.

Now maybe travel bores you. Or you're allergic to horses. All you want is to be the richest man in your small community. To do it, all you need is a reasonable plan. To achieve that goal, your daily activities should always be related to achieving your objectives. Eventually you'll make it. If you schedule time, establish priorities and stick to plans, there is no way you can not achieve your goals. To think like a tycoon, however, once your plan is in effect, you must stick to it. You must acquire the patience to see it through, plus the flexibility to alter it if the original premise on which the plan was based changes.

There always have been and always will be negative people who say, "These things can't be done." Or, "You're doing it the wrong way." What you want is too 'abnormal' or whatever. Remember Charlie Brown and Lucy? You must not drift, deviate or be discouraged, regardless of what others say or think about you and your goals. You know best. Success speaks for itself. Remember, tycoons like us are the 'doers' of the world. We are the caretakers of life's abundance.

Capitalists do it a lot of good too. We create jobs for people less creative or dynamic than us. We produce better products, better places to live. We achieve more than 'social' engineers, academics, theorists, do-gooder social workers or fuzzy-thinking leftists. Any or all of whom, by the way, will criticise our actions.

As the world has seen, even the communists have realised how much they can benefit from tycoons. Before this change, I personally visited the Soviet Union. That neon light in my head started to flash overtime. The needs were shocking. Most apartment buildings were in the same bad shape as the worst public housing projects of the West. Driving between Moscow and Leningrad, there wasn't a single decent place to eat, not even borscht, much less a cheeseburger. Functioning gas stations were hundreds of miles apart even on the most-travelled roads. Consumer goods of all types were in dreadfully short supply. If you wanted to buy chewing gum, ballpoint pens, a silent-tick alarm clock or 99 per cent of the consumer goods we all take for granted, forget it!

When, at last, a McDonald's opened in Moscow a few years after my visit, people waited hours to get a Big Mac. That should tell you something about the quality of the other food available! The fact of the matter is, as most of the communist regimes have now realised, communism just isn't practical. Unless the average Joe can see that there is something in a deal for him, he's not going to do a whole hell of a lot for it. Profit motivates people. A tycoon would never let his apartment building slowly fall apart. Such careless inaction would drastically affect how much he could rent or sell it for. When the state owns all of the apartment buildings in a country, why should one little civil servant, not paid a whole lot, care about one particular building that he has never even seen.

The road to capitalism will undoubtedly be long and difficult for the former communist countries. However, if they stick with the programmes they have started, as any good tycoon must, these countries will surely be better places to live in 10 or 20 years' time. This is, of course, assuming that the struggles and tumults by the power hungry politicians and bureaucrats don't create a nightmare situation of staggering corruption. In the meantime, these countries offer massive opportunities for the strong-of-spirit tycoon, one that can handle the almost overwhelming array of rules, restrictions and bureaucratic bungles, a remaining remnant from communist days.

While I have few kind words for the former communist governments, much the same applies to most western governments. At this point, US government officials are confiscating a large percentage of the gross national product in the form of taxes. In most of Europe, the situation is even worse. The things which taxes pay for are almost always pure waste. What could be more useless than the billions we spend on military goods? The equipment abandoned in Vietnam two decades ago still represents the third largest weapons arsenal in the world. Many tycoons have already arranged to buy all this army surplus and resell it to other trouble makers. They have made several billion on these deals. I personally would never deal in arms, but used guns and tanks are how many wheelers and dealers make their piles, all thanks to careless government spending with your tax money.

Get A Little Help From Your Friends

Have you ever heard of Reverend Ike? Reverend Ike is a black preacher who operates mostly out of New York City and talks to his congregation about material success, prosperity and making money. One of the things he says is that you should go out of your way to cultivate successful, powerful, intelligent people. People who are the way you'd like to be. The Bible according to Reverend Ike says, "If you hang around street-corners with losers, you are a loser." You are judged by the company you keep and you'll end up with the values, morals and net worth of your peer group.

Where can you get role models if your friends are all deadbeats or jailbirds? Interestingly enough, I found that most successful people have avidly read biographies of other well-known people in the fields in which they are interested. One example was the late Mr L, a legendary figure on Wall Street. I was privileged to be his house guest many times and to get to know him fairly well, because his son was my college roommate. While at his house one day, I was surprised to see that his personal library consisted almost exclusively of the biographies of men and women who had made a success of themselves in finance, on Wall Street or in Europe. No trashy novels for him.

When I asked Mr L about his choice of reading matter, the man replied, "Many of my best ideas were variations on deals I read about in historical biographies of tycoons." Mr L also told me that he learned something special from these biographies, "Virtually everyone who made a big success of themselves had been the protégé of a winner!" In his own case, Mr L made an effort to become the protégé of the senior partner of a big respected Wall Street firm. Mr L came up with some good ideas in the field of arbitrage – that is, buying and selling the same stock or commodity in two different places at the same time to take advantage of international price differences. He made the firm big trading profits by borrowing an idea from the biography of Bernard Baruch who'd made similar deals 30 years earlier. Soon L became a senior partner of the most prestigious firm on Wall Street. He later became chairman of the Board of Governors of the New York Stock Exchange.

Mr L owed a lot to the tycoons he met only in books. Maybe you will too if you read some of the selections on my book list. Reading a selection of books is recommended for important reasons. Potential tycoons cannot only apply the same principles these people did to make the right deals, but also, with the benefit of hindsight, profit from where these tycoons went wrong.

In reading biographies, you should gain greater understanding of economic history and the role of the tycoon in history. You'll learn that the possibility of acquiring great wealth has only been around for the last 100 years. Before then, unless you were born with a silver spoon, you usually ended up in a poverty trap. Virtually all fortunes today are made from scratch. Prior to the Industrial Revolution, there were only a few dozen self-made millionaires in the entire western world. They made their money in shipping, whaling or slave-trading. Perhaps the first national property tycoon in America was Hetty Green, whose investments began with the birth of the railroad. She invested her small whaling fortune in industrial slums all over the US. Her property was low-grade, low-rent tenements. Hetty was such a tough negotiator and tightwad that she earned the nickname *The Witch of Wall Street*, which is recommended reading.

Another early property developer was Vincent Astor, who got his grubstake together as a fur trapper. His family motto was 'Never Sell the Land.' He bought only first-class property in busy business locations. Both Hetty and Vincent made well over a 100 million dollars each. This happened over a century ago when a million was really worth something.

The American Civil War caused great industrial expansion in North America. There was a building boom in the cities. Throughout the world, the period from 1840 onwards was a time of rapid social and economic change. Ever since, technology and opportunity has made it possible for ordinary people to acquire greater wealth and status than nobles or kings had in earlier periods. First the stagecoach was replaced by the iron horse as railways and steamboats crisscrossed the world. But money was made mainly by people out 'of railroads' (like stock promoters) rather than by people 'in' them (like investors). Bankruptcies and lawsuits involving the new 'public companies' were common. Wealth changed hands rapidly.

Land, before the growth of industry, was incredibly cheap by today's standards. Roads were poor and there was so much uncultivated property around in the New World that governments gave away trillions of acres to homesteaders. To buy several thousand acres near a city was no big deal. But railroads meant mobility and changed the nature of the property market. Urban land prices soared worldwide as people moved out of the country into sooty cities where good-paying jobs were available in steel mills and other new industries. Cornelius Vanderbilt made his first million transporting immigrants and these newly-mobile masses. He sent his 'clipper' sailboats from Europe to New York City and from New York to California via Nicaragua. The discovery of gold near Sacramento caused the California Gold Rush, a human stampede the likes of which America has not seen since. Vanderbilt found a need and filled it. He made a deal with the locals in Panama to allow his passengers to cross overland on his trains. They were transferred to another Vanderbilt clipper waiting on the other side. The Vanderbilt clipper route was faster and cheaper than going overland. Boats were much safer than going by covered wagon. Vanderbilt made it easy for would-be bonanza kings to travel from the East Coast to California.

Now we come to my favourite book, *The Robber Barons*. The most colourful robber baron of the 19th century was Big Jim Fisk. He was a complete opportunist. Dumb. Crude. No special talent except for making money. Jim eventually took over the Erie Railroad. Being especially fond of lady singers, he built the opera house in New York City so he could become its 'casting director.' Unfortunately for poor Fisk, one day he got it on with a cute soprano and ended up murdered by the lady's lover. Moral: tycoons should steer clear of sopranos. Or anyone else with jealous lovers.

In this same era, another robber baron, John D. Rockefeller, made half a million in the leather business. Like all great tycoons he then diversified. He bought oil wells and started selling kerosene, used for lamps in those days before electricity. Those were also the days before cars. Finding he wasn't making enough profit from kerosene – did Rocky give up? Of course not. He put his brains to work and came up with a deal that thousands have been copying ever since. What was he trying to sell? Kerosene. What uses kerosene? Lamps. So Rockefeller gave away the lamps. All over the world, customers were so delighted with their free gift standard oil lamp that they bought their fuel from, you guessed it, Rockefeller's Standard Oil Company. Gillette did the same thing with razor holders. And then sold his blades by the millions. The so-called 'Robber Barons' were actually great innovators and social benefactors. Fuzzy-thinking liberal leftist journalists gave these men and capitalists in general a bad name.

This is a valuable lesson for all modern tycoons. Both Rockefeller and Gillette saw a need. How to fill it? By giving away a product that depended on refills only *they* sold.

This technique is still used today. Melita coffee pots and filter holders were originally designed to use no other filters than their own brand. So anybody using the cheap Melita coffee pot had to buy their filters from – Melita. The same with Hoover and their vacuum cleaner bags. Have you made your fortune today? Get your free ideas from people who have!

Biographies exist of hundreds of great tycoons. I highly recommend you read all you can get hold of. These men and women had several characteristics in common. They stole or should we say 'borrowed' ideas from each other. All found a need and filled it. In the case of cosmetics and cigarette magnates, they created needs with advertising. Most started from scratch. Historical biographies of tycoons who made it are inspirational. Practical. Fun. They're also free if you go to your public library.

Besides cultivating and studying people who can do them good, another admirable characteristic of many tycoons is that they speak well of other people. There is an old saying, "If you can't say anything good about someone – keep quiet." I've found that to minimise the number of enemies and keep friends to a maximum, it's a good idea to praise people to others wherever possible. If you can give someone a sincere compliment, give it! If talking about ex-lovers, ex-employers or ex-business associates, try to be positive about them, not negative. Even if the experience you had with a particular person was unpleasant, if you speak well of them, it will probably get back to the person in question. Then they will be more likely to speak well of you. To paraphrase the Golden Rule: speak about others as you would have them speak about you.

Tycoons must be optimistic. About friends, about finance, about the future. That does not mean that you should ignore obvious risks, but given a choice between visualising a future of rosy progress and one of gloomy fiasco, you will be better off viewing the future positively and acting accordingly. There are always going to be gloomers and doomers. Predictors of disaster are often 'gold bugs'. They are right-wing lunatic fringe types who for the last 60 years have been sure that the world-as-we-know-it is about to come to a grinding halt. The way to survive into the future, say the most fanatic 'gold bugs', is to leave the country now or take to the hills. Bury stashes of gold coins, keep an arsenal or two of automatic weapons and lots of food.

In my opinion, there may be a need for all that someday, but these negative guys are missing the big opportunities. Even when there is an economic collapse, somebody has a chance to get rich. I would spend only a very small portion of my energies on disaster preparation. I'd much rather believe that over the next five years things are going to get better – that profits will continue to be made in the free enterprise system. The drastic changes we are seeing in the former communist states of the Soviet Union and Eastern Europe will probably lead to a new era of European prosperity. A trend away from the socialist welfare state we've been drifting into during the last 50 years bodes well for the aspiring tycoon. In my opinion if one wants to be prepared for disaster, the way to do it is by insuring your mobility with a spare passport (i.e. dual nationality). You should establish offshore business interests or stash some of your assets half way around the world. People who shut themselves up in fortifications with weapons, coins and food call themselves 'survivalists'. But they are using strategy suitable for the Middle Ages. Mobility and electronic funds transfer is the castle and moat of the 21st century. But that is the subject of *PT*, another book of mine. Here, our focus is on how to acquire wealth. PT is 'Preserving Treasure'. That comes after you have become financially independent – next year! Don't even bother reading *PT 1* then *PT 2* until you have made your first quarter million. Make your fortune first, then preserve it with PT, a Perfect Technique.

Do It, Don't Talk About It

Another thing you will notice about the way tycoons think and act is that they avoid unnecessary conversation. Some time-wasters merely sit and shoot the breeze for hours on end. They discuss the weather. The fortunes of their favourite ball team. "And hey – did you hear that Mabel went home with Henry last night? Robin was so upset she called her old lover Harry and then Blanche came in. . . " Tycoons don't gossip. They don't 'make conversation'. Silence gives the impression of strength and knowledge. But when tycoons do

Most folks stand around watching other people acquire wealth. They'd be amazed at what they could do by getting into the game and making an offer!

How about exchanging squares tonight, baby?

speak, they have something important to say. A tycoon does not brag about himself either. He doesn't have to toot his own horn. Success speaks loud and clear.

The Tycoon's Morality

Much of the business inspirational material I've read has made a great deal of 'morality'.

Many people feel that being a womaniser, a drinker or dope-smoker are pit-stops on the road to failure. But, based on the many tycoons I have known or created, the fact that they indulged in occasional immoral delights has had no effect on their financial success. Of course, the key here is moderation. If entire energies are devoted to close encounters of a physical kind, then obviously there isn't enough time in the day to be successful in business. Of course, once you are rich you'll want to read the book I have recently finished, *Sex Havens*. But sensibly spending a moderate amount of time on 'vices' probably won't make a bit of difference to your future. Of course, a 'vice' can be viewed in many ways. When people talk about drinking too much, I always remember the story about the Temperance League.

Once, in an anti-drinking demonstration, a Temperance League lady exhibited to her audience of bums, a can of worms. She put half the worms in one glass and poured water on them. Then she took the other half of the worms and poured 90-proof vodka on them. The worms in water wriggled around, but the worms marinated in vodka curled up and died almost instantly. The prohibitionists ended the demonstration by asking the question, "Now what does that tell you about drinking?" Someone stood up in the audience and shouted, "If you drink a lot, you'll never have worms."

You can see that what is considered a vice by some may be considered beneficial by others. So be tolerant. Remember: as a property tycoon, you may find yourself buying a house from someone who drinks too much. Lecture to them about the evils of drink, and you'll blow the deal. But like the time you spend on sin, a reasonable amount of missionary zeal expended on your favourite morality crusade outside of business hours, should likewise not inhibit your business success. Who knows – it might even add to it. Take religion for instance . . .

Become A Transcendental Tycoon

Don't laugh. A few words on meditation isn't as out of place in a property book as you might imagine. Some years ago, the Harvard Business School recommended it for relieving stress in executives. And who can argue with the "B" school? You don't have to wear white robes or chant exotic mantras. You can meditate effectively right now. Here's the secret:

Whenever you have a problem or just lack a sense of well-being, place yourself in a horizontal position in a darkened room. Get comfortable. Eliminate distractions and banish all thoughts. Breathe in a regular manner. Concentrate on relaxing each part of your body, from toes to ankles to calves and so forth, until you have consciously relaxed all your body. At the same time concentrate on breathing. Silently repeat a meaningless word. It should be a word that has no particular association, such as 'abracadabra' or 'alhambrabamba'. Silently repeat this word over and over. Do it in rhythm with your breathing. For instance, breathe in – *abra*, breathe out – *cadabra, abra, cadabra* . . . If you can do this successfully in a quiet place, with near total relaxation, you will achieve a particularly satisfying state of mind. Some would say it eventually lead, to a 'religious experience'.

Meditation can be utilised a number of ways. Use it simply to get to sleep or practise it in the middle of the day instead of a cat nap. It'll clear the mind. You might even find solutions to many of the troublesome problems of the day. A 'natural high' some call it. But whatever it is, meditation creates an altered state of consciousness that is invariably beneficial. It's cheaper than alcohol or dope, and, like I said, it's recommended not just by me, but by the Harvard Business School.

In case you're now too relaxed to remember, here's a quick summary: persistence and enthusiasm are a tycoon's most important tools. You learn how to do right only by doing it wrong first. View all mistakes with a sense of humour, as experiences that will do you some good. Every mistake, every 'failure' is a valuable experience. Problems are just exciting challenges. Laugh a lot.

Pay no attention to negative people. Ruthlessly cull the people who tell you "it can't be done" from your address book. When you're really depressed, don't dwell on failure. Think about what you did right, not what you did wrong. Never worry! If you use meditation to clear out your mind, you will often find that your subconscious will work out creative solutions that will magically surface when you come out of your higher consciousness.

No one ever made a big success of themselves without failure. Winston Churchill, in World War I, was the instigator of a disastrous plan to invade Turkey at Gallipoli. It was such a massive military failure that Churchill was forced to retire from public life in disgrace. He wrote, studied and made no attempt to come back for many years. But he was preparing to be a leader again. He did not give up. Remember your biggest successes will come only if you persist, and usually only after your biggest failures. A tycoon is never a quitter!

A tycoon is always alert for changes in the economy. He always asks, how can I profit from the coming events? When he looks at a sausage in a store he doesn't see a sausage, he sees 'a deal'. For example, relating to property of course, if you see a major employer in your area is having problems, that means the lay-off of a lot of people. Local unemployment will cause a temporary depression in the market. It might be the time to sell or trade property when everyone is selling and prices are depressed. Property sells below replacement costs during depressions. When interest rates go to abnormally high levels, many property owners feel that they must dump everything. The tycoon knows it pays to buy when everyone else is panicking. Naturally, a tycoon will negotiate special deals where interest payments are waived for a few years. Depressions do not last forever. They are windows of opportunity. The difference between a poor slob and a tycoon is simply that the tycoon sees an 'opportunity to be creative' while the poor slob sees only an insoluble problem.

A tycoon always has historical perspective. He knows that a big boom is always followed by a bust, as the buying frenzy of the late 80s was followed by the current recession. After a very healthy rise in the stock market or the property market, there's a period of levelling-off, or even declining prices, called a 'correction'. During that "correction" (a bad one is called a depression), the tycoon must be prepared to wait for the waters to be safe again. Remember, the time of biggest opportunity is when everyone else is running scared. After every bust there is a recovery. Alternatively, the tycoon can move on to more lucrative areas, even different countries, if necessary. A tycoon is ready to go where the action is.

For the mobile tycoon with several passports and banking connections in several countries, deals are possible which are off limits or illegal to citizens of just one nation. For example, it is possible to borrow money in Swiss francs (from a Swiss bank) at half the interest rates charged in other places, but you must have foreign accounts to know of such possibilities. I cover a lot of this international material in *The Passport Report*, also available from Scope International. See the back of this report for more information.

Avoid Being A Consumer

Finally, I must outline the most important rule for a tycoon, and that is: don't be a consumer. If your mind is always focused on how to blow the next few hundred you earn, you'll never accumulate the capital you need to be successful.

These are my three rules to avoid being a consumer. If you see it in a store and are about to buy it, ask yourself:

CAN I LIVE WITHOUT IT?
IS THERE SOMETHING I CAN TRADE FOR IT?
CAN I GET IT CHEAPER SOMEWHERE ELSE?

Hopefully, the mental process you go through with those three questions, will make you forget about any consumer product and cause you to look for more remunerative uses for your money. Like where to invest funds and get back two for one, in a year. Not where to spend and get nothing except a memory. Whenever possible, don't even think about consumer goods like cars, vacations, pets. Nor any sports activities requiring your valuable time or expensive trappings. You're independently wealthy only when you've enough money coming in from your investments to enable you to quit working. Then, the surplus left over from paying for basic necessities can be spent on consumer goods. Once you have an income from your investments rather than your work, you can take up ballooning or other expensive hobbies. Don't put the cart before the horse.

Not only does a tycoon not consume, he generally pays little or no taxes. Under their confiscatory tax policies, most governments are our 50 to 90 per cent partners. Most tycoons don't pay much in taxes because we spend (far too much) time figuring out how to legally shelter income. Most of us do this by making business deals that create tax or paper losses. This is much easier to do when one has complex multinational interests. It makes it much harder for any local government to figure out how much you are making when you are a one-man multinational.

Some companies pay taxes by simply charging more for their products. The fuzzy-thinking leftists of the world don't realise that when an outfit like General Motors pays about 50 per cent in corporate income taxes, it only passes these taxes along to the consumer.

Take the typical small car, for instance. It could sell for US $3,000. But does it? Of course not. 'Consumers' shell out $8,000. Why? Because $5,000 is needed for taxes. Companies must always raise the price of their product to cover all costs. This way they get the needed return on their investment. Companies don't pay taxes, people pay taxes; In reality, taxes are always just another add-on cost for the consumer. Fuzzy-thinking leftists, when they say 'tax the corporations' are always just raising the prices of goods and services provided by those businesses. The same is true when 'greens' or others impose costly restrictions or regulations. There is no free lunch. The users pay.

If you're going to be a tycoon, you will have to keep clear not only of taxes, but of flakes, frauds and red ribbon deals. The red ribbon rule is to avoid a deal presented to you all wrapped in a red ribbon, your only requirement being to write out a check, sit back and watch the profits flow in. Don't do it. The deal will never happen. Avoid sucker investments.

The best business deals are the ones you create, where you personally see a need and are willing and able to do what it takes to fill it.

Double ESSers

No matter how good a deal sounds or what guarantees you're offered, never get involved with a person of bad reputation. That person will find a way to do a 'double S' on you. Screw and Sue, in other words. 'Double eSSers' are people who want to get something they are not entitled to. They get you into lawsuits which are a waste of much money and valuable energy. Always find a way to settle quickly with a double eSSer, then never have anything more to do with him. Go on to something more productive.

Women in a divorce situation are often double eSSers. One lady I knew, let's call her Sue Screw to make the point, was married to a wealthy fellow named Sam. The marriage fell apart and Sue hit Sam with a vengeance. She contacted famous divorce lawyer 'SS Castrator' who sought a court order for Sam to pay her a huge alimony cheque each month. Sam refused such a high sum. He offered half as an out of court settlement. Was Sue Screw satisfied? No. She would rather fight! Things dragged on for years, with Sam refusing and Sue screwing, but Sue fought on. Sue didn't realise that 80 per cent of all alimony orders are in default, anyway, within two years of the alimony award. Eventually the case was decided, after five years of agro and 10 years of income spent on court costs. Sue Screw was awarded the alimony she wanted. Sam moved to Israel and became a kibbutznik. "I'm broke and I can't pay a penny," he wrote to the judge from Israel. She never got a pfennig. If only she had accepted Sam's original offer, Sue could have bought property and been a lot richer both financially and emotionally. So, the Bill Hill rule on double eSSers is: forget it. Stay out-of-court – settle quickly. Do something productive instead. The only one who wins in a lawsuit is the lawyer. Double eSSers exist in business too, and they come in all three sexes. So always be sure the people you rely on in a deal are dependable and of super reputation. The same rule applies to you.

Don't be a double eSSer!

From time to time, for very good reasons, you may have to be technically a 'lawbreaker'. But never take what isn't yours. It's just that sometimes the laws of the country or a community make no sense. Number one priority has to be 'look to your own survival'. When a place like Rhodesia (now Zimbabwe) prevented Rhodesians from simply picking up their chips and moving to safety, it was necessary for intelligent people to circumvent the law.

Governments are immoral, cynical and inhumanly interested in their own self-perpetuation. Always at the expense of their citizens – sometimes at the expense of the lives of their citizens. As Voltaire once said, laws are passed so that the 'in group' can push around everyone else.

On a less dramatic level, if the building code in my town makes it impossible for me to complete a necessary repair or alteration on one of my buildings, I may find it necessary to make that repair anyway and take my chances of getting caught. Economic survival on a day-to-day level is as important as my personal survival. My feeling is that you should respect the laws of your country or community where you can, but when they get ridiculous, follow your own conscience.

I remind you again that every tycoon, certainly when he starts out, should prepare written plans. Set forth your goals and what it is you want to accomplish. The world steps aside for a man or woman with a plan.

Have complete confidence in yourself whatever you're doing. Recognise that if you're well-prepared, well-educated, well-organised and have a plan, you will not fail to achieve your goals.

After you become a tycoon and are financially independent, ask the question, what would I do if I had only six months to live? Then do it. With financial independence, you finally have the power to do whatever you want. Real power, i.e. the freedom to determine your own destiny. While on one level I talk about how to make money, at a deeper and more philosophical level, I'm talking about this freedom. You get freedom only when you don't have to work at a job you hate – or live with a spouse just because he or she is paying the rent.

When you have no money problems, you can expand your horizons, consider foreign opportunities and have time to smell the flowers. You can pursue the opposite sex and enjoy life. Enjoying your family more might be one of the unexpected benefits, because the reason you will be with them is that you want to enjoy them, not that you have to stick around.

Once you've made a lot of money, look beyond your home town and think about protecting your fortune by diversification. You must be ready at any time to transport yourself or your business into other areas, even other countries. It never hurts to start your diversification programme from a position of success.

Don't wait for the boom to bust. While still doing well in property dealing, set aside funds abroad to establish reserves or, even better, look for different business ventures. Anyone who can relate to what I've discussed in these pages has the capacity to become financially independent in one to three years. And to keep it, you don't need luck. Luck always comes to those who think like a tycoon.

The choice of whether you do nothing, apply yourself moderately or make it big, is yours!

"Life is a banquet," said Auntie Mame, "but most people never get near the table."

The choice is up to you. Are you ready? Let's take step one of the tycoon plan: tomorrow morning, at 9am, go and see a banker.

Chapter 7

YOU AND YOUR BANKER

You have probably often heard the saying, 'it takes money to make money'. This little expression is certainly true, but despair not if you have no money of your own (why else would you be reading this report), for that financial truism doesn't stipulate whose money it's talking about. As a general rule, the tycoon must borrow money. The more the better. You want to borrow money at low interest to acquire things and also to acquire education in developing saleable skills. The fees and commissions earned as a doctor, lawyer or plumber in your ordinary job, and the rents received from your property, will build slowly until the time comes when you're rich enough not to need an ordinary job. In the meantime, the money debts you have accumulated can be paid off with ever more worthless currency even in times of low inflation. Let me explain more about debt. If eggs were money, they'd be getting cheaper every year.

Suppose you borrowed 100,000 eggs to buy an apartment building this year. With a typical loan you have 30 years to pay those eggs back. It's easy to see why property is such a good investment. You can estimate that 30 years hence, the property may be worth one million eggs, but the borrowed eggs used to finance the property can be paid back with just 100,000 eggs. Sell the property and you get 900,000 eggs free. Get the point? Borrow today to buy an asset today. You pay back a lot less than you borrow in terms of real money. How do you pay the interest back each year? Not out of your own pocket! But with the rent or income from a business.

Due to low or moderate inflation, the quoted value of all property and businesses will increase, yet debts are paid back with cheaper and cheaper currency. With each passing year, all other things being equal, the debt you own becomes less and less burdensome, while the property and business you bought becomes more and more valuable. Obviously, the less money you put down to make a deal the better. This can be arranged by either reducing the price of the property (and thereby the required deposit, a percentage of the buying price) or by borrowing a greater portion of the price. The less of your money it takes to make each deal, the more deals you will be able to make. The more buys you make, the more assets you acquire and the wealthier you become. The nitty-gritty of my techniques on how to buy repossessed property, and how to buy property with little or no money down, are fully covered in later chapters of this report.

Some people would say that if you have big mortgage debts and you owe money to a lot of people, then those lenders can come after your other assets if you default. Actually the truth is often quite a different story. In the deals I like, you the buyer can just walk away from a deal that doesn't work out and tell the lender or seller to take back the property. These rules vary tremendously from country to country and should be looked into. In the UK, for example, personal liability often attaches to a mortgage, making you personally liable for a debt unless you know how to structure a deal properly. Of course, if you're what is known as 'a man of straw' (you have no personal assets or money now anyway) you really do have nothing to lose.

Thus, it is the goal of every tycoon to acquire as much income property and productive assets as possible. Needless to say, there will be occasional disappointments, but if you have the tycoon mentality, you will emerge from these a better, stronger person.

As most budding tycoons don't have access to the sort of money it takes to build a property empire, the help of a friendly banker is required. Even if your family or a friend does have money, you will undoubtedly feel much better about yourself, and look better in the eyes of your family, by 'going it alone'. Time to visit your local banker.

The Banking Mentality

Unfortunately, it seems that bankers all go to the same class to learn the basic rule of their trade, namely, never lend to anyone who actually needs money. In the old days, before I learned this secret, I walked into a bank cold and asked to borrow. They requested collateral in the form of some asset worth more than what I was asking to borrow. The banker asked me to pledge bank accounts or marketable stock worth double the amount I needed.

In these old days I tried to explain that, if I had a savings account for more than I wanted to borrow, I could use my own money and not have to borrow. If I had stock of double the value of the hoped-for loan, I could sell half my stock to get the money I needed. Several times my unsecured loan requests were refused. I was always left frustrated. But that was a long time ago, before I learned how to get unlimited money. Now I get whatever I want, from any bank.

Let me share this unbelievable simple secret. It will get you a million or a hundred million, whatever you need in unsecured credit – whenever you need it. The bankers will court you and ask, "How much can you use?"

Before I learned how to do it myself, I made some wrong assumptions about how unsecured loans were made. I figured that family ties, school contacts or some clubby-social considerations made the difference between outsiders like me and the favoured few who were extended unsecured credit. I was very wrong. Banks are interested in making loans to almost anyone. The only reason they refuse to make a loan is they are (rightly) worried about getting the loan paid back. If you can convince a banker there is no risk, you will get their money. If your ability to pay is unknown or in doubt, you will get the cold shoulder. Here is how you can establish credit:

First, open a checking or current account at any large bank. Put enough money in your current account so there will be no service charges. Be sure your new account is classified as a business or commercial account. Do that by calling yourself "John Yourname and Associates".

Once your account has been opened, wander over to the section where the bank officers sit. You'll notice the two flashing signs that say "Smartie Desk" and "Idiots Report Here". You may have trouble seeing these signs because they are invisible to the uneducated eye. But if you ask: "Who handles consumer loans?" and "Who handles commercial loans?" someone at the bank will tell you.

Consumer loans are used to buy consumer goods, like a new car that will be a worthless, rusted hulk in five years. The interest for foolish loans on disposable consumer products is much more than the interest rate on commercial loans. Idiots report there. Commercial loans are used, or at least should be used, to invest in deals that will bring you back twice the amount that you borrow. Now do you begin to see the flashing lights?

Walk over to the Smart Desk, the chap or lady who makes commercial loans, and say something cute, like, "Hello, I'd like to have a relationship with you." After their initial puzzlement subsides, explain that you are starting the John or Joan Yourname Business. While you do not want a loan immediately, you want to establish a rapport today. You want to know their commercial credit requirements. Explain further that you want your potential banker to know you and to be aware of your probable future needs for credit.

Establishing, rapport with an intelligent and reasonable bank officer on your wave-length is of the utmost importance. If you are an attractive young lady-tycoon-to-be, perhaps your best banker will be an old fuddy-duddy. You can flatter him with your attention and charm. Fuddy-duddy might turn a wheeler-dealer like me down in an instant, but the attractive Miss Leggs could do very well with him. A young and aggressive black man might do better by seeking out a female loan officer with the latest model African hairdo. Mr Fudd says "no," to trendy young studs, especially if they are not members or potential members of the establishment.

Unfortunately, some prejudices, both positive and negative, do exist. It is up to you to exploit them to your own advantage. A Chinese vice-president, for instance, might be more understanding to a Chinese customer than a closet neo-Nazi who feels all non-Germans and Asians, in particular, are inferior beings. But racially prejudiced bank loan officers are relatively rare in my experience. Old school ties, family connections – all these things may help but are by no means a major factor. It is important that the bank officer starts out liking you. As I said, try to get one on your wave-length.

It may appear that I am telling you to forget your principles and pander to the base instincts of dirty old men (in the case of Miss Leggs) or give up your legal rights to equal treatment (in the case of Mr Afro). That is one way of looking at it. You could, as a female or black, seek out a bank officer who instinctively dislikes you and vice versa. Then when he or she refused to make a loan, you could sue. 10 or 15 years later, your civil rights case might be decided. You might win. You might lose. But many years of expending negative energy would have gone by, and your plan for becoming a millionaire would, at least, have been sidetracked.

This book is about the world as it is or at least as I perceive it. It's not a fairy story of how it should be. Getting ahead will definitely involve being agreeable, even charming, to people that, socially or intellectually, you might have no use for. It will involve going round obstacles rather than fighting staunchly for 'your rights' and thereby spending your life in frustrating confrontations – or waiting for your case to be decided in courts of law. More than anything else, being successful financially involves the constant application of common sense. If your goal was to be a great medical doctor, kissing the shoes of a hospital administrator who is balky about signing your certification may be necessary if you don't want to go back to driving a cab. Once you have overcome the certification barrier, you have the freedom to proceed according to your own values.

This book is about freedom. A net worth of a million dollars, or even a quarter million, buys freedom. Making a million in a few years is not easy. It may involve compromises and sacrifices you don't feel should be necessary. It will almost certainly involve cultivating people you would rather not deal with. It will involve exploiting every talent you have and grabbing every opportunity you come across. Thus, the example of a black friend of mine. He refused an executive partnership because it seemed his potential partners wanted him as their token black. He was a fool! You must get the job, deal or loan first. Then you can prove how good you are. Your boss, partners or bankers will soon become colour-blind. If you have the tycoon mentality, you will have to exploit all your assets to the fullest. Negative people may call you an "opportunist". But all successful people have pressed on and taken advantage of situations they either observed or created.

Getting back to the narrower issue of loans. Whatever your financial needs are, do not be afraid to shop around for banks and loan officers until you find one or more you can relate to. Bankers are just employees trying to do their job. That job is to make solid loans to reliable people; and to get the loans paid back as agreed, on time, with interest.

A bank couldn't stay in business for a month if it was not able to lend out its capital and deposits. That's their business. They need borrowers. They want you to succeed. But no matter how charming they are, no matter how much your new banker likes you, their job is also to protect their capital by keeping alert for telltale signs that will indicate how reliable you are likely to be. Do you bounce cheques? If you do, forget about ever borrowing a penny – or change your habits. A person sloppy enough to be writing unauthorised overdrafts is automatically labelled irresponsible and a poor loan risk.

Do you make regular deposits to your account that indicate a steady source of income? Do you make occasional larger deposits indicating that you are a successful wheeler dealer? You should create the appearance of success from the start. If you appear to have a regular income or seem to be a successful person with a cash flow, you establish credibility. The record established at your neighbourhood branch with the bank manager, and ultimately with the big shots at 'head office' is what gets you a million, unsecured. If you think it can be done in a week, forget it. This is a one to three-year program. Patience and the approach outlined here will get you all the credit you need. But the necessary confidence-building could take a couple of years.

After establishing a rapport you are ready to apply for your first loan. Remember the bankers' rule on first loans is that you will not get it if you need it. Thus, your first small loan of say 500 is only to establish credibility. You want to establish a record that you pay back on time or, better yet, early. If you do not have any good deals to invest in, create a not too fanciful story about 10 cases of rare wine you can purchase at a bargain price for sale to local wine connoisseurs at a 100 per cent profit. Or perhaps you can invent a deal involving an antique dining room set that you can buy for 500, refinish in your basement and resell for 1,000.

When applying for your first loan, offer to transfer 500 from your current account to a savings account to stand as security for the 500 you want to borrow. Or be ready to pledge some shares or stock.

Remember, even when you borrow 100 per cent secured, the loan is still to you. If the loan officer suspects he will have to grab the security, he would rather not make the loan. Bad loans are a headache and cause public relation problems. If you do not service your first loan as agreed, you might as well move your account somewhere else and start all over again. You also might just as well forget about being a tycoon. Every successful entrepreneur will need the backing of a banking community that perceives him or her as a responsible and worthy customer.

Rule: during your first year of borrowing, pay off every loan early! Assuming you have made that all important first bank loan for a term of three months, go in and pay it off in three weeks.

The small gift rule: a small or token gift can be given after some service has been rendered. It is not a bribe. You already got your loan. You go into the bank on payoff day with your cheque. You effusively thank the banker for his help and tell him about all the money you made on the chair deal or the wine deal. You happen to have with you a sample chair or bottle, which you give the banker to show him the product you were trading or producing. You say, "By the way, here's an extra (or factory second). Why don't you keep it as a souvenir of our first successful joint venture?"

Once I (really) invested in a soap factory. When the loan was paid off everybody in the bank got a bar of cucumber-flavour glycerine soap. To this day, the tellers, clerks and loan officers remember me as the 'soap guy'. For five years I got super service at that branch. The most important thing about the small gift rule is that your banker will remember you. You stand out among the sea of applicants he must listen to every day. Effusive thanks or buying your banker lunch is a variant on the small gift rule. It psychologically conditions your banker to expect a goodie or some strokes for himself at the same time he marks "paid in full" on a good deal for his employer. Verbal praise can mean as much as material things to some individuals.

For your second loan, which should be requested soon after the first has been paid, ask for at least double the amount of money of the first loan. Have another 'good deal story' ready. You may have to do the 'savings account as security' bit again, but it's likely that if your current account balance is more than the amount borrowed, you can, for loan number two, merely informally promise your banker that you will keep your account balance over the amount of the loan.

Before the loan is due, handle the payback, small gift and effusive thank you scene as before. The third, fourth and each succeeding loan should be for more money, longer terms and with less security than previous loans. You may have to provide financial statements, copies of income tax returns and so on once you get over 5,000, but by then the banker, with whom you have established a rapport, will help you prepare statements and documentation that will look good to his higher-ups.

Your loan officer should become a firm ally within six months. You can, by the fifth loan, even confide in him that your first loan was not really used for a wine deal, but that you were just establishing credit and your relationship with him. He may confide in you that he, too, read this book and knew what you were up to all the time. Needless to say, by your third loan, you should have found some genuine and profitable uses for borrowed money. The whole purpose of this exercise is to establish a credit line so that you can pick up bargain deals, products or businesses for cash when opportunities present themselves.

Around the time of your third or fourth loan, consider going through the whole process of establishing rapport a with another banker at one or more different banks. You should not tell the first banker about bank number two or three unless he asks. Bankers do not like what they call 'double-borrowing'. But here is how it works:

Assume you went through the same process of building confidence with a series of secured, then unsecured loans of increasingly large sums at a second bank. While you will have to meet interest payments out of personal funds, you can borrow 10,000 from bank number one. When it is due, you repay with 10,000 from bank number two. When that comes due, pay it off with a new loan from bank number one. If you want to get complicated, pay that loan off with a loan from number three.

The result is that your 10,000 is always rolling over between banks. The full 10,000 can be in deals out there working for you – hopefully earning 100 per cent a month while your loan interest is only 15 per cent or so per year. As mentioned, banks do not particularly like this double or triple borrowing mode of operation. Yet all big companies and all tycoons sometimes operate on borrowed money from multiple lenders in much the same way. This handbook is just making you aware, as a future tycoon, of what is going on in the real world. Once you make your first deals with borrowed money, refinements in your system of paying back loans will come from your own experiences. Your borrowings will be scheduled in accord with your own needs and in line with the requirements of your banks or other financial backers. A word of caution, always try to be liquid enough to clear up all your short-term loans at once every year or two. If your double or triple borrowing is discovered, admit what you are doing honestly and candidly. You may be surprised, as I was, when banker number one said to me, "You don't have to go through all that nonsense with three banks. We will give you whatever you need, up to five million. Just clear the decks every now and then to show us that you have the ability to pay off all your short-term loans from time to time."

After that, for several years, I did all my short-term commercial borrowing with one bank, and they did indeed give me whatever I wanted. It took me three years, but by paying my debts on time, taking my banker to lunch and establishing social and personal contacts with higher-level bankers in the same bank, I eventually got carte blanche. If I could do it, so can you.

Bankers now invite me to lunch and ply me with small gifts. If times get tough and it's impossible for you to repay a loan on time, don't be afraid to ask for an extension of the payback time. If this happens on your first, second or third loan, it will be harmful to your credit. But after a dozen loans or a year of dealing with the same banker, you will have established enough credit and credibility to call your banker and say things like, "I have written a cheque for 50,000 to acquire a property worth 100,000. In line with our previous agreement, will you cover it with an unsecured loan until I line up a long-term loan? I'll have you paid back in three months." With established credit, you can make a partial payment in three months and get the loan extended for another three months if necessary.

DON'T BE A DEADBEAT

The most common or deadbeat way of handling a cash flow or a bouncing cheque problem is the worst. At the first sign of trouble the deadbeat puts a pillow over his head and does nothing.

Even worse, he disappears. Goes fishing. His phone is disconnected for non-payment of bills, and mail is returned to creditors unopened. As a result, any normal banker will get all upset. The banker makes a bad debt report to the higher-ups and instantly the deadbeat borrower has zero credit. Even if at a future time the borrower belatedly pays back the loan, the sour taste of irresponsibility remains. How much better and simpler it would have been if the embryo tycoon went to his banker, explained the problem, received the standard permission to extend the loan, or even if he didn't get an extension, made regular token payments until conditions improved.

If you cannot meet a loan payment, or cannot resist an opportunity to make a deal with what would otherwise be a bouncing cheque, you must always call or stop in at the bank and explain quite truthfully what has happened. More importantly, you must tell your lender what you are going to do about it. If, over a period of years, a businessman never had any temporary cash binds, he'd be a most unusual character indeed. You become an even better risk if you show skill at extricating yourself from occasionally difficult positions. Obtaining a long-term building society or savings and loan-secured mortgage (due in 20 or 30 years) is my favourite way of paying off short-term debt. If you own property or a business, getting a long-term mortgage loan or doing a sale-leaseback can usually raise needed cash.

Bankers hate lawsuits and foreclosures. They would much rather give you a chance to settle up on terms you can live with. They do not want to terminate a good relationship with a bad lawsuit. To sum up, this is how to borrow a million unsecured:

1. Always borrow from the commercial loan department. Never have anything to do with consumer credit.

2. Establish a relationship with loan officers you have a rapport with. Start with just one bank.

3. Borrow money you don't really need on a secured basis. Repay loans early to establish credit and credibility. Remember the small gift rule.

4. Establish credit at more than one bank.

5. Always borrow more than you need. Use extra borrowings to repay.

6. Always pay back your loans a bit early.

7. Each time you apply for a loan, borrow more than your previous loans, even if you don't need it.

8. Deposit unused funds in other banks, as reserves. At a certain point, move a nest egg abroad, beyond the reach of creditors, ex-wives, tax collectors, etc.

9. Always keep cash reserves of at least 25 per cent of your loans.

10. Establish bank friendships on levels that are appropriate for your level of operations. You should aim to be on a first name basis with the bank CEO (Chief Executive Officer) within one year.

11. Meet your obligations punctually. Remember the small gift rule and you will be remembered.

12. In times of difficulty, after you have established credit and credibility, never appear irresponsible. Never disappear. Always stay in contact. Prepare and show creditors or investor partners your plans for solving any problems. If you are reasonable, a bank will always grant extensions. Occasional financial difficulties are an expected part of all business operations.

High finance is not a mystery. It always involves the steady build-up of unsecured credit to create in the minds of others an apparently credit-worthy person. You, as a tycoon, will use other people's money in many ways, as explained in other chapters. With a good line of unsecured credit you can take advantage of special situations that less credit-worthy individuals can't handle. Cash is king, and when a financially troubled company or disgusted property owner wants to sell in a hurry, you will be able to pick up bargains. You cannot be a tycoon without investor backing or a substantial line of unsecured credit. Visit the Smartie Desk today.

Chapter 8

PREPARING FOR YOUR FIRST INVESTMENT

L et's go to kindergarten! The first thing you must do is toddle out into the real world and see what's on the market. Although I mainly talk about property in this chapter, the same principles apply to the purchase of any asset or business. There are a lot of bargains out there.

Most property is marked "for sale" at a high nominal price. Only a tiny fraction of what's available is known to most, including you and your potential competitors, other buyers. What's 'advertised' or openly listed with brokers is like the tip of an iceberg. Most people investing in property, business deals, motels or whatever, never get below that tip. In the next few chapters you'll learn about the vast untapped market below the surface, but for now just buy a magic marker and your local weekend newspapers. Get property lists from the various brokers in your area. Exploring only the tip of the iceberg will be quite enough to keep you busy for the next few weeks. It will be your basic training.

Once you've bought the papers don't waste time with the sports pages or news. Throw out everything but the classified section. Turn to the property ads. Circle every ad for apartments, homes and investment property located within half an hour from where you live. Look at them carefully. Go over expense and income figures with sellers and their agents. For at least a month, look at a minimum of 25 offerings every weekend. Spend weekday time after work looking at more deals if you can. This first exposure to the conventional market is your kindergarten. Don't get carried away. Don't buy anything. You are not educated yet – not until you have seen one hundred properties. Just look! Ask questions. Don't worry about a great deal getting away, there's always another waiting around the corner.

Assume that sellers and their agents are lying to you. They are! Values and rental incomes will be exaggerated. Expenses will be grossly understated. But you can ferret out real figures. Check everything. Don't be afraid to check public records for property taxes. Review tenants' leases. Follow up 'for rent' ads. Pretend to be a prospective tenant to discover true rent levels in your chosen area.

Also, during this educational or looking phase, don't neglect to prepare yourself intellectually. Finish reading this report. Take an elementary tax and basic accounting course and consider going to college for an evening course in property appraisal. Be extroverted and expand your contacts.

You can attend most courses at local continuing education colleges. Basic contracts and commercial law are useful and inexpensive. The only problem is that many college instructors go by the book. They learned from a book and have never been out trying to put together deals in the real world. I know of very few teachers who make any money wheeling and dealing. As George Bernard Shaw said, "People who can, do. People who can't, teach. People who can't teach, teach teachers!" That's why after you've learned the basics, the best ideas will not come from books or courses, but from looking at many properties and negotiating in the field. The courses are very much secondary.

To repeat, suggested college courses in the order of importance are 1) accounting, 2) property appraisal and 3) tax. Courses will do you more good and give you more usable ideas after you have educated yourself in the field and understand what opportunities are on the market.

Make no serious offers until you have looked at at least one hundred properties, tempting as it may be. Then, make a low offer or a no-money-down offer on every deal you look at! After looking at one hundred properties you will recognise or be able to create an outstanding deal when you see it.

Until you become an expert, here's one rule of thumb to tell you what a property is worth if you are going to hold it for income. Take the monthly gross rent you expect to get (not necessarily the existing rent) and multiply by 80 to get 'the value'. For example, let's talk about a duplex (two apartments) that rent for $600 per month for each unit. That's a total of $1,200 per month. Now to apply my rule of thumb, take those monthly rentals of $1,200 per month and multiply by 80. That will give you $96,000, as $1,200 times 80 is $96,000. In many areas, if you shop around, you can buy a two-unit property earning $400 per month for $32,000 in an average neighbourhood in average condition. That may seem like an incredibly low price to those who have been looking at property in expensive areas, but in many parts of the world, six and a half times the gross annual rent or 80 times the gross monthly rent is a high valuation. It is necessary to pay a premium for apartment buildings with condo-conversion potential or in areas perceived as more desirable than average.

If you expect to make an income from any property, you should never pay more than one hundred times the gross monthly rental. The $96,000 property we are talking about must be purchased for under $120,000. If bought for more than $120,000 it would be a bad deal because it would need cash from your pocket each month to meet expenses and mortgage obligations, unless you could raise the rents quickly and substantially.

Naturally, the rental figures that you could use in this rule of thumb should be realistic rents you can expect to collect. Actual rents could be too high or too low for the existing market.

Many investors use a multiple of the annual gross as their rule of thumb to determine if a deal is worth making. You can earn a positive cash flow with a price of five to seven times the annual gross rents. At prices above eight times the expected annual gross, unless the property is in a spectacular location, pass the deal! There are still many properties available at bargain prices if you know how to find them. In my 'heyday', I was making about three deals a week. Most required little or no cash investment. Even with no money down, all my deals were scheduled to break even or produce a small cash flow within a few months. Don't ever buy a deal or property that doesn't carry itself. If you have to feed or subsidise it, it's a bad deal.

To judge your performance, if you are closing less than one deal every six months, you are not operating anywhere near tycoon levels. It may take six months for you to get rolling in the business. One deal a month should be your initial goal. One good deal a month will make you a millionaire in two to five years.

In addition to following the classified ads, simply walk around a neighbourhood you feel comfortable in, particularly in springtime. You'll see people working, painting houses, planting in yards. You can be sure they are not tenants. Tenants never work on their houses or gardens. Anyone doing beautification is probably an owner. Ask a person working in his yard about his place, particularly if he's older and near retirement. Once you start talking, you may find that he has some interest in selling and moving. Don't be too disappointed if in your first few conversations nothing materialises; it could take six months until you get rolling. But if six months go by and you still haven't bought anything, you are doing something wrong.

Expect to make one hundred cold contacts to get five hot prospects. Five live prospects may yield only one or two deals. To make your first super-deal will take much effort and persistence. Getting acquainted with older people in your own neighbourhood is a good way to spend part of those first months. If they like you, you will make many useful contacts. Eventually you'll get several direct (no agent) deals at reasonable prices with good terms.

By following the basic steps of this simple plan, you will soon be on your way to financial independence. It is not unrealistic for you to expect to make $20,000 from one deal alone. What would you make on 50 or one hundred such deals? Get used to multiplying and having your results come out in million plus figures. You will soon be earning between one and three million per year.

Of course, sceptics will say, "You can't do that. It's not that easy." Well, don't take my word for it, just ask anyone you know who bought a house or apartment 10 years ago, ask any homeowner! For example, a place I bought when the price of an average home was $25,000 required a down payment of $2,500, the standard 10 per cent. A loan for $22,500 at seven per cent interest was easily arranged and voila… just look at my little home today, less than 10 years later. The average selling price of that same property is close to $100,000, but the loan I took out is now paid down to $13,000.

What is the equity in such a home? Equity is the market value less the loan balance or the anticipated net cash receivable if the property is sold. In this average no-exceptional-tycoon-skills-required deal, the equity is $87,000. Thus, $2,500 invested 10 years ago in a very average home has turned into an $87,000 equity. That's the easiest money that I or all those other homeowners who bought 10 years ago made in their lives. If they had bought a dozen, all they'd have to do to count their piles would be to multiply $87,000 by 12. Owning a dozen dinky homes makes you a millionaire.

As you can guess, most people who invested $2,500 in a home purchased 10 years ago probably did not shop too hard. They didn't know the secrets or tricks of the trade explained here, such as how to eliminate closing costs. They were not good negotiators. They had low ambitions and no motivation to make a fortune in property. They didn't have the drive to look at one hundred deals a weekend and pick out only the three best ones. They just wanted a place to live. Still, the average homeowner picked up from $80,000 to $90,000.

What did that same guy save at his wage-slave job? What did you save while working at your eight-hour-a-day job? The average guy is lucky to save $1,000 a year! In 10 years that totals $10,000, if you don't dip in and spend along the way. Years ago $10,000 could have bought a new Cadillac. Today, we're talking a used Volkswagen at best, and that's after years of struggling.

The moral should be clear. You can't get ahead working for a wage or salary, but you can make a great deal of money using borrowed funds to buy property. The same exact principles apply to acquiring going businesses, large and small. I've done it. My associates are doing it. You can certainly do it. If this sounds inspirational, like a pep talk, that's what it's meant to be. Negativism is sure defeat. If you feel you can't make it, that attitude will bog you down and prevent you from taking the first step.

You can make big money through property without quitting your present job and without risking anything except time you would be wasting anyway. If you enter the marketplace with a positive attitude and make enough offers, you'll be surprised at the exceptional opportunities waiting like ripe fruit to fall into your lap. But you must get out there and circulate. You must get out there today and start making deals. There's no way that you can fail! There's no risk!

If you put little or no down payment on properties, the most you can lose is your time. If you put 10 per cent down, you will soon get your money out in the form of tax savings or refinancing. Of course, if you put no money down in the first place, there's no risk at all. In California, for instance, lenders cannot go after your personal assets if you default on a purchase-money property loan used to buy four units or less. These laws vary tremendously from state to state and country to country, so make sure you look into them.

Now I'm not telling you to default. But if the world turns to ashes or the current recession turns into the worst depression the world has ever seen, it's comforting to know you can walk away from a property deal. It is possible to walk away and still hold on to whatever else you may own. If you buy in the name of a corporation, trust or straw man, you can escape personal liability in other jurisdictions.

Can you make a lot of money in property today? Probably, yes. Not everybody can do it. If you are very rich, you may have problems. Rich folks are generally not hungry enough to get out in the rough-and-tumble market and make deals. Rich people always seem anxious to make a big down payment or maybe even pay all cash. They are conservative. This is not the way to do it. Let me explain, if you bought a $100,000 property for all cash and it went up in value 10 per cent a year, all you get is 10 per cent profit on your money. But if you buy 10 $100,000 properties for 10 per cent down and they each go up 10 per cent, you make $100,000. Over 100 per cent on your money. Rich people do not seem to understand that using leverage or debt is how money can make money. Creditors lose their shirts.

Also, to make big money you can't be too smart or intellectual. If one thinks too much about the pros and cons and intellectualises endlessly over 'to buy or not to buy' a particular property, someone else will turn the deal before you even make a decision. Action, not agonising, makes tycoons.

So, by now you're probably thinking, what about the future, what about the next five to 10 years, what about the recession? As we prepare to go to press in early 1994, the world seems to be slowly moving away from the much-talked-about recession. Prices are lower than they have been in years. In other words, the time is ripe for aspiring tycoons to move in and scoop up some truly outstanding deals.

What will happen over the next five years? Will inflation rise again to make you the same money it made me through my modest home of the mid 1980's? What if it doesn't? What if it drops to half? Simple. You'll only make $35,000. That would not be too bad a return on a $2,500 investment without risk. Remember also that for a tycoon the idea is to buy so cheaply that market fluctuations don't affect you. (There will be more of this in the next few chapters.)

To understand the recession, you must understand that periods during which property values remain static, or actually go down and stay down for a few years, occur with cyclical regularity. If you 'buy right' and can rent your property out to cover debt service, your patience will be rewarded. Don't panic because some guru predicts property will drop in value by 98 per cent overnight. He is wrong. It may continue to be hard to get top dollar or even to sell at last year's market price for the next year or two, but the market will rebound. It always does. In fact, it is better to start out in property at a time when everyone is depressed and the market is 'slow'. No time is as good as the present.

Of course, you cannot be lazy. If you have a problem with a stopped-up drain or a tenant complaint, you have to get out there and snake out the obstruction or otherwise fix it. If you just sit back, pay no attention to your properties, let the tenants get behind in rent or don't stay on top of their collection, property will not work out for you. Keeping up with the maintenance of your properties, getting along with your tenants and doing repairs promptly is not only simple, it's necessary!

Property is not a lazy person's business. Sure, after you've been in it a few years you can hire managers, bookkeepers and handymen. They will be your buffers. But for the first few years you will have to work like you have never worked before. If you are too lazy to get off your butt, look at properties and keep them up once you own them, you won't make it.

Quit watching soap operas on television. Take that TV set and put it in the closet. Leave it there for three years. Get out, start looking at property this weekend. Inertia is the greatest problem. Get off the time-wasting TV treadmill. Quit wasting your time. This month look at one hundred business deals or properties! All your spare time should be devoted to looking at deals, starting now. After you've looked at one hundred situations, make a low-down or no-money-down offer on every single deal you look at. You can make no-money-down offers and know that you are doing right because once you have looked at a hundred deals you will know what every deal is worth. Being successful is like being an athlete. The more you work at it, the better you get. If you get out there and negotiate to take over a property or business, you'll get an education. You'll soon have many contacts. If you make a lot of offers you'll make deals. Once you become an entrepreneur, if you make the effort to effectively manage your acquisitions, you will get very rich, very soon.

The heart of this little pep talk, to repeat for the tenth time, is that you should get out there. Now! Live, sleep, think and eat deals. Talk to everybody you run into about their businesses or property. Talk to everybody that knows anything about deals. If property is not exciting for you, look at other business opportunities in any field where you have some expertise. In this way you will be getting a good education. After looking at all the deals on the market in your community, you will be as good an appraiser as anyone else. Once you've looked at one hundred deals, you'll develop a good sense of what things should sell for. More importantly, you'll recognise the motivated seller who'd rather sell out and get an IOU than abandon his property or business. When a bargain comes up, you'll be able to recognise it. That's probably something you can't do right now.

Making An Offer

Now there are timid souls out there reading this report. They think that if you offer a 10-year note for $100,000 on a property and things do not 'work out' you will have big problems. By not working out I mean you've changed your mind and don't want to buy or you are not able to pay. Timid souls think they could lose 'everything' just by making an offer. 'They' would come and 'they' would take their home, bank accounts and car.

Nothing could be further from the truth. When you make an offer using my suggested methods and the seller accepts it, guess what? The seller must sell to you, but, if you do not want the property before the deal closes, you walk away from the deal with no loss, no penalties and no cost whatsoever. In most deals, done my way, even after the deal closes you can always walk away from it with no loss whatsoever. So let's get into a sample offer right now. Let me show you how to fill out a standard purchase agreement. In most countries, you can draw up a contract in a way that ties up the property so the seller can't get out of the deal, but you can. (See form on following page).

First of all, fill in the line 'Received From' with your name (Bob Buyer in our example), your address, your town and your phone number. In every detail there is a lot of communication that has to go on. If the seller does not have your address and does not know how to get in touch with you, all sorts of things can go wrong. It can blow a deal out of the water. These days everybody thinks they are a celebrity and has unlisted phone numbers. If you can't get in touch to arrange for the lender to get in to appraise, it's very frustrating indeed. Naturally you want the seller and any estate agents involved to have your name and number just as you need the seller's and his agent's names, addresses and phone numbers. The best way to keep that information handy, right at the start of negotiations, is to put everyone's name, address and home and office phone numbers on the offer and acceptance form.

The next thing for you to fill in is the 'Sum Received as a Deposit' line. There is no reason to give the seller a cash deposit, even if the broker does insist that doing so is 'customary'. As it is preferable to not tie up any real money, write in 'Loan Note'. Such a note can either be made up, or perhaps more easily obtained, at any stationery store in the US or legal form store in the UK.

As you can see, this practice allows you to make a dozen offers a day without putting up one penny. There is no reason for the seller to not accept a note instead of a more traditional payment, as real money is usually held by a broker or escrow company anyway. The seller

Offer to Purchase Real Estate

RECEIVED FROM: *Bob Buyer, Yourtown, Your state*

TELEPHONE: *(333) 444-5555* or his assignee, hereafter "Buyer," THIS SUM RECEIVED AS A DEPOSIT: *$1,000* Personal Cheque, (   ) Cash, (Cashier's Cheque, (   ) Deposit to Escrow, (   )

Other: *Note*

ON A TOTAL PURCHASE PRICE OF: *One Hundred Thousand Dollars*

For real property situated in the city of *Bigtown* county of *Globe* state of *California* ADDRESS: *1 Bargain Ave., a duplex with 3 garages, assessor's parcel #12345*

SUBJECT TO THE FOLLOWING TERMS AND CONDITIONS: *All terms subject to survey*

Note: Buyer is acquiring property for long-term investment purposes, not for resale.

ADDENDA:

PERSONAL PROPERTY INCLUDED WITH THIS REAL ESTATE: *Drapes & wall-to-wall carpeting in living room, 2 gas stoves, 2 GE refrigerators, washer & dryer, assorted garden tools, 6 potted cactus plants on front deck.*

ENCUMBRANCES: all liens against property including bonds or assessments are to be paid by the seller. Taxes to be prorated to date of sale. Clear title to be provided by seller.

CLOSING COSTS: Escrow charges and "points" to be paid by the seller.

DEPOSIT INCREASE: Not applicable.

TITLE INSURANCE POLICY TO BE PAID FOR BY: (X) THE SELLER (Binder Rate) (   ) THE BUYER.

OCCUPANCY DATE: (   )_____*(X)* UPON RECORDATION OF DEED.

The date of closing shall be *Feb. 2 1994.* If seller remains in possession after the closing and buyer has performed fully, seller shall pay buyer *$30.00* per day from date of recording to date possession is delivered.

Seller shall leave in escrow *$750.00* as a security deposit for cleaning, damage, and rent payable in the event possession is not delivered at closing.

RISK OF LOSS: Shall be Seller's until date of closing.

PRORATIONS: Shall be made as of date of closing as per custom in the area.

MAINTENANCE AND CONDITION: Seller agrees to maintain and deliver all heating, sewer, electrical, plumbing appliances and equipment in good working order, to maintain and deliver the grounds and property in clean condition with no broken or cracked glass and all debris and personal property removed.

CODE VIOLATION: The seller warrants that he has neither created nor has any knowledge of legal violations relating to this property.

PEST CONTROL: Inspection report to be obtained at expense of 1. *(X)* Seller; 2. (   ) Buyer; 3. (   ) Seller agrees to have all needed pest control work done at his expense and to deliver a termite-cleared property; 4. (X) Property is to be taken in its present condition to buyer's approval of termite report.

TIME IS OF THE ESSENCE IN THIS CONTRACT.

Bob Buyer

Barbara Buyer

BUYERS

DATED: *Jan 1, 1994* TIME: 9 AM

doesn't get it. In those rare deals where you are forced to put up real money, keep the deposit as low as possible. The price of a good dinner, for instance. I seldom make a deposit of more than the value of town dinners no matter how big the deal is.

In most countries, a deposit has to be paid in order for a contract to exist as "there can be no contract without consideration". However, 'consideration' can be a note, as I suggest, or a peppercorn. You might also wish to add "subject to survey" as a way to get out of the deal if the deeds, title or anything is not in order, or even to your liking.

Freehold Versus Leasehold

This little difference in terminology probably won't affect most of you, but if you encounter either of these terms while you are out hunting for deals, it will certainly help to understand them. Freehold is simple enough. It is the sort of deal that you'll encounter with most property. Like the name implies, if you hold or buy the freehold on a property, you own it free and clear. It is yours to let or sell or pass on to your heirs or to do with as you please. The property will always belong to either you personally, or your estate, unless you sell it, of course.

Leasehold property involves a different arrangement altogether. Budding tycoons in the London area will encounter this sort of property. Generally, if the property is a leasehold, the estate agent will fill you in on the details. However, in a nutshell, a leasehold is a property that is let out on a long lease, generally for a hundred years. When the lease expires, the property will return to the freehold owner and, most likely, another long lease will be arranged.

During the period of the leasehold, it can be bought and sold in the same manner as a freehold would be. In the beginning, when the leasehold is first arranged, it is sold for a price almost equal to that of buying the property free and clear. As the years diminish, the price comes down, although little effect is felt until the leasehold drops to less than 50 or even 40 years. Also, during the course of the leasehold, a small ground rent is collected by the freeholder, usually from £100 to £300 per annum.

This concept was developed primarily to benefit large, land-owning aristocratic families. They realised a few centuries ago that, rather than keeping all of their money tied up in their property, they could play with it by leasing the property off periodically. Every hundred years or so, the leaseholds on their property expire, and presto, they can sell it again. Leasehold property is almost all that is available in some of the more exclusive parts of London. The Duke of Westminster and a few of his noble friends own the freehold on almost all of W1 that's the postcode for downtown London for those of you that don't know.

Whether the leasehold concept is good or bad depends entirely upon your perspective. You can sometimes find some great bargains on properties with only a few years, less than

20, remaining on their leasehold. If you can make a rental profit out of such a property with a small up-front expense, the cost of the remaining few years on the leasehold, how can you lose? You may also be able to play with the aristocrats and leasehold off some of the property on which you own the freehold. This is a fantastic way to generate needed capital without permanently parting with an asset. You may also want to consider a variation of the concept by selling long-term leases, say for 20 years with five-year revisions, on some of your property.

Of course, if you plan to buy and then re-sell property over a fairly short period of time, two or three years say, whether you buy freehold or leasehold will make little difference.

As a final word, legislation has recently been introduced in England that will allow the leasehold owner of a property to buy in its freehold if he chooses to do so. Meaning that if you were to own the leasehold on a property you could be guaranteed the right to buy in the freehold and thus granted another option from just letting the leasehold expire. Again, whether this legislation is good or bad depends on your perspective. The successful introduction of such legislation certainly hasn't put a smile on the Duke of Westminster's face. But if your leasehold property fits the requirements, you now have the right to acquire the freehold.

Time For Action

Well, enough talk for now. It's time to get down to the nitty-gritty of seeking out and arranging deals. It's not difficult. In fact, it's about the easiest money that I or anybody else ever made.

The big question that people who think they're smart always ask me is, "If it's so good, why doesn't everybody do it?" The fact of the matter is that although 60 per cent of families own property and nearly 20 per cent of all people own their own businesses at some point during their lives, most heads of households are timid souls. Property owners usually own only the home they live in and maybe one other property. A mere five per cent own several investment properties. Wouldn't you like to be a member of that small group that owns several properties?

Worldwide, it's a big club. In absolute numbers for the US and Europe, there are millions of big-time entrepreneurs and property owners out there. You can and should become one of them! Or perhaps you'd rather be a member of approximately one third of the population that does not own any independent business or property. For all practical purposes these people are economically imprisoned. They are wage-slaves or completely dependent on public welfare, the 'underclass' who for the most part choose to be 'victims' of the system rather than its masters. For them, things are going to get worse in the coming years. The ongoing taxpayers' rebellion, and the restructuring of the dole to minimise its almost crippling effect on the so-called welfare state, will reduce them to less than adequate subsistence.

I think making the choice to be rich rather than poor is pretty easy. Getting started involves nothing more than getting off your butt and beginning to look at properties and business opportunities. Once you're comfortable, start to make ridiculously low offers. Get an education. Don't be afraid to read and study. Learn how to make offers, how to negotiate and how to look at deals and properties. You can teach yourself. You can learn everything you'll need to know. Even if you do nothing more than read this book, you'll have learned the most important secret. You have to get out there in the real world.

First step? Start reading the classified ads in any big city newspaper. Call up the advertisers. Let them try to sell you their wares. There never was and never will be a shortage of promising deals. If you know this basic secret, you are in a position to start your own financial advancement programme today.

There are no convenient excuses for a tycoon's failures. The nature of business makes it impossible to blame failure on anything but your own laziness. No one discriminates against producers of goods and services or property traders on account of sex, colour, social class, educational background, religion or handicaps. Some sellers may not like you. But if I sense that someone does not want to deal with me for reasons of personal prejudice, I simply send in a friendly ringer. If a black seller does not want to deal with me because I am white, you can be sure I'm not going to court and waiting five years till my civil rights case comes up. I simply send in a black friend to negotiate on my behalf. He closes the deal and then transfers title to me. Then I owe him a favour on his next deal.

The only way to be a loser in property is to think of yourself as a loser and to sit at home doing nothing but watching the boob-tube. If you get out there and use the tricks of the trade in this book you'll make your million in one, two or possibly three years. If you do everything wrong, but keep at it, you'll still make a million within five years. You only have to get out and make offers!

There is more to learn. The fine points. Tricks of the trade. They can make or save you an extra million or three during the next five years. It's cheaper to learn about mistakes to avoid from someone like me than to make my costly mistakes all over again yourself. Finish this book and look at deals and properties. Read all you can but consider the source. 'How To' books that you take seriously must be written by people who have done what they are writing about. Fiction won't help you succeed in business.

If you could read and relate to this chapter, you've got what it takes to be a tycoon.

Chapter 9

BUYING DISTRESS PROPERTY

D istress property is an often overlooked part of every property market; always has been, always will be. The banks, trust companies, public trustee, public administrator, auction houses, and even the tax people of most communities, almost always have a large number of foreclosures or distress property for sale. The recession has brought much attention to this type of property, but don't be fooled into thinking that it created these incredible deals or that when it goes so will they. The fact of the matter is that distress property is produced through a myriad of events that are quite simply just a part of everyday life – divorce, death, unemployment, health problems, etc. Unless something truly astounding happens in the next few years, people will continue to get divorced, to die, to lose their jobs and to fall into bad health, producing a continuous stream of distress property. These situations are definitely unfortunate, but as tycoons we help no-one by sitting around sobbing into our hankies at the 'cruel irony' of it all. However, we do help people by buying this property, repairing it when necessary and making it ready as a place in which another person can live a happy productive life.

Distress property is known by many different names, such as probates, conservatorships, partition suits, foreclosures, tax sales, HUDs, FHAs and REOs. The auctions at which it is sold are referred to varyingly as Trustee's Sales, Sheriff's Sales, Judicial Sales, Bankruptcy Sales and just plain old Property Auctions. The reasons behind these differences in nomenclature are more technical than practical in nature, but basically involve either a different finance structure for the property or a different lending institution. To make things easy, just understand that distress property is property that has been repossessed and will be sold to the highest bidder at auction. For now, don't let this multitude of titles and formalities confuse you. No matter what it's called, the bottom line for distress property is the same; property at 20 to 50 per cent below market value.

Undoubtedly, the recession has added a great deal to this already lucrative area. It is estimated that in the UK alone, 1.4 million people are in negative equity, where their property is no longer worth the loan secured against it. There are also between 200,000 to 300,000 houses in the UK on the market waiting to be sold, and an unknown but large number of borrowers have fallen behind in their payments. If this all spells gloom rather than opportunity for you, you're reading the wrong report. Put it down now (no sense in wasting any more time) and go plead with the boss for a raise. Maybe you'll even get one!

If, on the other hand, opportunity bells are ringing so loud in your head you can hardly concentrate, this chapter is for you. The time has never been better for the prospective property tycoon. It's a buyer's market! Needless to say, property will continue to come up for auction, producing incredible bargains. Also, as a tycoon who understands the market and scoops up deals at 20 to 50 per cent below market value, you have little worry of falling into the problems of negative equity. In fact, the minute you buy a property using my suggested techniques, you create a substantial amount of positive equity, i.e. you could almost immediately sell your property for more than you paid for it.

How To Find Out About Distress Property

Discovering the location and availability of property to be sold at auction is even easier than finding bargains through the classified ads in your Sunday newspaper. While squinting at the small type in search of the perfect deal, let your eyes relax a bit and wander across the page to the large display ad under the section titled, 'Auctions'. Phone these people, and they'll send you a catalogue.

Large auction houses, such as Allsop & Co or Stickley & Kent in England, auction off property that has been repossessed by various lending institutions. About a month before each regularly scheduled auction, they distribute full colour catalogues, often offering in excess of 200 properties. Such auctions are frequently advertised in the major Sunday newspapers for your community. It is also a good idea to get on the mailing lists of these companies. Some charge a small fee, but it's well worth it for all the great deals they'll pass your way.

There are several other ways that you can learn about distress property. Most county courts have bulletin boards where all Probate Estates (the estate of a deceased person who did not leave a will) and Trustee's Sales or Sheriff's Sales (foreclosures) must, by law, be posted. They must also be advertised in a newspaper of 'general circulation'.

In every community, there is an obscure legal paper that almost nobody reads. It will have a name like the Law Bulletin or Legal Advertiser. In the UK, try the *Estates Times* and *Estates Gazette*. These magazines and newspapers are the favoured places for publishing notices of distress sales, often advertising commercial auctions where property can be acquired at 'wholesale' prices. Check the postings and read the newspapers containing legal notices for those pertaining to property. If you call the law firm mentioned in an ad or posted notice, you will get details or the appraised value, location and problems for the properties up for auction.

Real Estate Owned (REOs)

REOs are another little-known area with massive earning potential. REO stands for Real Estate Owned, meaning property owned by a lending institution. An REO is a property that has been repossessed and put up for auction. At the auction, it failed to reach the minimum required bid or published minimum reserve. (I'll explain more about this later in the chapter.) When this happens, the property is not sold, but is withdrawn from the auction. Hence, the lending institution ends up the proud owner of this property desired by no-one else. These lending institutions are usually banks, but can be any business or individual that offered a loan for a property which has since been repossessed.

Naturally, these properties can usually be purchased for only a fraction of their value. If you're at an auction and the property that you desire is withdrawn because it could not generate the minimum bid, you're in a wonderful position. You are guaranteed that the property will be yours for at least that minimum bid, probably for even less.

In addition to finding out about REOs through attending auctions, you can contact banks and lending institutions directly. Due to the recession, most banks are carrying many REOs on their books. Remember, though, don't get too cocky and become convinced that you're doing the bank a favour by taking a much-neglected property off their hands. The bank is in business to make money and will only let the property go if they think the price you're offering is reasonable. Individuals, however, who end up in possession of an REO may indeed consider ridiculously low offers, particularly if they live out of town. Again, it's just a matter of getting in there and doing some homework.

HUD, FHA And VA Auctions And Foreclosures

Another category of auctions will not be posted in the county courthouse. In the US, you can get on the federal government's mailing list or find out what sort of deals they have by keeping in touch with the local office of the federal government's department of Housing and Urban Development (HUD), the Federal Housing Administration (FHA), Veterans Administration (VA) and your local housing authority. These institutions all lend money to qualified applicants and thus end up with repossessions and foreclosures like any other lending institution. Who knows, you might even qualify for one of their spiffy low-interest loans.

In every Western country, there are myriads of loan programmes, subsidies, gimmicks and give-aways subsidised by the taxpayer. To catch the gravy train and get your share, just call up the local numbers listed in the phone book or ask at your local library. It would take another book of several volumes to go through all the government and estate programmes. For our purposes, I just want to make sure you are aware that if you have a low income, have a handicapped child or elderly person to support or are blind, deprived or disadvantaged in any way, the government probably has a special give-away programme just for you.

For ordinary, unhandicapped folks, there are plenty of opportunities too. For instance, when a US government loan is foreclosed, the home or apartment building in question is often refurbished at government expense, to high FHA standards, before it is put up for resale. The deal to the buyer often involves little or no money-down with goodies like a 40-year, three per cent loan. The government always pays a commission to any broker who represents the buyer, even if it's a no-money-down deal. If the broker is your wife or business partner, you can see that the family could close a deal and be net cash ahead! The main job of all governments is to take away money from other people (in taxes) and drop it in your lap. All you need do is simply take the time to study how they 'redistribute wealth' and then proceed to put yourself on the receiving end.

Preparing For The Auction Day

The first thing to do is to sit down and select the properties up for auction in which you are most interested. Obviously, you will want to go and inspect these properties. In most cases, the telephone number of the estate agent or broker representing the property is provided, and you can arrange a viewing time through them.

In some cases, group viewing times are set in advance to accommodate large numbers of people over the short period of time leading up to the auction. These provide an excellent opportunity for you to assess how much competition is likely at the auction. They may even offer you the chance to meet up and form partnerships with other budding tycoons. For those of you still fulfilling the 'One Hundred House Rule', you can easily reach that number through these set times with no need to worry about being eternally branded a time-waster. Although remember, you never hurt anyone by asking a stupid question, but you can fall prey to enormous mistakes or errors in judgement by neglecting to ask those very same 'stupid' questions.

In some rare cases it is not possible to actually gain access to the property. I would suggest that you avoid bidding on these properties while you're just starting out. Wait until you have a little experience and full knowledge of the prevailing market under your belt.

Also, it is a good idea to attend a few auctions during this preparatory stage simply to get a feel for how they operate. Then, when you are ready to bid on your first property, it's unlikely that you'll encounter any surprises.

Determining What To Bid

Deciding what to bid is probably the easiest part of buying property at auction. It's simple; bid as little as you have to. Most property for auction will have an established minimum bid or published minimum reserve. If you were not sent a list of these prices with the auction catalogue, contact the auctioneer. These prices have been established as the minimum price at which the property will be sold at auction. If this amount is not reached, the property will be withdrawn and fall into the hands of whoever or whatever repossessed it.

Some auction houses provide what are known as guide prices. These are a slight variation of the minimum bid in that two figures are provided, a top and a bottom price. The bottom price is the published minimum reserve. The top price is, well, actually nothing. It is, however, expected that the property will sell somewhere in between the two prices, but as you will see after attending just one auction, anything can happen and there are no guarantees.

Determining the top amount at which you should stop bidding and let the property go to someone else is also more or less straightforward. As you are going through the extra hassle of buying a property at auction and the risks it involves, never bid more than 80 per cent of the market value of the property. If at the auction, Iwannabe Homeowner and Notifaycan Helpit dive into a feeding frenzy most piranhas would shy away from, pushing the price up to 120 per cent of its market value, pull out! It's better to let the happy homeowner have it. Tycoons can't compete with Iwannabea Homeowners. The motivation is completely different. You want a nice sound investment, they want a warm cosy place to live.

Of course, the auction house loves such a feeding frenzy. That's how they make money. You can be sure that the auctioneer will do whatever possible to create just such a situation. Don't be sucked in; set your price and stick with it. Remember, homework is never wasted and whatever time and effort you put into assessing this one property will undoubtedly bear fruit in future deals even if things don't work out this time around.

Determining Market Value

Fine, you might think, so I'm not supposed to bid more than 80 per cent of market value. That's no problem. The problem is, what on earth is market value and, more importantly, how does little old me go about discovering it?

Well, the first step is obviously to follow the 'One Hundred House Rule'. After looking at one hundred properties, you should have developed a pretty good ability to determine what is worth what where. Some of the basic criteria that determine the value of the property are the number of rooms in total as well as the number of bathrooms and bedrooms specifically. Of course, the size of the property, the size of individual rooms and never forget, location, location, location are also important. It is often helpful to break the property down into a price per square foot.

As you start looking at properties, you will probably encounter some rough rules of thumb, such as $100,000 per bedroom in Sydney or £50,000 per bedroom in London. Don't believe them! Property is such an imperfect market with much brought into consideration to determine its value. Obviously, the state of repair and the location of a property will have a massive influence on the amount it is worth. There is no way that a bedroom on the outskirts of town costs as much as one right in the heart of it all. Also remember, property sold at auction operates outside the normal market. It is not unreasonable for you to expect to pick up bargains at half the price you could turn around and sell them for.

Another good way to determine the market value of a property to be sold at auction is to look at recent comparative sales in the area. Contact local estate agents or brokers for lists of their recent sales. Remember, though, that moving two blocks in one direction or another can have a massive effect on the perceived value of a property, even if it and its neighbour are both relatively the same size and in the same state of repair. These are all factors with which your tycoon senses will quickly become accustomed.

Dealing With The Necessary Financial Enquiries

Unfortunately, no matter how wonderful you become at accurately assessing the value of property in your area, your talent will go unrecognised by your friendly banker unless you take the trouble of going to school to receive a nice little piece of paper recognising you as a qualified property surveyor or appraiser. Almost all banks will not lend money for the purchase of a property unless they receive a report from a qualified surveyor or appraiser which shows them that the property is worth more than the amount you have asked to borrow. Also, most banks are only willing to lend 90 per cent of the purchase price on property bought at auction.

Under normal circumstances, these requirements don't cause drastic problems. The cost of having a property officially valued is a standard part of the transaction and can simply be factored into the overall price of the property. The problem with buying property at auction is that after, having the property appraised and then arranging for it to be financed by your bank, you have no guarantee that the property will even end up yours at the end of the day. On the other hand, if you are the highest bidder, once the hammer falls, the property is yours, whether your bank will provide financing in the end or not. It is your responsibility to come up with the full payment of the entire purchase price within a fairly short period of time, sometimes as few as 28 days.

Hence, you are left with two options: 1) Have the property valued by a professional before the auction and pre-arrange financing on a conditional basis with your bank or 2) Wing it, trust your tycoon instincts and ability to pull everything together after the fall of the hammer. Which route you choose is entirely up to you. If you'll sleep better at night laying out the small amounts required to have the properties you're interested in surveyed, then do so. It may be helpful just to factor in the cost of these appraisals, both for the properties you buy and those you let go, as a normal part of buying property at auction. However, if you trust your instincts and are prepared to take a chance, do so. Remember, you must be prepared to possibly lose the deposit you have placed on a property (usually 10 per cent of the purchase price) if you are unable to secure financing for it in time.

I would suggest that in the beginning you pre-arrange financing before going to the auction. As you develop more experience, your instincts will become finely tuned and you'll be less likely to make a mistake. Also, by keeping bids low and avoiding the piranha bowl, you increase your chances of arranging financing easily as the amount you will need to borrow is also kept to a minimum.

Dealing With The Necessary Legal Enquiries

Before bidding on a property, you must find out its legal position. Auction catalogues not only come with glossy pictures of the lots for sale, they usually also have an equal amount of small print. Read it! Make sure you have read all of the "General Conditions of Sale" and "Special Conditions of Sale". When you buy a property at auction, you buy it 'as is'. These are small words, but they mean a tremendous amount. Make sure that there are no outstanding liens or encumbrances secured against the property. Don't be afraid to stop by the town hall or local council to make sure that the information you have been given is correct. Also, as you examine each property look closely for signs of structural damage, such as termite problems or water leaks, because once you buy, it's yours.

It is also a good idea at this time, before the auction, to establish relations with a lawyer or solicitor who can represent you when you are the successful bidder. It need not cost anything, particularly if you can convince him or her that you are the up-and-coming local tycoon. Don't forget to make use of contacts through family or friends. You may also be able to arrange to have property appraised at reduced costs, maybe even for free, through these methods. Perhaps by offering these people a 'piece of the pie', you can get the ball rolling for almost nothing. For more hints and tips on how to assemble your successful team, see the chapter, "Get Yourself Organised".

One other final preparation that you will want to make is for housing insurance. Once the hammer has fallen the property is yours, meaning that it is at your insurable risk. If there is a freak fire, perhaps one set by the irate previous owner from whom the property has been repossessed, it's your loss. By making arrangements ahead of time, the property can be insured almost as soon as the hammer falls.

Making an Offer

Now that you have done your homework and are more than prepared for the upcoming auction, you're probably content to sit back and wait for the excitement of the big day. This is the worst course of action you could possibly take. Once you have found a property, tentatively arranged financing, determined its value and from that determined the 80 per cent you are willing to bid, it's time to make an offer, just like you would on any normal property.

Unless someone else makes a bigger offer, which would be above your 80 per cent limit, the worst that can happen is that your offer will be turned down and the property will go to auction. This will happen if the auctioneer feels that there are several separate parties interested in the property and a feeding frenzy is likely to ensue. Otherwise, the auctioneer will probably let you have the property, assuming that your offer is above the published minimum reserve. You see, the auction house would much rather not have the property go up for auction at all. Why else would they spend all of that money advertising through a full colour catalogue? They want to sell the lots, if at all possible, before the auction.

This works to your benefit as well. By securing the property before you go to auction, you no longer need to worry about the uncertainty of whether you will be the successful bidder or not. If they accept your offer, it's yours. Some tycoons regularly offer less than the 80 per cent they are prepared to bid, hoping to scoop up a super-bargain. This may or may not prove to be successful, but the way I see it, picking up a property for 80 per cent of what it's worth is pretty good no matter how you look at it. There's no reason to get greedy.

Last Minute Preparations

So, the big day is finally looming. Your bid has been turned down, the property is going to auction and your palms are starting to sweat with eager anticipation. Well, don't sit back now, there's yet more homework to do. A few days before the auction, contact the auction house to make sure there have not been, and are not likely to be, any final changes to the contract of sale. Also, make sure that the lot or lots in which you are interested have not been withdrawn. Generally, once you have contacted the auction house and expressed your interest in a certain lot, they will make an effort to keep you updated on developments in its status.

Before going to the auction, you must also look into the conditions under which it operates. There are technical rules for each type of sale. Most auctions require that you pay a deposit, usually 10 per cent, before leaving the auction. A few require that the entire purchase price be paid. These payments must almost always be in the form of either a cashier's cheque, a banker's draft or good old cash. Before the auction, make the necessary arrangements for such a payment that will cover the deposit (or purchase price if you have a wealthy partner) for the maximum amount you intend to bid. You may be required to show such means before being allowed to bid.

If you are only required to pay a deposit, the closing can generally be scheduled for 30 to 60 days after your successful bid is accepted and confirmed. At that point, you will need to make the payment of the balance of the purchase price.

At the Auction

The big day is finally here. All that is left is to show up at the allotted time and hope for little competition. As you arrive, you will probably be handed an addendum or some other type of notification of last-minute alterations. A few final changes may have still come into effect. Read this information carefully! If you have any questions, make sure you clear them up before bidding. On that note, if you are unclear about anything at all concerning the lot in which you are interested, it's best not to bid.

It generally takes only about three to five minutes for each lot to be offered; so much homework for such a brief moment of glory. This is the time in which you must reap the benefits of your patience and planning. Remember to not be swept into the piranha bowl and gobbled alive. Don't be intimidated by the other bidders, they probably haven't even done a fraction of the preparatory work that you have. Set your top limit and stick with it. Don't start thinking that another $500 surely can't make that much of a difference, because before you know it $500 will be $5,000, which does make one hell of a difference. With a little luck, you'll soon be the proud owner of a fantastic investment property at the price you want it for.

If things don't work out, don't worry about it. Every tycoon experiences a number of setbacks along the road to success. Just remember that by closing only one little deal you'll be generating $10,000 to $20,000 in positive equity, never mind the steady revenue you can generate from rental income. If four of five properties pass you by before you are a successful bidder, you have still earned from $2,000 to $4,000 per lost deal on average. That's not bad for a few days work! Also, by buying property at costs significantly below market value, you ensure your eventual success by not falling into the easy trap of overbidding.

A Few Final Thoughts

At some auctions it is possible to bid by proxy, meaning that you need not be there in person. Under this set-up, you deliver your sealed maximum bid with the required deposit to the auctioneer before the auction. Of course, this method of operation puts you at a serious disadvantage in comparison to your competition. If at all possible, go to the auction in person. The only reasonable excuse that I can think of for not actually attending is if you're tied up at another auction. Nonetheless, if you can't 'pull a sickie' at the office, this may be your only option.

As mentioned earlier, a few properties will fail to reach their published minimum reserve. Pay special attention to these deals, you'll probably be able to scoop them up at super-prices.

If the lot you are interested in is withdrawn, contact the people in charge immediately. State your interest in it and offer the smallest amount you think it will take to make the property yours. In such cases (often occurring in a half-finished construction project or vandalised building) it may even be possible to negotiate either an option or a large mortgage to be carried back by the seller. Of course, if you were the final bidder for the property during its three minutes of glory, you will at least be written up as the most interested party, even if your final bid was below the minimum-required bid.

As a final word of caution, beware the redemption period. This is an archaic law that allows the previous owner the right to buy back his or her repossessed property. This law varies from country to country and state to state, not even existing in many, so look into it before losing any sleep. However, in some cases, these previous owners are allowed the right to buy back their property for as much as one year after the auction. Considering that the previous owner must pay cash plus interest on your investment, it is highly unlikely that much harm can be done, otherwise why would the property be repossessed in the first place. Still, just thought I'd warn you.

Sam The Postman

One potential tycoon who read this chapter and decided he was going to make his fortune through distress property was a friend of mine in London. So as not to embarrass him, let's call him Sam, not his real name of course. Sam was the sort of guy who never seemed to do incredibly well in life. He left school early, hating the endless monotony of yet another useless geometry lesson. After travelling Europe for a while on a backpacker's budget, he decided that it was time for him to settle down, take life seriously and hopefully, somewhere along the line, earn some decent money. That's when he encountered my reports.

The idea to earn some 'decent' money quickly transformed into that of stacking up "a nice pile so I can retire early". Sam, unlike many people today, has no worries about occupying his time even if he retires at the early age of 30. As he sees things, the world has more than enough beaches and pretty young things to keep him occupied well into his late 80s.

Sam is 26 now, and as you may have already guessed from my clever heading for this section, he is currently employed by Her Majesty's Royal Mail Service, or to put it more bluntly, the Post Office in good old England. Sam doesn't mind his work too much. While delivering the mail, he at least gets out in the fresh air and doesn't have to worry about an irate boss breathing down his neck. The Queen, actually, only rarely checks in to see if everything is going all right.

The other benefit of his work is that Sam gets to look at property all day, every day. As a result of his daily rounds, he has become finely attuned with what's happening where. Within his district, he knows what's for sale, what the asking prices are, what has sold and what the prices are that were finally agreed upon; an excellent variation of the 'One Hundred House

Rule', or flats as it may be in this case. He is also friendly with many of the elderly people in his district and hopes that some day these important contacts will help him put together a valuable deal.

The major problem with his work is a common gripe – the pay. Sam makes a meagre £11,000 ($16,000) a year. The banks in England, being the cooperative folk that they are, are willing to lend him up to three times his annual salary if he puts up a 10 per cent deposit. That gives Sam the capacity to borrow £33,000, not an incredible amount when one considers that a standard one-bedroom flat in London sells for a minimum of £50,000. Alas, as Sam was eager to get into the property game, and knew that it would be impossible for him to quickly come up with the £17,000 difference between the cost of a small flat and the amount he could borrow, Sam started to look into distress property.

The first few deals that he pursued, four to be exact, turned up nothing. Sam carefully and diligently did all of the required homework, got his hopes and expectations up and entertained the thoughts of fortunes rolling in to only end up leaving each auction disappointed.

However, Sam did what every good tycoon must. He stuck at it, hoping that sooner or later things would work out. He refused to give in and bid an excessive amount for one of these properties. He knew that if he were to do so, he would never be able to get the figures right and make money out of his property. He tried not to think about the fact that he had already put up in excess of £1,000 in surveyor's fees and had nothing to show for it. He maintained his confidence that it would all work out in the end.

For his fifth potential distress property, Sam located a three-bedroom ex-council flat in Battersea, just south of the River Thames. It was an enormous flat spread across two floors with large, spacious rooms. In addition, the place was in good repair. Its only problem was its location. It was stuck in the middle of a large sort of Orwellian block of flats, one the local council had put up in the 60s. Also, the public transport train (or tube as its called in London) ran by the front windows every so often. Sam, however, was not deterred because the truly amazing thing about this flat was its published minimum reserve, a staggeringly low £18,000. Apparently, the flat had been in search of a new owner for quite some time.

Sam decided to go ahead and have the property surveyed. (He always has been and still is the cautious type.) The value came back at £35,000; very cheap for a three-bedroom flat in London, but still twice the price of the minimum bid. Using this figure as a guide, Sam calculated his top bid to be £28,800, 80 per cent of £35,000. This left plenty of leg room for him between his top bid and the minimum acceptable bid. Hopes high again, Sam went ahead and offered £28,000 for the property. His offer was quickly and unequivocally turned down, it seems that the auction house was under the impression that a piranha bowl was brewing for Sam's favoured lot.

Still not deterred, Sam went to the auction. The three minutes went by so quickly that at the end of it Sam was slightly stunned to realise that he was the top bidder, better still he had bid only £26,500, surprisingly £1,500 less than what he had offered two weeks earlier. The paperwork was all quickly taken care of and financing easily arranged. Sam was only asking to borrow £23,850 (the purchase price of £26,500 minus his deposit of £2,650) which was well within his limit of £33,000. In the end, Sam's payments came to a meagre £190 a month for a 20 year loan at eight per cent interest. The bank was not willing to give Sam a 30 year loan for "such a small amount".

Two weeks later Sam moved in. A further £1,000 for new carpets, some furniture and a washing machine, combined with much effort and work on Sam's part, got the flat up and running in another couple of weeks. Sam now lives in the smallest bedroom, understanding that the extra space would only make him buy extra stuff with which to fill it. He rents out the other two bedrooms for £40 per week each, which works out to £170 per calendar month per room. Hence, at the end of the month Sam is now £150 ahead (£340 rent for the two rooms minus his £190 mortgage payment). However, this positive cash flow is not the real benefit that Sam got from buying his new property. Remember that by being persistent and refusing not to overspend, Sam bought his flat for less than 80 per cent of its market value. Sam paid only £26,500 for a flat worth £35,000. He has now acquired £8,500 worth of positive equity, all of that in the middle of the recession. If he were to sell again tomorrow, he would come out far ahead of the amount he spent on his deposit and surveyor fees. Anyway, Sam has no intentions to sell at the moment. He's getting on well with his roommates and finds the daily trains rolling by outside his window to be rather amusing. He plans to wait until property prices push up slightly, then he'll sell and pull out somewhere between £10,000 and £15,000.

For now, Sam is concentrating on finding his second distress property. He is confident that this time around, won't take him as long. Sam is able to live quite comfortably on the revenue generated from his flat alone. (He never did recover from the beans and toast diet forced on him during his backpacking days). As a result, it will take him no time to save the necessary money to acquire his second property. He also looks great on paper with all of that positive equity and anticipates little problem in arranging further financing. In a few years, he's confident that he will have graduated into the world of champagne and caviar, sitting on a nice beach somewhere, of course.

Generating The Necessary Cash

The major problem with distress property is that it is generally impossible to get a seller to help with the financing by carrying a back loan for part of the purchase price. Usually there is no room for creative finance or strange barter offers in negotiations with trustees or estate administrators. They merely put property up for the best all-cash bid in what amounts to a private auction. The nature of distress property is that the seller needs all cash in order to pay his or her own debts or to make distribution to heirs. Thus, until you have a line of unsecured credit, it is necessary to bid real money to take advantage of the generally lower than market prices of distress property.

Those of you particularly adept at mathematics will realise that although Sam's flat was a super-bargain, it did not come cheap. Sam spent approximately £4,500 on his deposit, surveyor's fees and repair costs. Granted, he doubled that amount (with his £8,500 worth of equity) the minute the papers were transferred. Also, purely as an investment, this amount is quite small when one considers that it bought Sam room and board for a lifetime, if he were to stay in his flat. Still, this sort of investment is more than the average Joe tends to have lying around. Sam managed to save it gradually over a six-month period, thanks to both the help of a few surprise gifts and his beans and toast diet. Although leading a frugal lifestyle is the best way to get started, there are other ways to generate the needed cash.

For example, most banks in the US are just itching to give away their credit cards, particularly if you are enrolled as a full-time student at a university. It may be worthwhile 'signing on' with a local community college just to pick up the goodies. Once you have the credit cards, ask the issuing banks to send you cheques that can be written against them. It's then just a matter of piling the money up in your bank account. Although the interest rates are incredibly high for these so-called cash advances, it is an easy way to raise money on a speedy basis. A friend graduating from college recently stacked up $80,000 of such unsecured credit.

Another way of raising the necessary start-up costs is simply to ask for it. It's amazing the results that can be generated from a classified ad with a catchy title, such as, "Cash Required Urgently for Lucrative Business Prospects" or more simply, "Money Wanted".

If you are a homeowner, look into the possibility of taking out a home improvement loan. Banks rarely check to see if the money is actually used for what you say it will be. Partnerships, perhaps with the vendors you will be using to assess or repair your properties, can also prove to be most fruitful. For more ideas on the lucrative side of teaming up, see the chapter "Partnerships Can Make You Rich".

If the company for which you work has a credit union, look into its lending facilities. You may even be able to strike up some sort of deal with your boss, if he or she is the understanding tycoon type. You will also want to look into the possibility of borrowing against your life insurance or pension, if you have such generally useless perks. If you have a decent job, you may also be able to borrow the start-up costs from one of a myriad of small finance companies. Lending money is big business, and there is plenty available for you if you can convince them (the lenders) that you are dependable and will pay the money back, with interest of course.

There are plenty of opportunities to generate the small amounts of money needed to start off in the distress property game. You merely need to be creative. Of course, don't forget the easiest and, perhaps, the best source of revenue – your parents, family and friends. Such simple contacts have started off many a tycoon.

Cheap Is Cheap

When you get property cheap, it can be very cheap indeed! At a delinquent property tax auction, I once bought a half acre in fashionable San Anselmo, California, for $10. At the time, similar-sized lots were selling for $30,000! Why was this one so cheap? For starters it was landlocked, meaning there was no access to it from the road. No road could be built because most of the surrounding properties had homes on them. All the adjacent owners refused to give an easement to pass over their land. Equally significant, at least half of my lot was under a creek in a community that did not permit construction on underwater lots. Other people at the auction though it was worthless, so I bid the minimum of $10. For such a small amount, I figured, how wrong could I go?

I didn't go too far wrong, because two years later I sold that lot for $10,000. I did it by picking up an adjacent parcel with a home on it, at a fair price. Now I had access. Combining two sub-standard parcels, I created one excellent creek-side apartment building site. The two sites together had proper square footage and enough above-water land to get a multi-unit building permit.

Moral to this story: If you watch all the published and posted legal notices plus auction announcements and check them out carefully, all sorts of opportunities will come your way.

Auctions, foreclosure sales and public land dispositions produce all sorts or weird slivers of land that nobody seems to be interested in. They can be picked up for peanuts. I generally bid the minimum of about 10 bucks on all of them, figuring that if worse comes to worse, I can grow a weed garden or use them in a trade (see the chapter "No Money Down Deals"). What usually happens is that the owner of an adjacent property will pay me at least one-hundred times my 10-buck investment. In the story I just told you, I made a return of one thousand times my investment. In the property business that sort of thing happens every day. Just keep your eyes and ears open, read the notices, go to the auctions and bid. Think creatively about what you can do with these properties. The money will start rolling in faster than you can count.

Chapter 10

BUYING PROPERTY
WITHOUT MONEY

In addition to buying property inexpensively, such as at auction, another way to quickly become the leader of your own little property empire is to acquire property for little to no money down. In a no-money-down deal, you acquire a property without putting up any money of your own. In other words, you get something for nothing; well not exactly nothing because such arrangements do require a lot of work on your part. To rephrase, you get something for nothing, but time, and as the Irish say, the man who made time made plenty of it.

Now, concerning the no-money-down deal, some property agents will say, "I've been in the business 20 years and I have never seen a deal like the one you want." The unfortunate fact is that most estate agents would not know how to make a no-money-down deal if it fell on them. Agents seldom know how to create anything but very standard financing arrangements, i.e. 10 per cent down payment and 90 per cent financing. In my opinion, most agents are just not very creative at their trade and, hence, not a great deal of help. It is fair to estimate that in any locality 20 per cent of the estate agents earn 80 per cent of the commissions. The problem is that until you've become a serious buyer, the best ones, those estate agents who have all the good deals and could arrange no-money-down purchases, won't want anything to do with you.

So what is a budding tycoon to do in the meantime? Why would a seller ever want to accept a no-money-down deal? I'll tell you why. Because what is a no-money-down deal to you as a buyer will not necessarily be a no-money-received deal to the seller. Say a seller owns a $100,000 business or property with no mortgage or other encumbrances secured against it. If you bought it from him subject to obtaining a 90 per cent first loan, then he gets $90,000 cash when the deal closes (from the new financing). If you owe him $10,000 that's only a small per cent of the total purchase price.

You, as a buyer, might make a no-money-down deal if a second mortgage lender agreed to lend the $10,000 down payment. Thus, what is a no-money-down deal to you may yield the seller 100 per cent of his sales price in cash. Many sellers, particularly older people, can even be convinced to carry back interest-yielding mortgages.

Typical estate agents do not like no-money-down deals. They expect their commission in cash. Look at a $100,000 deal. A broker wants his commission when the deal closes. Naturally, the extra cash for his three to six per cent commission has to be generated somewhere, and better indirectly from you than directly from the seller, who he is supposedly making money for. So, usually it's harder to make a no-money-down deal with a hungry agent in the picture than if you are dealing directly with the seller.

For the moment, assume that you have found a good property and a willing seller (a little old lady with a nice four-plex in a neighbourhood you have decided is convenient and desirable). You negotiate a price with her of $100,000. The terms are no money down, including a 90 per cent bank loan with the seller carrying the remaining at 10 per cent interest for 10 years. With current worldwide interest rates plunging below six per cent, 10 per cent is better than most banks could do with her savings, meaning that she'll make more from you than she would from simple bank deposits.

Sometimes a seller or lender will give you the argument that if you don't have any money in a deal, you are likely to walk away if times get tough. Supposedly, you have nothing to lose. It may take a little convincing to overcome that fear on the part of the seller. You have to show the seller, the little old lady in your case, that perhaps you have had the same job for quite a long time and you are a steady person, a family man. Whatever works! After 20 visits, a few small gifts and a lot of conversation, hopefully you can convince the seller that your motive is not to get her property and then walk away from it, but rather to keep it and improve it. Of course, that truly should be your motive. You must convince the seller you will provide the dependable monthly cheques she needs.

Of course, if you do not pay the $10,000 debt back, she can always take back her property and sell it to someone else. That is what a second mortgage is all about. It is not as if the seller is getting nothing. She is getting $90,000 cash from the proceeds of the first mortgage and an additional $10,000 from you. The note itself has a cash value and could be resold at a discount by the seller. Discounts on second mortgages typically range from 20 to 40 per cent of the face value. So there's only a limited risk in making a no-money-down deal with you. Still you always have to convince sellers and lenders that you are reliable.

You mean that with this book and nothing else
I could own that building, for no money down?

Bill Hill: **Yes! Yes! Yes!**

Now let's analyse a typical deal. We'll take a $100,000 four-plex and assume the fair rents are $300 a month on each of the four units that you just bought. An income of $300 for four units is a total of $1,200 per month. 80 times that is $96,000. So $100,000 fits my rule of thumb as the fair market value of that particular property. I told you that the gross rents per month for all the units combined is $1,200. If you multiply that times 12, you will get an annual gross rental income of $14,000 per year. Six and a half times the annual gross is about $99,000.

Your payments on the first mortgage would be at least $10,000 per year. Your taxes in that deal would probably be under $2,000 while your upkeep and maintenance would be another $2,000 a year. Naturally, these figures must be massaged to fit the facts of your particular market. A rule of thumb in Argentina may not be appropriate for the London market.

Property taxes in most Western countries are usually just about 10 per cent of your gross rent. In France, it will be a lot less. In Monaco or Andorra, there are no property taxes and no taxes on rental income. Naturally, real estate prices will be higher. Back to our example. Other expenses in round numbers will be about 20 per cent depending on the age and condition of the building. The rest of the rental income will go to the amortisation of the loan. That figure, of course, will be different in every case depending on what arrangement you made for financing. But in the case we are talking about, the loan amortisation or mortgage payments would be over $10,000 per year. The expenses and taxes altogether would be about $4,000 a year, totalling $14,000. With a gross rental income of $14,000, the net cash flow would be only $400 per year. But remember, this was a no-money-down deal.

Seeing this small figure, you might ask, "What's so terrific about spending a lot of time negotiating a deal, running the property, putting out a lot of work and effort, improving the property and collecting rent?" Maybe if you are very lucky and have no vacancies or major repairs you will take out $400 a year. You say to yourself, "I didn't put up any money but what's so terrific? $400 a year? That's peanuts. How is that kind of deal ever going to get me financially independent? I can see that it might possibly make me a millionaire in 3000 years – but what's with this two years Hill talks about?" Well, the cash flow in property, so long as you break even, is the least important consideration. Let's talk about what's really important. How do you make money?

The main benefit of buying real estate is not the cash flow. (Cash flow is what you have left from your rents after you pay the mortgage, taxes and operating expense.) The main benefit you are going to reap from owning property is the price appreciation resulting from inflation. We talked previously about the negative effects of a five per cent inflation rate on the worker, saver or rich person with money in the bank. The same five per cent decline in value of money or a wage-slave's purchasing power will make the buildings that you bought for $100,000 worth at least $5,000 more paper money a year later. The real value of the property in terms of chickens or gold coins may be the same – but because of your high indebtedness you make out like a bandit. When you bought a building for no money down in year one, in year two with five per cent inflation you would be able to sell that building for a $5,000 cash profit. Since that $5,000 would be taxable, you'd no doubt prefer to refinance the property and pull out $5,000 in tax-free cash by borrowing, yet keeping the property.

Let's consider the tax-free borrowing power that will be yours once you own property. You bought a $100,000 duplex a few years back. It's gone up in value to $120,000 just as a result of inflation. It was a very average deal. Nothing special. You did no work, made no physical improvements. Because it has gone up in monetary value from $100,000 to $120,000, you will be able to borrow around $15,000 more than your original loan against the property. That manoeuvre is called refinancing.

How does refinancing work? Once you borrow money using property you own as security, that bank isn't concerned with what you do with it. You can spend it on a lover or give it to the Red Cross. You can fly around the world, buy yourself a yacht or do whatever turns you on. Refinancing proceeds are like disposable income because you can spend the money any way you want. But because it is borrowed, most tax authorities do not consider it taxable income. So one of the best things about property is that it gives you more and more borrowing power as the years pass.

The next logical question is, if you borrow money, don't you have to pay it back? The answer is you don't have to pay it back because your tenants will pay it back. What's more, under your expert management and continuous upgrading, rents can (hopefully) be increased at the rate of 10 to 20 per cent a year above local inflation rates. Inflation will, in a few years time, make your loan payments insignificant.

The next thing to consider is your reward for creativity, good management, initiative, and skilful negotiating. This is even more important when the investment property is not just a standard apartment or house, but is a hotel, business or something that can be made to produce a much greater cash flow because of your input. A hotel, restaurant or service-oriented business always succeeds or fails because of your input. A hotel, restaurant or service-oriented business always succeeds or fails depending on the personality, taste or skills of the owner. Many times, a property you buy will be run-down and painted an ugly colour. You may choose to paint it with super-bright graphics. Or you can give it charm by mere cleaning, adding geraniums, window boxes and bright ornamental shutters. Cosmetic improvements, tastefully executed, can make your property worth infinitely more than it was when you bought it. Then too, the fact that you looked at considerable amounts of property before you committed yourself to any particular one deal means that you probably bought right, or below market value. If you also negotiated hard and received good financing terms, these efforts alone will make your property work more. Most buyers do not expect to get a no-money-down deal. Thus, if you did get 100 per cent financing, other buyers will beat your door down to take the deal off your hands for a premium or profit to you above the loans. If you did not get better than average terms, you should have been able to negotiate the seller down to a price of at least 10 per cent below market value.

As you can see, the real benefit on our $100,000 deal is not the pitiful $400 cash flow you might have available to spend, but the invisible benefits:

Creativity and Management – The reward you have earned by carefully improving your property and managing it well. Possible resulting improvement in value on your first property may well be $10,000.

Initiative and Negotiation – Property is an 'imperfect market' say the economists. As a result, if you search carefully and negotiate hard, it is to be expected that properties you acquire will be bargains worth $10,000 more on the open market than what you paid.

Inflationary Price Increase – In a highly leveraged property deal, because of the decline in the purchasing power of any paper currency, the fixed-debt amotisation payments become less of a burden because they are made with upward rising rents. The underlying market values of income properties increase at something more than the inflation rate. Assumed one-year gain on first deal may be as much as $10,000.

Total up these three factors and you will see a possible increase in your net worth, only one year after your very first deal, of $30,000! While this figure is arbitrary, it represents a composite, and a very conservative composite at that, of typical results. Total idiots, people who can't chew gum and drive a car at the same time, have achieved similar results over and over again.

Working With Options

Another type of no-money-down deal involves the use of an option. People don't tend to think of options as a way of getting property for no money down, but it certainly is a way of doing just that. Using options to get control of property is one of the least risky and most profitable ways to deal in property.

An option is the right to buy a given piece of property for a set period of time, whether it be six months or five years, at a fixed price. Any item, whether it's property, a personal possession or stock, could be the subject of an option. Every option has a definite time period. It gives you the right to buy a specific property, business or 'thing' in the future for a certain time period, for a certain price, both of which are clearly stated in the contract.

You could, for instance, get control of a $100,000 property for $100 (or even $1!) and tie it up for a year. During that year, if you are able to sell the parcel to a third party for $150,000, you could make $50,000 on your investment. Results will often be that spectacular! So, options are a method of 100 per cent financing with which you should be familiar.

Let me give you another example of how to use an option to make big money. Suppose that you are about to become a tenant in a three-flat building in Yourtown. At the time that you move in, the property is worth about $70,000. In the process of negotiating with the landlord for a two-year lease, you say to the landlord, "I would like the right to buy this property during the term of the lease for the price of $70,000." The landlord may be willing to give you that right, or he may say, "No, I'd sell only for $80,000." He may charge you $1 for the option, $100 or even $1,000. Often the price of the option will be deductible from the price of the property. However, it won't be unless you provide in the contract that the amount paid for the option is to be applied against the purchase price.

In a more typical option between landlord and tenant, you, the tenant, might lease a single-family home for a period of two years at $1,000 a month rent. During these two years the landlord might agree by writing on the lease that you have the right to buy that home for $100,000. The consideration (there always has to be a consideration for any contract) is the fact that you are leasing it and paying rent. You don't really need to pay an extra $1 to the landlord to have the right to buy the property in that two-year period. But it is a good idea to always pay at least $1 extra for a separate option. That way, if you default on the lease by missing a rent payment or moving early, the option is still good.

How do you get a lease option? You simply ask for one. Tell the landlord that you would like to buy his property. Ask, "What would you sell it for?" Merely by asking any potential seller for an option, you may get one. Perhaps the seller is willing to sell to you for $40,000, but at the moment you are not able to qualify for a loan or you don't have quite enough money for a down payment. Then you ask your seller if he will give you a few months to raise the down payment or arrange a mortgage. Very often the owner of a property will be willing to give someone a six-month option in this type of situation, hoping that with time the deal will come together. The details of the option are limited only by your (and the landlord's) imagination.

In many cases where an option is negotiated, the rent charged is the fair rent, and the entire fair rent is deductible from a reasonable option price if it is exercised during the first year. That sort of option is a very good deal for the tenant. The landlord may want to raise your rent as consideration for the option. But he may also give you credit for the extra rent off the option price. You could counter by asking for a cumulative monthly credit. There's no limit to the ways of working out an option contract.

When you get an option contract from a landlord it is very important that you have it on a separate sheet of paper from the lease or rental agreement. It must be notarised and recorded with the county recorder of deeds or registrar. In the UK, it must be caution registered with the Land Registry. Why? Because recording protects you against the seller's change of heart.

Let's say you have an option to buy a property for $40,000 and during the course of the next year the landlord simply forgets about it. It slipped his mind, perhaps because he got a better offer from an outsider of maybe $50,000 and, as a result, totally forgot about your option to buy the property for $40,000. If you didn't have your option notarised and recorded, the new buyer would own the property free and clear. You might have a claim against the landlord. You would certainly have a good lawsuit, but as we said before you want to avoid lawyers. If you've had the option contract recorded, a new buyer would be on notice of your right to buy the deal and only be able to get physical control of the property by buying you out.

Now, suppose you have an option on a property at $40,000. You've been lucky. It's gone up in value to $60,000. If you are able to negotiate long-term options, this sort of price appreciation will not be as unusual as you may think, particularly if your option is held against a commercial property on which you also hold the lease. You may have had a long-term lease as well, perhaps for five years. During a three to five-year period, a price rise from $40,000 to $60,000 isn't unusual at all. Best of all, you may exercise this wonderful option to buy a $60,000 property for $40,000 even if you do not have $40,000.

At this point you have several choices. Of course, you could let the option expire, doing no good for anyone except your landlord. This course of action, in fact, would be very foolish if you are at all interested in your own financial betterment. You would not own the property and the landlord would regain full rights. (An option must be exercised before it expires!) In this case, by letting the option expire, you will lose $20,000, your potential profit.

A second, much better, alternative is to go to the seller, your landlord, and say, "Mr Seller, let's take out a loan to refinance your property. Now that it's worth $60,000 you won't have any problem getting a loan for $50,000 on it. Then I will take over the property and assume your new loan."

The seller may say, "Why should I do that? What's in it for me? You have the right to buy my property at $40,000. If you want it you can have it. But why should I borrow for you and sign a note for $50,000?"

You will have to make it worth the seller's while. You may want to offer him $5,000 extra for his property. If your seller got a $50,000 loan under these circumstances, it would be in your favour too. You could walk away with an extra $5,000 at the close. All you do is assume the seller's new loan of $50,000 and make all payments on it thereafter. Result? You bought a property worth $60,000 with $45,000 that the seller borrowed and came out $5,000 net cash ahead. To get your seller to cooperate with you, you will of course have to convince him that you are a reliable person and won't default on the newly-arranged $50,000 loan.

Another, more typical course of action available to you if you have an option on a property for significantly less than what it is worth, is to simply put up a 'for sale' sign and sell it to a third party. Perhaps you will be lucky enough to find a buyer at $60,000. Then $40,000 will go to the landlord and you will make $20,000 on the deal. All that profit is your return on the price of the option.

You may ask, "Is all this legal? It seems to good to be true." The answer is, "Yes, yes, yes." These sorts of deals are what options are all about! You do not have to own a property to sell it if you have an option on it. An option is transferable during its entire time-period. So, you could sell the property to someone else, or, more directly, you could just sell the option.

An option contract is very simple. Here's how to prepare one; just take a blank sheet of paper and title it: **Option Contract**

Or if your seller is unsophisticated and afraid of the word contract – then just call it:

Option

I, Larry Landlord, for the sum of $1 *(or other agreed sum)* **hereby sell to Tom Tenant an option to purchase my house, flat etc at 44 Blank Street, Town, County, for a full price of $40,000 from this date until January 1st, 1997.**

Terms: All cash to seller

---

*Larry Landlor*d   **Date**

Accepted, *Tom Tenant*   **Date**

Some people will tell you that, as the buyer, you don't have to sign the option contract. This is true. However, I recommend that you always do sign it. This indicates that both you and the landlord (option seller) had a 'meeting of minds', so to speak, and that you both knew exactly what you were doing. Larry Landlord, your seller on the other hand, must sign it. If he or she is married, the spouse must also sign it. The option contract might be enforceable without a spouse's signature, but it could get you into court. The most important thing about court is to avoid it at all costs. Once the contract is publicly recorded, no one else can buy the property without being on notice of your interest in it.

One of the first deals in my career involved the use of a kind of option. One of the hundred houses I looked at during my self-education period was a little summer hiker's cabin in the woods. To some, it was a 'yuck' house because the floors tilted at 10 degree angles and the heavy redwood plank walls were of a single thickness with cracks and knot-holes, admitting plenty of wind and rain. The fixtures and fittings looked as if they had been installed in about 1895. But the cottage had charm. The lot was an acre on a sunny hillside in an area which had become the setting for many a wealthy family's mountain hideaway. The average price for a little old summer cabin was $75,000.

Here was a charming little unliveable cabin for sale at an asking price of $25,000. It was liveable perhaps if your name was Thoreau, but I imagined that it would be pretty difficult to rent. I made enquiries about the property with neighbours and local estate agents or brokers. It seemed there had been a few offers near the asking price, but all were dependent on 80 per cent financing. Unfortunately, no bank or savings and loan would lend anything unless the buyer came up with architect's plans to put in a new foundation, expand the house from one tiny bedroom to a more conventional three bedrooms, put in a garage and, in the end, spend about $50,000. Since a ready-built home in the area on a less attractive site could be had for $75,000, I was told that no-one wanted to tackle a major construction project. All the paperwork of getting building permits, environmental impact reports and other red tape had apparently driven off all potential buyers. So now the house sat vacant.

As you should know by now, when a property has been on the market for a long period of time, the owner is usually amenable to 'unusual' offers that would initially have been rejected. My first step was to talk to a local lender.

"Would you lend me anything on the place if I put in a foundation, straightened up the floors, made the place liveable, and was able to sell it for $34,000?" The banker said, "Because of its unusually good location we'd go to 50 per cent." That was banker-talk meaning that he would let me have a loan of up to $17,000.

I knew I could get the place into shape for $3,000 with my lightning 'emergency repair' technique in a weekend. I knew the building inspector wouldn't catch me. No permits need to be applied for where 'emergency repairs' are made. Was a foundation and an extra bedroom an emergency repair? For a dumb, inexperienced guy like me, they were. My next step was to contact the owner. My offer, shown at the top of the next page, had a personal cheque for $300 attached.

My offer was much lower than the asking price, but it was direct and would be principal to principal. Without the usual six per cent commission, it worked out to be the same as an offer worth an additional $1,000 but made through an agent. I stressed this point to him. Furthermore, I explained to him what he already knew. The property had been on the market for six months. People who would be poor enough to want to live in and fix up a house of its nature would not have $16,000 cash. They also would not qualify for a loan. If, on the outside chance an interested buyer did qualify, the banks would, in the end, refuse to lend on his property unless the potential buyer agreed to spend a fortune on a new foundation and various other improvements. Finally, the county would never grant permission for the needed improvements unless one went to many meetings and filled out forms for a year or two.

Here is the offer agreement I proposed:

Offer to Purchase Real Estate

The undersigned, William Hill, hereby offers to purchase the house at 10 Redwood Lane, Pleasant Valley, further identified as Assessor's Parcel No. 4545, for a full price of $16,000, all cash to seller.

The sum of $300 is attached herewith and may be cashed by seller upon acceptance of this offer. Upon acceptance, possession of the property shall go to buyer in order that buyer may put in a foundation and otherwise make emergency repairs and improvements to said property in order to qualify for a bank loan which will enable him to complete the purchase within six months.

In the event that the balance is not fully paid to the seller for any reason within six months, the seller shall have the right to repossess the property, retain any improvements made by the buyer, and keep the buyer's $300 deposit.

Accepted

William Hill   **Sam Seller**

My plan was to buy the property for $16,000 with only $300 down. I would then improve it by working on it myself and spending about $3,000. I was going to get back those costs and more by taking out an $8,000 home improvement loan on the place where I already lived. After I completed the improvements, my plan was to get my promised loan of $17,000, rent the place out for $275 a month and have enough rent coming in to pay off both the $17,000 first loan on the property and the $8,000 home improvement loan on my place. Here is how the cash flow would have worked:

Cash Outflow		Cash Inflow	
$300	For down payment	Home improvement loan	$8,000
$3,000	For improvements		
$16,000	Price of house	First loan	$17,000
$1,000	Closing costs, reserve		
$20,300	Total	Total	$25,000

Yes, within six months I would end up with almost $5,000 in my pocket. The loans would all be paid back by the tenant. At the end of it all, I would own the property, be cash ahead and get tax benefits that would shelter other income.

That was the plan, but something even better was to happen as a fluke. I put up a little card inside a front window so that it could be seen from the outside. (If you post notices outside, someone is sure to pull them off.) The card said:

For information regarding
the sale or rental of this property
contact: W Hill, owner.
Phone 777-7777

Why make it hard for people who might want to make an offer you can't refuse?

Here is what happened. The old owner signed my contract on a Thursday morning. I posted the sign at about noon. At three o'clock I got a call from Helen, a property lady I had dated occasionally and knew pretty well.

"I heard you've got an option on Redwood Lane for $16,000." She made me a firm offer. "I'll take it over from you for a thousand profit. I'll give you $1,300 today for your option."

I explained to my friend Helen that I would like to deal with her, but that I had a plan for fixing up the property and hoped to sell it for around $34,000. I hoped to make a profit of more like $15,000.

She told me that I was crazy, that it wasn't worth it. Helen then got abusive. She said, "I've had my eye on the property for over six months and now you've stolen it from me." She said she was getting all set to offer $17,500 all cash to the seller, and I would be the meanest cruellest man alive if I didn't sell to her at once. Now Property Helen was no dummy. She was into house speculation two years before I was. I felt if she was willing to offer $17,500 real money in cash, I must have pulled off a coup by getting it for $16,000 on an almost no-money-down deal.

I told Helen to cut the hysterics, that I hadn't even known she was interested and that consequently I had not "stolen" her property. If she was getting all set to make an offer, she should have made the offer instead of keeping it a secret. Helen slammed the phone down and has been bad mouthing me in property circles ever since. Moral of story: You are bound to make enemies even if you're trying to be a nice guy.

In any event, as soon as Helen hung up on me, someone else called. He had seen my card on the property and had also been planning to make an offer when the owner was more desperate. He too was planning to offer $17,500. I told him that I had a firm contract to buy the place at $16,000, had received an offer of $17,300 just a few minutes earlier and had turned it down without hesitation because I hoped to sell the property for $34,000 as soon as I had it fixed up. This chap then said he'd offer $18,500, all cash. I said, "I will consider it and call you back."

An hour later, another, even higher, offer came in. I wondered why all these offers had been hiding in the woodwork. Later, when I asked, the answer was that people were timid about 'insulting the seller' by offering so much below the asking price of $25,000. However, once they heard that I had tied the property up for $16,000, they felt very good about offering me a quick profit. Thus, my advice to budding tycoons is never be afraid to make a low offer. Forget your timidity or psychological problems; just make the offer. The seller may be delighted that someone is even interested in his property at all. If he refuses, what did you lose? The same technique works for any proposition, including an invitation to come to bed. All anyone can do is say "yes" or "no". If the answer is "no", you can either walk away or make a better offer.

Getting back to our tale, the property I had bought at $16,000 was absolutely the lowest-price home in town. The next house in line, offered on the multiple listing service, was $35,000. Thus, every buyer searching for a cheap house had seen Redwood Lane, but everybody waited until my deal went through and then got interested.

I had the hottest property in town. In the next three days I got a dozen or more calls and eventually sold my contract for a $5,000 profit. The lady who bought it from me (at an effective price to her of $21,000 cash) didn't do a thing to the property. She just rented it for $200 a month. Three years later she sold it for $34,000.

As for me, I invested $300 and got back $5,300 in a few days. I had never made that much return in such a short space of time in stocks, commissions or anything. From this point, I was hooked on property dealing.

One Hundred Per Cent Financing

Another method of getting property for no money down is with 100 per cent loans. A few years ago I came across some charming old cabins in the country. They were very rustic, surrounded by redwood trees near a stream and very run-down. I had heard that the owner, a retired gentleman of about 70, was interested in selling. He had told neighbours, "I'm really tired of fixing up that place and running after tenants for rent. There's always something wrong. I'm working all my days repairing things and sick and tired of it all." I knew that on this particular property, lenders would not give a conventional loan because it consisted of run-down 60-year old cabins. Lenders and bankers don't like charm. Only tenants do.

So I went to the seller. We talked. The most important thing you, as a buyer, should always do is quickly find out what the seller wants. I simply asked, "What are your plans if you sell this place? What do you want to do?" Basically he wanted to move to a retirement community and have a comfortable extra income in addition to his pension. That was his real need. By telling him about my career and engaging in friendly conversations during the course of a number of visits, I won his confidence. I let him know I wasn't a flake, that I had some other property and was regular in my mortgage payments. He soon realised that I was a dependable person. He felt that if we did negotiate a deal and he carried back a mortgage loan, he could rest secure in his golden years, he could depend on my cheque coming in every month.

At first he hummed and hawed about possibly having to chase me for late payments. I countered with, "Look, I am prepared to give you post-dated cheques for two years on these mortgage payments. As you know, it's a criminal offence to pass out bum cheques, so will give you whatever payments we agree on in the form of two years worth of post-dated cheques. You will have a big stack of them and be very secure that they will be paid on time. When you get half way through your stack of cheques, I'll give you another stack of twelve monthly cheques. That way you'll always be at least a year ahead." That offer seemed to turn him on.

Then we had to negotiate price. We established that the present rents from the property were about $750 a month. (For the sake of this example, let's assume this was net, after expenses). So I said to him, "Look, wouldn't you like to get exactly what you're making now in the form of loan payments? I'll give you that $750 a month without you having to do any repairs, meaning no work, no vacancy problems, no chasing tenants for rent. In other words, you'll be getting exactly what you're getting now, without any work, for the rest of your life. That's my offer."

"Great," he said, "but for how long do I get that $750 a month?"

I said, "Look, you're 70 years old now. How does 10 years sound?"

The owner said, "I might be around in 10 years, in fact I hope to be around in 30." In the end we compromised at 20 years.

Then we checked the amortisation tables and looked for the figures $750 and 20 years.

That came out to a 71/2 per cent loan on $93,000 fully amortised or paid off over 20 years. Basically that's how we set the price. We agreed on a dollar amount of $93,000 paid off by 20 years of monthly cheques at $750. My seller got exactly what he wanted, $750 trouble-free net cash every month. I became the proud owner of a project I immediately named the Dipsea Rustique Cabins.

Why was I willing to give him exactly what he was getting in rent with the buildings in such rough shape? Because I knew that if I improved the cabins just a little, I could easily raise those rents up from $750 a month. From the very beginning, with no money down, I would have a little profit each month for myself.

Three years later, I still owned the Dipsea Cabins. By that time, I had raised the rents to $2,750 and as a result was making a $2,000 net cash flow out of a property I had bought with no money down. At the same time, I was paying off the loan I had arranged privately with the previous owner. Had I stuck with the property for another 17 years, I would have become the proud owner of the Dipsea Cabins, free and clear. And just think what the rents would have been then!

The seller was well pleased. He settled up in his wine-country retirement home, secure with a steady payment of $750 a month and reassured by my post-dated cheques. Even though he sold to me for no money down, by providing a 100 per cent loan, he couldn't have been happier. We had long since become good friends.

As mentioned, I bought the Dipsea Cabins in rough shape. During my period of ownership I built up what I call a sweat equity. In other words, I went out there personally on weekends to take care of what needed doing. I took out rotten boards. I put in some sun decks. I added ivy. In a nutshell, I took good care of the place, seeing to all needed repairs and painting. When it came time to sell, the place was in much better shape than it had been when I first stepped in.

I never did see what those rents would have become under another 17 years of my ownership and supervision. 10 years after the purchase, I put the Dipsea Cabins up for sale at $2,000,000, yes that's two million. A bargain-hunter offered me half price subject to his arranging a 100 per cent bank loan. Having become somewhat tired of property and ready to let a new tycoon get on the treadmill, I sold out for a million net to me and turned the remaining balance of my loan with the original owner over to the new buyer. That's the story of how I turned a few afternoons of gabbing into a cool million. During that same year, I sold off all my assets and became a PT. However, this is getting slightly off the beaten track as PT is a different story and, hence, in a different report. Once you've made your million, see the back pages of this report for information on how to live out this next chapter of tycoondom with minimal stress and hassle.

Now, going back to those original purchase negotiations, supposing the same seller liked everything I proposed but said, "Bill, I just have to get some cash out of the closing. Can't you come up with some cash? I would like to get at least $40,000 up front to buy my new retirement home free and clear." If I had a fairly good credit standing, I could have gone to the bank with the seller, co-signed on his loan and probably could have arranged for him to borrow $40,000 on a first loan. He would then have got his cash. I would have made the payments. Then I'd have made arrangements with the seller to give me a $60,000 second loan. So I would still have got the net effect of a no-money-down deal, except that I would have then owed one loan payment each month to a bank and one loan payment to the seller. That's how to deal with this type of situation, when the seller wants money up front.

Arranging For Seller Financing

Here is another variation. Let's assume your credit is bad. Until now you have been a slow payer or a nonpayer. You don't have a good reputation and lenders would consider you a bad risk. (Incidentally, change your ways. If you want to make it as a property wheeler-dealer you must develop a good reputation for meeting your obligations.) Here's a little gimmick you can use to get the seller the cash he wants. I could have said, "Before we make the deal, Mr Seller, you get the property refinanced." In other words, get the seller to go to a banker, preferably one he has a relationship with, and get whatever loan they will give. Here, we're talking about a $93,000 property. Even when money is tight and things aren't so good, you can always get a 20 per cent loan or a 30 to 40 per cent loan. It's the 80 to 90 per cent loan that you don't get when money is tight or the property is run-down.

So the seller could have gone to his friendly bank to say he wanted some cash just before he sold to you. He could then have refinanced the property using his credit and not yours. In that case you might want to be a co-signer. But if your credit is really bad, you don't want the bank to even know your name. You could then take over the property from the seller on a contract of sale. With a contract of sale, which I will talk more about later, the seller retains legal title. In every other way it is a sale. You collect rents and you take all the deductions.

The secret of 100 per cent financing or 120 per cent financing is finding someone who will carry the loan. Most often it will be the seller who carries the entire loan, but sometimes a bank or building society will make a first loan, and the seller will carry the second. Sometimes outside lenders can be brought in. But the key to making a no-money-down deal is a 100 per cent loan.

Suppose you found an owner who has a building for which he wants $100,000. You are going to get an $80,000 loan from a lender, but you don't have $20,000 for the down payment.

You could give the owner a $20,000 second loan secured by properties you already own. Obviously this suggestion can apply only to people who already own property. In other words you can create a lien on your own home, or another property you already own, shortly before the closing. The seller would give you his cheque for $20,000. You give him an IOU or note for $20,000 secured by property you already own. Then you use his cheque as the down payment on the new place.

Everything in the world is negotiable. The seller might say something like, "I don't really want to take a second mortgage on your home as a down payment. I want $10,000 cash. I don't care how you do it." A lot of sellers just don't want to do fancy deals. You can show him that at the closing he would be getting $80,000 cash from the bank. Nonetheless, some sellers may still not want to lend you the $20,000 for the down payment.

Here's one way to get him 'all cash'. You will still need the seller's cooperation. You give the seller the second mortgage on your property, as in the last example. Only this time you raise it to $25,000. You tell him the truth – there is a big market for second mortgages. People are trading second mortgages at a discount all the time, especially in the US. All you have to do is look in the Sunday newspaper or the phone book to get a long list of people who are active in the second mortgage business. I would say, without doubt, that you could always sell a relatively short-term $25,000 note for at least $20,000. Generally a 10 or 20 per cent discount is what you'll run into in discounting second mortgage paper. So you tell your seller he'll get his $80,000 from the savings and loan and he'll get his $20,000 out of that second mortgage. I always personally guarantee that my $25,000 second mortgage can be sold at a discount to a third person.

Many small loan or finance companies will issue a written commitment to purchase the second loan, such as in our example for $20,000 cash. So, there should be no reason why you shouldn't be able to raise that $20,000 by creating a new $25,000 second mortgage on property you already own before the deal closes. As mentioned, there are plenty of people out there dealing in second mortgages. Like property or the stock market, trading in small loan paper at a discount is a very big field in itself. There are a surprising number of older people who don't want to deal with the tenant problems inherent in rental property. But they love wheeling and dealing in second mortgages at discounts. An ad in the paper might bring them in. Once you get involved in the discount loan market, you'll get familiar with it. So, you can produce a lot of interest, especially if the rate of return you offer is attractive, by putting an ad in your local newspaper which says something like, "Second mortgage, $25,000, 20 per cent interest, two years, well-secured, will sell for $20,000."

Of course it would be much more convenient and cheaper for you if your seller would take the $20,000 note at face value as the down payment. But if he is not willing to do so, you can always raise the face value of your note and discount it to a third party to come up with the $20,000 that you need.

There is another problem that can arise. The seller may say to you, "Look, I know and love the property I'm selling to you. I'm prepared to take a second loan on the property, but I don't want a second on your own home or any other property of yours that I don't know anything about." You can go along with this. It poses no problem for you and gives you a no-money-down deal. However, your lender will probably have a problem with this sort of arrangement. Often the bank or savings and loan who's making an 80 per cent first loan will not finance a no-money-down deal if they know all the details. They seem to feel that people who don't have anything invested will walk away from deals to leave the bank holding an empty bag.

I think the lenders are dead wrong with this attitude. If I were a banker, I would rather hold a first loan in a situation where there is a second loan held by a wealthy seller. Why? Because the holder of a big second mortgage will pick up the property and make the payments on the first loan if the owner goes under and the first goes into default. If the seller doesn't keep up payments, he loses the money that is due him on the second mortgage.

In the case of the seller who wants a second mortgage on the property he is selling you, here is how to handle the deal. You issue him the note and trust deed as in our previous example. The security is property you already own. You write on it, "This trust deed is transferable at seller's option to the property on Oak Lane at any time after 30 days."

So we solved the problem of getting the $20,000 cash down payment you needed to buy the $100,000 property. You got that $20,000 by creating a note and trust deed on property you already own. As before, you have to own property already in order to make this deal. Now the seller has never seen your home, but he does know and love his own place. He's willing to take a second loan on that, but you can't give him a second loan simultaneously because the bank that's making the first loan won't let the deal go through if you do it that way. They don't usually want to make loans on no-money-down deals. You start out instead by creating a note or trust deed on your own property or home. That's legal. The bank won't object to that.

You make this deal with the seller. A month after closing, he can transfer security for the note from your home to his. That means he releases your home and has the same note secured by a trust deed on the place he's selling you. If you do that manoeuvre any time after the closing of the new property, it will work out. After the title to the house is in your name you get the lien released from your old property and placed against the new property you just bought.

A title company will show you exactly how to handle the technicalities of releasing one property and putting a loan against a second property. A good title company will always help a customer on any such paperwork problems without charge.

Keeping Transfer Of Ownership Confidential

Sometimes you may make a deal with a seller to take over a property and continue to pay his obligations. If you have what's called a 'contract of sale', the lender is allowed to call this loan in, which could be disastrous. For this or another reason, you may simply not want the lender to know that you have sold or acquired a property or are subleasing a rent-controlled property. You may also want to keep the transfer of ownership confidential so that a 'less qualified' buyer can step in and take over payments on a favourable loan. This way the previous owner can relinquish his management duties, move away and take what amounts to a down payment from a person with a 'black' income, for instance.

The buyer is someone who can probably keep up on the payments, but can't qualify from the lender's point of view as his tax returns and employment income 'on paper' are insufficient. This sort of anonymous arrangement is legal in the US, but may or may not be in your country. Look into the particulars of local legislation before proceeding. Anyway, here's how to do it:

Suppose the lender or owner is ABC Bank. You go along with Sam Seller to a different bank and you, Bob Buyer, open up a joint account with Sam Seller at the XYZ bank. You tell ABC to automatically withdraw all mortgage payments from that XYZ account. Then, all you, Bob Buyer, have to do is make regular payments into that savings account. This can also be done automatically from your account in your regular bank. The ABC bank will never know that anyone other than Sam Seller is paying the rent or loan. Clever, eh? Legal title is left in possession of the seller while equitable or beneficial title goes to the buyer. In other words, the deal should be structured so that title does not pass on public record, but possession and all the rights and duties of ownership do pass.

Of course, there are risks involved in such an arrangement. The risk to the seller is that Bob Buyer may default on the loan payments, and then the bank would come after Sam Seller who remains personally liable on the mortgage. The risk to the buyer is that Sam Seller may get into some financial problems unrelated to the property and that a judgement against Sam will become a lien on the property in front of Bob Buyer's rights. Another risk is that Sam Seller might die or become arbitrarily disagreeable and refuse, or be unable, to deed over the property after Bob has made all of the payments for many years.

Bob Buyer will eventually want to either:

1. Sell to a third party.

2. Take title for himself or a nominee company.

3. Refinance.

Sam Seller will eventually want to get his name off the mortgage so that he is no longer liable for the debt. However, if Bob Buyer defaults on the payments and Sam does have to come up with back-payments, he will want to get possession of the property back.

The way that both parties can achieve their objectives is for each to provide a 'quit claim' deed to a third party or escrow agent. This third party is usually an independent solicitor. He should be provided with detailed instructions that if Bob Buyer defaults on bank loan payments, he (Bob Buyer) will vacate the property and the property will revert to Sam Seller. The deed for the property, also held in escrow, will also go to Sam.

On the other hand, as Sam Seller's deed will automatically be recorded by the escrow agent or solicitor, the buyer will be protected if:

1. The loan is paid off.

2. The potential for a new deal to an outsider surfaces.

3. The buyer is unable to get a new loan to finance the property.

If any of the above conditions are met, the deed will go to Bob Buyer. Thus, Bob is protected against the possibility of Sam's arbitrary refusal to convey his legal title when the time comes. Also, as the property law of most jurisdictions protects one who has possession (living in or collecting rent for) of a property with an unrecorded deed, it will be difficult, if not impossible, for Sam to get a judgement against Bob or sell the property out from under him. Once again, laws vary widely from jurisdiction to jurisdiction, so check with a lawyer before proceeding with this type, or any other type, of contract. It is also a good idea to ask for a written legal opinion, as a lawyer will be more diligent in his research if he understands he will have to stand by his findings.

If the person in actual possession of the property, Bob Buyer in our example, is not protected in your jurisdiction, perhaps the deal could be structured as a 'Lease with Option to Buy'. Then, the escrow arrangements could be organised as outlined above.

Whatever happens, the point is that often a sale cannot close if both parties insist on a 100 per cent standard conveyance of title. The exact mechanics and wording of your particular contract of sale are not important. Just keep in mind that many arrangements can be made part of a creative property deal. Other possibilities could include leasing the property over a long period of time or arranging for the title to be conveyed subject to the seller keeping possession for life, or even to a third party keeping possession for life. The possibilities are endless.

You may want to consider sale-leasebacks, buy-back arrangements, loans against leaseholds, second, third, and fourth mortgages and so on. Whatever you hope to accomplish in a property deal is generally possible. A top-notch accountant or lawyer is essential. If, like me, you only rarely come across competent and responsible professionals who can help you make deals, you may want to consider taking night courses in local law or attending business schools that will cover just what you need. You may want to study just conveyancing and property law, for instance. Generally, you will quickly master what you need to know to represent yourself. No one will ever show the same degree of interest or creativity in your business problems as you will. Also, as an added bonus, the camaraderie, ideas and contacts found in a classroom situation often prove to be invaluable.

Avoid A Common Pitfall

The most usual and traditional way of getting a no-money-down deal happens to also be illegal. As it involves fraud, I strongly recommend that you refrain from using this method. Why? Because there are always legal ways to do almost anything you want.

Many professional property developers and bankers will agree to artificially inflate the price of a property so that a lending institution provides 100 per cent financing on a deal that it believes it is only financing by 80 or perhaps 90 per cent. For example, during the sale of a particular property, the buyer and seller come together and agree on a price of $80,000. The buyer will pay $80,000 to the seller, and the seller will turn over the property. However, while having agreed on a price of $80,000, they report an agreed price of $100,000 to the bank. So, on paper they draw up a phoney deal showing the price as $100,000 subject to 80 per cent financing, or an $80,000 first loan. The closing comes along. A non-existent $20,000 changes hands, and the bank lends $80,000, the actual total price of the property. As you can see, the bank has financed a 100 per cent deal, albeit unknowingly.

Things like this are done every day, but again I stress that you shouldn't jump on the bandwagon. This little manoeuvre is very simple, but it is also fraudulent. Granted, you probably wouldn't get caught on such a deal, known as 'pumping' or inflating the price, but it is possible that you could fall into trouble (loan fraud) down the line if you encountered financial difficulties and couldn't meet the required payments.

In most US states there is no liability on purchase loans on property. If things go sour, you can walk away from the deal with no personal liability, and the lenders cannot come after your other personal assets to satisfy the debt. They can only take over the property given as security for their loan. However, when there has been a fraud, they can protect against you personally. Thus, if a lender discovers that you made a fraudulent deal and got 100 per cent financing by giving him a false statement, he may try to grab your other assets or even send you to jail. Personally, I don't think the risks make it all worthwhile, particularly since it is not necessary to take any such risk in the first place. There is a way of accomplishing exactly the same result, legally.

Suppose you are negotiating for a property. The seller is asking for $100,000. You have a feeling he'll take $80,000. So you say to the seller, "Look, I'll take your property for $100,000." His eyes will undoubtedly widen. He was expecting you to offer much less. "Yes, I'm going to give you $80,000 cash but part of the deal is that I want you to buy from me my antique Wedgewood coffee set for $20,000." He says, "What are you talking about? I don't want a coffee set." Then you tell him, "I have these antique cups, an empty lot, paintings or an oriental rug." This item should be something that is of value to somebody but isn't necessarily of value to you. You tell the seller that it's part of the deal to use your antique cups as a down payment. "We will establish the price of the cups at $20,000. You want me to buy your turkey of a building for $100,000, so you've got to buy my turkey of a coffee cup set for $20,000."

The seller will think about it and perhaps realise that you are offering him the $80,000 he really wants and expects for his property. That is what lawyers call an 'arm's length deal'. If he takes it he will give you a $20,000 cheque that you hand back to him as down payment. Or you get a receipt for your coffee cup set for $20,000. Or he may give you a receipt saying he has received $20,000 outside of escrow as down payment on his property at Oak Lane. Now you go to the bank and show them the price of $100,000 and ask for an $80,000 loan. That will be legal because the price really is $100,000, even though it was negotiated at arm's length.

It just so happens that you used personal property in trade as all or part of the down payment. Your lawyer might raise an eyebrow at this, but I know that old hands in the property game do it all the time. Their favourite trading vehicle is an empty lot or perhaps some odd-shaped parcel of land they picked up for a song at a tax sale. Like a work of art, these parcels are difficult, if not impossible, to value. On your first trade deal of this type, you should confer with an experienced lawyer or agent and get an outside opinion on how to handle the paperwork. Escrow officers who have been around for a few years are always very helpful. They don't charge a fee for their advice and paperwork if you get title insurance through their office.

One Final Variation

There is yet another variation on the no-money-down theme. Actually, I picked this one up by accident. A few years back, I bought a place with the standard 20 per cent cash down, 80 per cent first loan financing. Naturally, the $20,000 had been borrowed unsecured, but that's another story. In this deal, when the seller moved out his possessions and I took over, I was shocked to discover that the floors looked like the English Channel on a windy day. That is to say they were seriously warped. The waves in the floors had been caused by annual floods, but the strategic placement of oriental rugs and furnishings by the seller had totally concealed this condition during my inspection of the place.

I wrote the seller immediately upon discovering the damage. "Dear Mr Seller, I am giving you a choice of taking back your building, El Warpo, or sending me $25,000 immediately as an allowance for repairs. I have just found out that you intentionally concealed material faults in the property including severely warped floors and a faulty drainage system which promises to flood the place each spring. If I do not hear from you in 24 hours, I will retain counsel and bring an action against you for recission of contract."

In real life, you never settle anything with one letter, but to make a long story short, eventually I got $22,000 out of the gyp-artist seller. Later, I did part of the repairs myself. I never spent anywhere near the $22,000 I received. After building a $1,000 concrete spillway to prevent future flooding, I was happy to keep the wavy floors, cover them with thick-pad carpeting and kid around with future tenants saying that these unique floors had been put in at great cost by Mr Wavy Gravy, a rock star. In any case, the net result of the deal was that I picked up over $21,000 tax free. Why was it tax free? Because recoveries of damage claims in lawsuits, or in lieu of lawsuit damages, are not taxed. Now doesn't that give you a lot of ideas?

You might have a similar situation sort of prearranged. For example, a sale is agreed upon at $100,000 but you make up a long list of expensive repairs that the seller is to take care of before the closing. You both value this work at $20,000. At the closing of the deal, guess what? The seller has not gotten around to doing the repairs he agreed to do. I can't see any legal reason why without telling the institutional lender a thing, he shouldn't simply rebate $20,000 to you. This situation is not the blatant fraud of establishing fictional contracts and a phoney sales price for the bank, while keeping the real deal in a separate secret contract. Just as in tax matters, the form in which a deal is done, its appearance so to speak, can make one transaction legal, while a second, involving only slight variations, can be labelled fraudulent. It is best, in my opinion, never to wave red flags in front of lenders. They like simple, easy-to-understand contracts and never want to wade through your side deals. You should therefore consider making some reference to repairs to be done or paid for by the seller so that the lender can't later claim he wasn't put on notice that some repairs were to be done. I would suggest something innocuous like a clause in the deposit which reads, "Seller agrees to put property into first-class shape before delivery to buyer." The private rebate agreement (the clarification of this clause) then spells out what first-class shape means, exactly what repairs are contemplated and provides that the seller is going to pay the buyer $20,000 if he fails to deliver up the property in first-class shape.

The way you can handle a no-money-down deal is limited only by your imagination. There are millions of ways of doing it since every property deal is different. Getting money back at a closing, meaning actually getting cash out of a deal at the start, is accomplished by the more aggressive use of exactly the same methods. The most important thing for you to realise is that it can be done, it is being done every day and you can do it. Get your mind working in the right direction! Soon you will control a highly-geared property or business empire having acquired it in exactly the same manner as countless other successful tycoons. Getting off your backside and overcoming inertia is all you have to do. You now have the knowledge!

Walking Away From An Unwanted Loan

Naturally, when dealing in property, it is best to avoid liability in the first place. This can be arranged sometimes through company ownership or by holding title in the name of a straw person without assets. However, I realise that many deals look so good that you don't mind taking on personal liability. I also recognise that to become truly rich, as quickly as possible, it is necessary to take some risks. Thus, the question becomes what to do if things go horribly and unpredictably wrong and you find yourself in 'deep doodoo' as it's known. How do you get out?

The answer is simple. Do the best you can. Rather than focusing on the black hole, concentrate on the doughnut of opportunities which surround it. Let's take an example. Suppose your goal is to walk away from a property on which you are personally liable for a mortgage loan that has a greater face value than that of the underlying property. There are a number of approaches you can take:

If the potential liability is truly horrendous, you might generally prepare for the situation as you would prepare for war, revolution or a 'take-no-prisoners' hostile divorce. Make all of your assets disappear offshore and become judgement-proof. Techniques for preserving your ass and assets against disaster are more fully explained in my PT series of reports. However, to simplify things, get your paperwork and finances in order so that you can disappear and start over with your remaining assets debt-free, lawsuit-free and as a new person in another country.

This is assuming that you already have substantial assets. If you are broke or nearly broke, another million or billion of debt will make little difference. Why? In most jurisdictions, you can simply declare bankruptcy, turn over all of your remaining assets to the court and then start fresh, although broke, a few months later. Most millionaires have been through bankruptcy at some point in their lives. It isn't the end of the world. What are your other options? Quite simply, you may be able to negotiate. Perhaps you can arrange it so that you only pay interest, or half interest, on your loan for one year. You may even be able to further extend this deal until things get better and you're on your feet again. Banks would rather compromise than foreclose, usually.

You may also be able to rent the property. If it's your personal residence, maybe you could take in bed and breakfast boarders. Can you turn the property into a 'timeshare' and sell individual weeks or quarters of ownership? Maybe you can find a qualified buyer who will take over the existing loan from you. You may even want to offer the new buyer a financial incentive in cash so that he gets the property, not only for no-money-down, but actually ends up with extra money in his pocket at closing. You would certainly generate some interest with an ad that says something like, "My beautiful home in Hampshire for nothing down. You walk away with £50,000 in your pocket!" In such a deal, the buyer would have to be financially qualified and not considered to be a financial risk. He would overpay a bit in return for a cash-up-front deal. When property in a particular locality is in a major slump, everyone wants to bail out at the same time. The outlook for owners seems to be bleak. On the other hand, major slumps, like the recession, are the times of greatest opportunity for buyers. If a developer has built 98 per cent of a project with £100 units, be they thousands or millions, but is forced to sell his remaining stock at auction for £50, you could pick up a super-bargain. You could then rent at half the price of your competition. What to do? Arrange the financing and put together a no-money-down deal for yourself. Perhaps you could even get cash back from the original distressed owner by arranging a private deal before the auction. If you have or can create a reputation as a turn-around expert, you will emerge from the recession as the tycoon of tomorrow.

No-Money-Down Deals – A Summary

A no-money-down deal is any acquisition of property or a business where you don't put up significant sums of your own money. I would put in this category a deal where you buy property for all cash with an unsecured loan and shortly after the close arrange for a combination of first, second and, possibly, third loans to arrive at the point where you have none of your own money in the deal. Many deals require little or no cash to begin with. Let's look at them in the order I regard as most preferable to the buyer:

1. Seller gives buyer option to purchase at a reasonable price for a lengthy period of time. The contract provides that buyer gets possession at a low rent during the option period.

2. Outright sale with seller carrying back a loan for the entire purchase price. Often sellers will insist that this be done with a contract of sale by which the seller retains title as security for buyer's meeting his obligations.

3. Sale with seller taking as down payment the buyer's personal or secured note – or a legitimate property in trade. The balance of financing (usually 70 to 95 per cent) comes from a lending institution.

4. Down payment borrowed from an outside lender by seller who refinances the property. Buyer assumes loan and seller carries balance due him in the form of another note or IOU.

5. Down payment borrowed from outside lender either on an unsecured note or secured by the property buyer already owns.

6. Property is 100 per cent (or more) financed by an institutional lender. The most common ways of obtaining such a loan are:

   A. Outright fraud by manufacturing phoney documents which establish a higher-than-actual sale price. This practice is emphatically not recommended, although you will probably find it to be quite common.

   B. Over-valuation of property or odd-ball assets used to put together a trade.

   C. Rebate for repairs from the seller or other imaginative schemes to transfer part of purchase price back to buyer or shortly after closing.

   D. Drastically increasing value of property by some action taken by buyer between time of contract and closing, for example: favourable re-zoning, lot split or issuance of building and planning permits; evicting undesirable tenants or establishing new and favourable leases; sub-dividing; establishing higher and better use for property. I personally prefer this option.

7. Property bought with substantial down payment (or all cash) with this cash recouped shortly after purchase by refinancing.

8. You use investor-partners for cash. They get half the profits on the deal for putting up all the money.

Why should you try to make a no-money-down deal? The answer is that with this method it is possible to acquire a large number of properties having a high dollar value in a relatively short time. In the Western US, the laws of many states make purchase-money loans non-recourse, meaning that if the deal goes sour you can walk away. There is no downside risk. No one can claim your other assets. In Eastern states, Great Britain and other countries, the same risk-free status can be obtained using land trusts, straw men, corporations, and other legal entities to insulate you, as the buyer, from personal liability. By acquiring large amounts of property over a short period of time, you will quickly become a millionaire. All you have to do is buy lots of carefully-selected property, sit back and wait. Your debts, reduced by the declining value of paper money, will become insignificant. Rents and property prices will go up. Your equity will soon grow to a million or more.

Nice Guys Finish Last!

Let's take a scenario. What if you had started buying property a few years ago, before the onset of the recession? Or worse, what if you start to buy property tomorrow and rather than the recession coming to an end, as the politicians are predicting, things continue to get worse and worse, meaning property prices and rents continue to drop? You come into a pinch and have problems meeting your various mortgage payments. You're still confident that things will work out all right over the long term, as you understand that you can expect an increase in value of 10 per cent a year on average, but the question now isn't about the long term. It's about the pinch you are feeling today.

As a result of considering this possibility, you may decide that it's best not to accumulate a lot of debt. You may think it's best not to overextend yourself so that income from your day job can see you through even the most dire of possible future consequences. You may think that the long term isn't particularly important right now and not likely to impress your bank in the event of a crisis. Well, to put it bluntly, you couldn't be more misinformed. Let's take a look at how two aspiring tycoons dealt with just such circumstances.

Mr Nice Guy believed his friendly banker's advice. He was told that it is better, safer and far more conservative to buy one four-plex (four unit building) with a large down payment than to 'speculate' in several four-plexes with the same amount of money. So Mr Nice Guy bought a $100,000 four-plex with a $30,000 down payment, taking out a $70,000 loan with the Friendly Bank. He didn't even consider the possibility of a no-money-down deal. As it happens, Mr Nice Guy bought in the late 80s, at the top of a period of escalating prices. Shortly after his purchase, the recession hit, forcing him to reduce his rents slightly. To make matters worse, Mr Nice Guy also lost his job, the insurance he was counting on. This combination of circumstances caused him to be unable to meet his mortgage payments of $700 per month. Mr Nice Guy can barely squeeze together $400 per month, meaning he is $300 short per each month.

At the same time, Miss Tycoon, who also had $30,000 cash to start with, decided to buy six four-plexes. She told little white lies to Friendly Bank and five other banks and thus was able to acquire six small apartment buildings, each for $100,000 with a $95,000 loan. Miss Tycoon was hit in exactly the same way by the recession, losing her job while at the same time being forced to reduce her rents. Like Mr Nice Guy, in the new economic climate, she is barely able to come up with $400 per month to make the payments on each loan. However, in her case, $950 per month is due on a total of six loans, meaning she is $3,300 short each month.

Property price levels have also dropped significantly. Her buildings could be liquidated quickly in the current market for only about $70,000 to 'all cash' buyers. She could sell, but only at prices 30 per cent below what she paid. The market value of her property is considerably below the amounts lent to make the purchase. Should she worry? No!

This is what happens in the real world. The friendly banker assesses the situation. Money is tight. The bank, like everyone else, needs money to keep afloat. The friendly banker has only one thing on his mind, "Where can I get it?" Money, that is.

He realises that with Miss Tycoon's deal, if the bank were to foreclose, it would get a $70,000 four-plex and thus only be able to realise $70,000 cash. Doing so would, of course, mean writing off a $95,000 loan and taking a $25,000 loss on the books. Under these circumstances, the friendly banker actually turns out to be friendly with Miss Tycoon. He offers to take lower payments of interest only until the economy recovers. In this way, the bank will not have to take a loss. Nobody likes to take losses, especially bankers who might lose their jobs if the stockholders object to their having made too high a loan relative to the security involved in the first place.

But Mr Nice Guy is in an entirely different situation. The bank can and does foreclose. They sell the property, receiving the same $70,000 cash. However, unlike they would with Miss Tycoon, they take no loss whatsoever. Thus, there is no reason at all to be friendly to Mr Nice Guy. This is what happens in the real world. Banks 'work with' tycoons and foreclose on nice guys.

A year or two from now, when the market recovers and four-plexes can be sold for $120,000 each, here is what will happen. Mr Nice Guy was wiped out. He started with

$30,000 but is now out of the game. He has lost his $30,000, and his credit is lousy. Why? Because he must now state under penalty of perjury on new loan applications that he went through a foreclosure.

On the other hand, Miss Tycoon will sell or trade up her six buildings for a handsome profit of $120,00 (6 x $20,000). The bankers will love her because she has 'staying power' and can help them ride through a difficult period by sticking with her properties. She also will not be the cause of any litigation or losses for them. On her $30,000 investment, she will make a 400 per cent profit. Everybody loves a winner! Do you get the point? It is better to have the banks and lenders as your partners rather than as your adversaries. This is accomplished by always being highly leverage or geared.

Chapter 11

FINDING SUPER DEALS

In this chapter, I talk about income property. But the techniques and mental attitude involved are just the same whether you are looking at business opportunities or 'things' to buy and sell at a profit.

Did you ever hear of Father Flanagan, the founder of Boys Town? He is famous for the quote, "There's no such thing as a badboy".Well, here is Bill Hill's variation on the same theme. I say, "There's no such thing as a bad property deal!" Every deal, every property, is potentially 'good' or profitable, but sometimes (read sometimes as usually) the price is too high. Yet, bought right and properly leveraged with good loans, any property could be an excellent deal. This is why, once you know the market, you should make an offer on virtually every property you look at. Much of this book is concerned with what sort of offers to make. Here we will deal with the process of ferreting out all the deals on the local market. More importantly, you'll learn to flush out deals that are not on the market, but can be yours exclusively.

Making big money in property is as easy as falling off a log. But if I told you to fall off a log this minute, you'd have a problem. First you would have to find a log. In most cities, that would be difficult. Then you would have to find a lake or stream. The third step, getting the log into the water, would involve a bit of work. Finally, the hardest thing of all, you would have to stand up on a floating log. After all that, falling off is easy.

Making money in property is as easy as falling off a log. But the problems in getting on are similar. First you must find suitable property. It might not be available in your

Making money is as easy as falling off a log.

Getting on the log is the biggest problem.

neighbourhood or even in your city. Then you've got to negotiate for it, arrange financing and close the deal. Finally, you must put the property in proper running order. Once all that is done, you'll make nothing but money. Finding the right property, negotiating the deal and staying on top of it is the hardest part.

Obviously you are nowhere until you find your first property. If you don't look you'll never find anything! Let me show you how to look for good deals and how to recognise a bargain when you see it.

How can you find or create that elusive first good deal? Do you think that if you sit in your living room and watch television, some salesman will come to the door and present you with a super-deal all tied up with a red ribbon? And all you'll have to do is write out a cheque and wait for profits to roll in? Unfortunately, any deal presented to you by a salesman with a smooth, memorised presentation and four-colour brochure isn't worth beans. You'll have to get off your butt! As a preliminary step you must educate yourself to the point where you can recognise or create a good deal when you see a promising situation. Educating yourself is easy. It costs nothing but a little time. The process shouldn't take more than four to six weeks. You simply learn and apply the Hill Hundred House Rule.

Look at a minimum of one hundred properties for sale. If you are interested in single-family houses, look at one hundred houses. Or you can look at one hundred small apartment houses, one hundred warehouses or one hundred motels. Look at whatever type of property you would feel comfortable owning and managing. I suggest that you concentrate your attention on run-down or half-vacant 'problem' properties. But also look at well-managed, clean, income properties commanding high rents and top-dollar asking prices. Ask yourself,

"How could I improve this particular sick property? How might I cure the problems to make this decrepit building worth more rent? What would my changes cost and what would they mean ultimately in terms of market value?"

Remember, until you have actually gone through one hundred properties, both physically and on paper, it's all just six weeks of looking, mere mental exercise. Do not make any offers. Just observe and ask questions. This is an educational time only. Don't let anyone sell you anything. During your hundred house period, explore different neighbourhoods. Visit nearby towns and communities. Observe where the growth areas are. By growth, I mean new construction, upgrading or remodelling. Which areas seem to be declining in popularity? Are undesirable elements (like bums or porno-massage-pinball parlours) moving into nearby shopping areas? Where are the trendy young professionals shopping? How much renovation is taking place? Check out different types of property. Be alert for special situations like the Dipsea Cabins I told you about in the last chapter.

Even though you may be preliminarily interested in buying small apartment units, don't be afraid to look at property containing stores on lower floors and apartments upstairs. This is called 'mixed use'. Look at homes, duplexes, apartment buildings, stores, offices, manufacturing buildings and warehouses. Notice which seem to be the best value for money. Where do you, from the point of view of a tenant, get the most square footage with your money? Compare prices for comparable properties in fashionable neighbourhoods and up-and-coming areas. Try to notice patterns of change. Consider the possibilities of converting abandoned warehouses into offices or apartments, apartments to offices or any type of property for alternate uses. Discuss your ideas with property agents, contractors, sellers and other people already in the business of owning, managing or remodelling. Look at failed

Watch out for special local factors affecting value.
Is there a new industrial park or shopping centre going up nearby?

projects, places with a lot of vacancies and those that have gone into foreclosure. What mistakes can they help you avoid? Perhaps you can take over an incomplete project once you have a little bit of construction and contracting experience.

To ascertain prevailing rents in an area, spend time posing as a prospective tenant. Seek to rent various types of property. If landlords are anxious to give concessions such as paying your moving expenses or giving free rent for three months, obviously the rental market must be soft. True rents are often not the same as scheduled rents. Scheduled rents are what sellers try to make you believe they can get.

How do you find one hundred properties to look at? The traditional method is to simply read ads in the local papers. Probably one-third to one-half of all property deals are initiated through newspaper classified ads. With a felt tipped pen, circle ads for interesting properties. Call. Make an appointment with the owner or agent handling the deal. Don't waste time. Arrange your schedule so there is order and flow to your viewing. In other words, look at all properties on the north side of town in the morning and on the south side in the afternoon. Stay organised! Don't spend time driving and going back and forth unnecessarily. Use time efficiently. Ask a lot of questions.

What's the local property market been like over the past 20 years? Over the past five years? Over the past year? Does it feel as if the effects of the recession are waning or are property prices still falling significantly? Are there more people anxious to sell than there are buyers or vice versa? How long does it take for a fairly-priced deal to sell? If the market looks as if it has yet to recover from the recession, you are probably best advised to wait a little before buying. Wait until prices are firm again. At the very least, operate with the understanding that you, as a buyer, are in demand and therefore will probably be able to negotiate all sorts of interesting terms and conditions.

You will also want to consider issues surrounding the local political and social structures. Where are the schools and churches? Does the town have a master plan? Is it likely that an urban renewal or, on the other hand, condemnation programme will be implemented in the near future? Are there any special grants-in-aid or subsidised government loans available for owners in the area because it is considered historical or otherwise worthy of preservation? Special tax breaks? Is a freeway going through?

What other new developments are going in? If expensive new apartments are planned for the area, it could be possible that the higher rents scheduled for these new projects will make the older units, by comparison, more attractive to prospective tenants. A new shopping centre or rapid transit stop could make all properties in an area more convenient and therefore more valuable.

What improvements made by other property owners are the most profitable? Perhaps installing a lot of skylights, modern kitchens and exterior shingles makes the difference between a $60,000 and a $100,000 property. It is up to you to ascertain the costs of value-adding improvements. Call up general contractors. Have them stop over at a property that you are considering. Let them give you their estimates and suggestions on restoration, remodelling, conversions or needed repairs. You may see indications that $10,000 in work could give you $30,000 in value. In many instances, merely cleaning up and painting could turn a lemon of a property into a juicy grapefruit. What work can you do yourself? Being your own contractor, carpenter and painter can save at least two-thirds on most projects.

The most important thing is that, by looking at a large number of deals on the market and considering all the possibilities, your creative mental juices will start circulating. You will begin to have original ideas on where to buy, how to make profitable improvements and how to best take advantage of the existing situation.

Why did I choose the Hill Hundred House Rule instead of the Hill Fifty House Rule? Is there any magic in the number one hundred, except, of course, for the fact that it sounds spiffy next to my name? Of course not! If you feel comfortable making your first serious offer after looking at 63 properties, do it. If you don't feel you know the market after carefully examining one hundred deals, then look at two hundred. Can you look at too many deals? Yes! As in the search for a spouse, it is impossible to find perfection. The perfect property deal doesn't exist. You can look forever and you'll never find perfection. There's always work to done, and no guarantees.

Once you are familiar with every property on the local market, unless everything is grossly overpriced, you have to take that giant step. Make an offer on the best deal available. You must get into the game! Rely on your intuition and do as well as you can on your first deal. Using my ideas you can't lose anything but time. You will gain valuable experience and self-confidence even if the deal is a dud. If you wait for perfection in a lover or a business deal, you'll die a virgin. In property there are plenty of virgins who have been 'just looking' for 40 years.

If everything that is local is so high priced that you would rather be unencumbered, it could be a good time to take a trip and see what sort of opportunities exist elsewhere. Before you begin your career as a property tycoon, it may well be the opportune moment to move to the area that you have always wanted to live in. Property investments, at least in the beginning years, will tie you down to a given locality. So you might as well acquire those first properties in a climate you are happy in. To make it big in property, you will probably have to put some roots down in a chosen community for at least a few years.

Finding A Good Agent

Earlier, I said that up to 50 per cent of all property deals are initiated by ads in the paper. If you were thinking and questioning, as you should be, you might have thought, "Well, where do the rest of the deals come from, or more to the point, is this other method or methods a

Good agents always have these pocket listings!

better way of finding out about deals?" Well, in a word, yes. Most of the best business and property deals are never placed on the market or advertised. In my experience, looking at properties with an average property agent or responding to ads is a wonderful way of getting an education, that is, doing the hundred house bit. But once familiar with the market, you will find that there are far better ways of ferreting out super-deals.

To start with, get a property agent who will do you some good. When you visit an estate agent or broker in response to an ad or just walk in off the street, casually ask whoever you are dealing with, "Who is the most successful agent in the office?" The agent on duty or 'floor person' will probably point out a busy, looking individual on the telephone with three people waiting to see him. Don't call him or waste his time during your hundred house period because he will rapidly size you up as a 'looker', not a buyer, and won't have anything to do with you after that. But keep his name and number in a safe place for future reference.

Once you have firmly decided the type of property you want, and the prices and terms you are interested in, call this agent. Also call any and every other top-notch agent at every other major firm in the area. Give them your requirements and explain that you are ready, willing and able to acquire large amounts of property. Any top-notch agent should already be familiar with tycoon principles as he and all his heavy-duty clients frequently use such techniques.

As a top producer, your new agent will have many clients who are interested in trading out of properties as they move up to bigger and better deals. These properties are generally available to buyers who make quick decisions and are known well by the agent. Many of these deals will never be listed for public sale. They are 'available' but not on the market or advertised for sale. You, as a buyer, will find out about them only by attending local trading sessions for professionals in property or getting to know agents who specialise in representing wheeler-dealers. These agents will invariably be the 'top producers' in every busy office. They have no time for amateurs, novices or lookers. They will be among the five per cent of brokers who earn 90 per cent of the commissions in an area.

Don't waste their time! Just remember that the best deals are often not advertised. This sort of deal is known as a 'pocket listing', probably because the seller is in the pocket of the agent and the agent keeps the listing in his pocket. He shows the best deals only to his favourite investor clients, entrepreneurs he knows will not pull out of a deal because of an irrational illness called 'buyers remorse'. The broker does not share his most worthwhile listings (and their potential commissions) with the other agents because he will earn a full commission on each deal by acting as sole agent. If such a broker knows exactly what you want, he will call only if a deal pretty close to your requirements materialises. The advantage of dealing with a top producer is that he does not waste your time showing you unsuitable properties.

I know several agents who only call me once or twice a year. When they do call, I know there will almost surely be a deal because they know exactly what I want, low up-front cash requirement, potential for improving the income stream and pots of money to be made in the ultimate resale or trade-up.

The most successful agents are successful for very good reasons. They know the market. They do not float around wasting their time with sellers who want outrageous prices or buyers who change their minds. They have no use for 'buyers' who are only lookers or clients who will try to chisel down or circumvent their commissions. Good agents will do their best to solve any problem as it comes up. They persuade lenders to loan during tight money periods. They convince title companies to waive objections. A successful agent cajoles building departments to approve permits or zoning if these are a contingency. If necessary to close a deal, good agents may be flexible about carrying back all or part of their commission in the form of a note. For such a consideration, they normally ask for, and get, the buyer's agreement to resell through him.

Thus the broker may sell the same property a dozen times or more in the course of his career. Whenever William Zeckendorf, the legendary broker in New York City, felt it was time to make another million, he would simply say, "It's time to sell the Plaza Hotel again!"

A good agent is worth his weight in gold. The only problem is that as few as one in 50 of all estate agents are any good. They probably earn well over $50,000 per year in commissions by handling in excess of 10 or 15 deals per year. If you are clear about what you want, they will let you know of good deals from time to time. You must be ready to move fast. If they call you on the hour, be ready to meet them at the property by quarter past and be ready to make an offer by half past. The best property deals are always snapped up on the day they are offered.

Naturally you are not in a position to recognise, much less make such a deal, until you know the market. The best way to know the market quickly is to use the hundred house rule. Once you have looked at one hundred properties, make low offers or no-money-down offers on every deal you look at. Remember, there is no such thing as a bad property deal! At the right price, or with good terms, any deal can help make your million.

Looking For Special Ads

How about other ways of finding super-deals? Going back to the ads, before we pass on to other methods, look particularly for ones that say "for sale by owner". In the trade, these are known as 'FISBOs'. Normally, owners have an exaggerated idea of what their property is worth. Often they start out asking well over market price. However, owners will sometimes accept terms that agents would convince them to turn down. Also, many sellers are what I call 'non-money-motivated'. So, if you can deal directly with a seller rather than through an agent, you may find that your seller has things other than money in mind when he begins to negotiate with you. A seller represented by an agent generally acts more rationally. In my comments on negotiating, coming up in a few chapters, I'll give you several hints on dealing directly with sellers. There are many different, creative techniques you can exploit in direct negotiations.

Another type of ad, which I call the 'hot tip' ad, will say something like "owner will carry loan". That statement, appearing in many ads, tells you that the seller may be willing to carry the financing on the property. The seller understands that if he takes a small cash down payment, or no cash, he will get certain tax benefits. He wants an instalment sale. In any event, you are at least assured that the seller is mentally prepared to lend you all, or a big part of the money it will take to buy his property. He will 'carry the paper'. For you as a buyer, this means that there will be no need to qualify for a bank loan. You only have to convince the seller that you are reliable. What's reliable? Namely, that you will make the required monthly payments to him on time for the mortgage he has carried back.

It may be possible for you to convince a seller advertising 'low down' to carry back a 100 per cent loan. Furthermore, the loan can be a single payment, interest-free 'balloon' all due in five or 10 years. If the seller receives no interest, he pays no tax. Of course, sceptics will say that it can't be done. I say don't knock it until you've tried it! Over half of my own several hundred deals have been no-money-down deals in which the sellers have carried the entire loan. There are many good reasons why a seller would be willing to do this.

For now, I am just stressing that where you see a "for sale by owner" ad, you will occasionally be able to get a property at a super-price. More often, you can negotiate creative financing that is very advantageous to you. Where you see "low down" in ads, it always means that the seller is willing to carry the financing. If you are just starting out, without two coins to rub together, are over-extended or if for some reason you find it difficult to borrow from financial institutions, the words "low down" may be your answer. They mean that you do not have to look too good on paper and can usually make the deal with a lot less than 10 per cent down. You only have to charm the seller, who seldom requests or requires even a financial statement.

Making Connections

Whenever you meet a seller or an agent through a newspaper ad, whether the deal advertised works out or not, never fail to ask if they have any other properties that you could look at now or coming up in the near future. Often, a property actually advertised in the paper turns out to be totally unattractive, but the owner will have another, better deal around the corner or up his sleeve. On several occasions, I bought this other, unmentioned property. Also, every owner or agent you meet is a good contact for the future. In property (as in any other business), having contacts who want to deal with you is of the utmost importance. A good contact in the business is far better than any one deal.

If someone in business appears to be exceptionally lucky time after time, you will find that his or her 'luck' is always other people. You'll often be presented with a deal or opportunity as a result of knowing someone who knows you are a serious, reliable buyer. Or they simply want to do you a favour. You'll be able to utilise that opportunity or take that deal because you have still more contacts to help you do it. In property, your contacts will range from sellers to handymen and construction people. There will also be potential tenants and financial backers and a whole gamut of acquaintances who can supply the pieces to make a deal work. During your hundred house period, you will not only be getting an education, but just as important, you will be cultivating a wide range of potentially useful contacts in the business.

Your preparation or training period should be complete within two months. Thoroughly familiar with the local market, you should at that point be able to do what I call a 'second gear appraisal'. You hear of a property for sale. You drive by in second gear. If you have done your hundred house homework, you should be able to look at any building from the outside and then, within a five per cent margin of error, estimate the asking price and the price it will actually sell for. Try it a few times. If you are way off, go back to the drawing board, the ads and keep looking and asking questions.

Once you can make successful second gear appraisals, you have arrived! You are as good as the so-called professionals in the area and should have full confidence in yourself. If you know the market, you can't make many mistakes.

Now that you are educated, you are finally ready to become a serious shopper and very soon, a buyer. Let's go on to the ways that insiders, people who really know their way around, get the very best deals.

Multiple Listings

So called multiple listings, the shared listings between agents, are generally the last place to look for good deals. Why? Because after an owner has unsuccessfully tried to sell his property on his own, he turns it over to an agent. The agent then shows it to all of his favoured investor clients. They refuse to take the deal because it is overpriced or because of some other fatal flaw. The agent advertises, but still no takers. Next, in desperation, the agent shares this turkey with other agents in his office. None of the other agents want such a stinker of a deal, nor do their clients. Finally, after exposure to several hundred buyers, the owner or agent decides to place the property with other agencies, the 'garbage can' as it is known in the trade. This is his last resort. The agent proclaims to the community, "I couldn't move this piece of crap to any of my own clients, so I'll pay half my commission to any other estate agent who can find a sucker to take it."

Getting multiple listings before the ink is dry.

Obviously the best deals never make it to the multiple listings. The best deals are kept tucked away safely in the pocket listings, the deals that never get listed at all. Are there exceptions? Can you ever get a good deal out of multiple listings?

I once bought a property through a multiple listing. The asking price was $50,000. I offered $18,000 cash. To my surprise, the offer was immediately accepted. I bought with an unsecured bank loan. In a few months, I repaid the unsecured loan because I had obtained a $25,000 long-term bank loan. Within three years, I sold the property for $88,000. Why did I get the property so cheap? There was a divorce going on. The wife wanted to keep the house as long as possible, so she refused to sign the contract unless it was over-priced at $50,000. She figured that pricing it out of the market would enable her to live in it longer. The property was actually (at that time) worth closer to $30,000. Six months passed. The husband moved out and didn't make payments. Later, the wife moved out. The mortgage loan people entered the scene. They had a problem – about $16,000 worth of a problem.

The place was a 'yuck' house. It was dirty, the yard was full of weeds and it smelled of cat pee. The lenders from Upright Savings and Loan told the wife she'd better take the first offer that came along over $16,000 otherwise they'd take over the property and she'd get nothing. Mr and Mrs Yuck could have sold at $30,000 and split an equity of $14,000. However, the wife was only interested in screwing her husband out of his half of a $14,000 equity. The husband was equally determined that she did not get any money out of the divorce. There were no assets besides the house. It was your typical divorce with both sides vindictive and angry. They let their assets go to hell. A good chunk went to their lawyers. But there's always a budding tycoon around to pick up broken pieces. You must put yourself in the right place at the right time, with the right offer. There are dozens of deals like this being made every day. For you to get your share, you just have to be there, looking and making offers. Divorces, debts and deaths of other people equal opportunity for you! Remember, the asking price on a deal is not the final selling price. Never be afraid to offer half or even less!

If you drive through almost any neighbourhood you'll see 'for sale' or 'to let' signs on property. For me, it's as regular a habit as breathing. I brake to a screeching halt, knock on the door and talk to the owner or the agent handling the deal. Every inquiry gives you more information on market prices, rents asked, etc. Just as important, it will create an ever widening circle of contacts. Never fail to ask the magic question, "What else do you have for sale or rent?" It will lead to other deals, further information and more contacts. Never stop asking questions! If it's a rental sign, ask the owner, "Did you ever consider selling this place

The 'Yuck' House.

so you wouldn't have to go through the bother of renting it?" If it's a 'for sale' sign and the deal is obviously not for you, ask, "What are the asking prices for comparable properties currently on the market? Are any of your neighbours thinking of selling or moving? Do you know the prices that other properties have recently sold for?"

One of my best deals resulted from going up to a door to read a tiny calling card with the cryptic message, "For information on this place, call – phone number." Hardly the way to get maximum exposure for the seller, but it permitted me to negotiate an excellent deal with a seller who told me he didn't want to be bothered with hordes of lookers. He figured that anyone who took the time to climb 20 stairs to read his little card would have to be a serious buyer.

Property is traded in what the economists call a very imperfect market. Every property is unique. Every buyer and seller has different peculiarities or motivations. You can regularly buy properties at well below their market value if: 1. You know the market. 2. You can learn of special situations through your network of contacts.

The Dirty Window Gambit

Would you believe that looking for dirty windows could make you a fortune in property? It has certainly helped me. I don't mean your ordinary garden variety of dirty windows. I mean really filthy, cracked or broken windows. They are usually found on a house or property that has a front yard full of weeds, peeling paint, signs of vandalism, graffiti or an abandoned looking car in the drive – in short, abandoned or neglected property.

The owner of neglected property may be in a nursing home, the French Foreign Legion or dead. The deceased may have heirs thousands of miles away who'd love to get an offer to purchase a property they might not even know they own. In one case, I discovered that the owners of a derelict property were scattered heirs, all of whom, when contacted, wanted to sell. But one heir in Poland, Vladimir Dzerwinkovitch, didn't answer my letters, telegrams or phone calls. I figured if I could buy deeds for three-quarters of the property and take possession, there would have to be a way to get the other one-quarter, whether the Polish heir wanted to sell or not. So I paid rather nominal sums, about $500 per deed, to three out of the four heirs. I recorded the deeds and went to the lawbooks. There were several ways to proceed. I had the choice of ignoring the interest of Vladimir for seven years, after which, if I took possession or rented out the property and paid my property taxes, the property would be entirely mine by virtue of the laws of adverse possession. But that seemed risky. The missing heir might turn up in the sixth year. Also, I'd be tied up for seven years. Another possibility was an immediate legal action against the Pole called a 'quiet title' or 'partition suit'.

So I filed suit. This involved publishing a notice in the *Law Bulletin* to the effect that Vladimir's interest would be sold on a certain day at the request of myself as his tenant in common. The law has always given a remedy to partners who don't get along. In due course, the property went up for public sale at my request. In this case, controlling three-quarters at the sale, I only had to put up cash representing one-quarter of my bid. Fortunately, I was the only bidder at $10. The Polish heir, good old Vladimir, was credited with a deposit of $2.50, which I assume the county treasurer is still holding for him.

If you had come to that auction, you might have bid me up to the $20,000 I was prepared to pay for the property. $20,000 wouldn't have been a bad price either, because three years later I put in on the market at $115,000. What was my cost? It included $1,500 to the heirs, $2.50 to the recalcitrant heir, $375 in legal fees and a lot of research, phone calls and running around. What was my profit? Give or take $112,000. All that for looking at dirty windows!

Think creatively!

Tax Delinquent Property

An uncared for property is often an unwanted property. What someone else throws away can make you a fortune. If a property isn't cared for physically, it probably isn't being cared for financially either. I have a way of finding those financially abandoned and unloved properties that is even more efficient than cruising the streets looking for dirty windows. As mentioned in a previous chapter, you should always watch the courthouse bulletin boards for notices of foreclosure and notices of default. A notice of default is publicly posted when a property owner doesn't meet his mortgage obligations under a trust deed or mortgage loan. Someone who can't pay his mortgage is a good prospect for a buy-out. But suppose the property is free and clear. There is no mortgage to default on. How can you discover financially-distressed owners of free and clear property? In most places you can go to the records of the local tax collector and compile a list of properties where the taxes or rates have been delinquent for a year or more. You send the owners (their addresses can be found on the public records) a friendly letter noting that their tax is delinquent and suggesting that you would consider making them an attractive offer for their property. I have found that a mass mailing to this particular list of property owners brings almost a 25 per cent positive response. When things are slow, it's one of my old faithful methods of stirring up a few hot deals. If you go beyond a mere mailing and trace owners whose mail is returned as undeliverable as well as telephone the rest of the non-responders, you will churn up even more prospective deals.

While you are tediously going through the public records for owners of tax delinquent properties, I suggest that you also prepare a list of out-of-state owners. Non-resident owners are often even more eager to sell so that they can re-invest proceeds in their own area.

Personal Contacts
Last and most important are personal contacts! They are so important that they deserve a second mention. My local Fuller Brush salesman makes about $10,000 a year selling hairbrushes and brooms door-to-door. He makes another half-million a year trading in property. He knows all the older people who plan on moving to Sunshine (Retirement) City. He's on a first name basis with all the pregnant women who will soon be pressuring their husbands to get them a bigger house. He is on top of job transfers, births, marriages, deaths, divorces and all the factors that cause people to make a change in their living or investment situations. His door-to-door selling job is literally worth half a million a year to him because it puts him in touch with everyone in the community.

You may not want to sell insurance, Shaklee vitamins or Avon cosmetics door-to-door, but nonetheless, you should consider a door-to-door sales job. You must make and keep up your contacts some way. Other alternatives included becoming a property agent and constantly doing appraisals for local lenders. At the very least, you should join the local National Guard, Masons, Knights of Columbus, Rotarians or Jaycees so that you will get to know lots of people. And lots of people must be made aware that you are interested in any property an owner might wish to sell privately before it is listed or advertised. Make a standing offer of a bottle of champagne for any such tip. Tell your friends that they will get at least $100 for any tip that results in such a deal. If you're looking for a business associate or have an idea with an international flare, you might want to consider placing a classified ad in Scope International's quarterly newspaper, *The Mouse Monitor*. You can thus make your pitch to a select international audience of potential and actual tycoons.

Put A Smile On Their Faces
Property agents, in the course of soliciting possible sellers for listings, will often find that an

owner is interested in selling but does not want to sign a formal listing contract. The property owner tells the agent, "If you can get me X I'll sell, but I'd rather not make too much of a fuss about it." The agent is then in a bind. If he alerts any client to a deal that has not been formally listed, it may prove difficult for him to collect his commission in the end. (The seller is traditionally required to pay six per cent of the closing purchase price.) Agents have been burned so often by this type of seller that they will usually not take any action to inform anyone of the potential deal. For every official written listing, an agent may know of 10 or 15 possible listings of the type just explained.

How do you take advantage of the situation and gain knowledge of them? Simple! Every agent you become friendly with should get the following offer from you, "Charlie, if you tip me off to a good deal, whether you have a listing or not, I'll put another smile on your face with another little bonus or I will list it directly with you." If you get a reputation for never trying to perform a commission-dectomy, where you cut an agent's commission on a deal that you close, but instead are known for always leaving these fine, hard-working ladies or gentlemen with a smile on their faces, your phone will ring constantly as your bird-dog brokers bring you more good deals than you can handle.

If you become a trustworthy wheeler-dealer, what happened to me once will happen to you.

Amos, an agent, woke me up at six in the morning with a phone call. In conspiratorial tones he said, "Bill, I've got a hot one for you."

"What is it?" I mumbled half asleep.

"I want $4,000 – if you buy it."

"The deal was $300. I offered you a flat $300 for hot tips."

"But this is a real hot one. Take it or leave it!"

"OK." I said. "I'll take it, but only on the conditions that: 1) I don't already know about it and 2) I only pay you the $4,000 if the deal closes and I buy the property."

"Done," said Amos. "I'll pick you up in half an hour."

Amos took me to a mansion I knew about. It had been on the market for years at $120,000. Very overpriced.

"What's the story?" I said.

"The mortgage has been foreclosed, and you can buy it at 10 this morning for $30,000 from the Bank of America. I want $4,000 cash at the closing. There's a public sale scheduled, but the time and place was given wrong in the papers. Only I know that the sale is on for this morning. You'll be the only bidder."

I almost didn't believe him, but as he had been a reliable source in the past, I toddled along with Amos to the Bank of America building, picking up two cashier's cheques as unsecured loans on the lower floor of the bank. One cheque was for $30,000 and one for $4,000. Amos introduced me to the trust office handling the deal. I made the only bid and handed $30,000 to the trust officer. At 10.02 I was given a trustee's deed to certify that I owned the property. It was easily worth $90,000. I slipped Amos his $4,000 on the way out.

The same day, I called a few of my own property investor friends and offered it to them at $64,000 as is, all cash, quick close. A week later, I sold the property at a $30,000 profit. I gave Amos another $100 bill.

Amos had a smile on his face.

I had a smile on my face.

I made $30,000 in a week, and I owed it all to knowing the market, having good contacts and having a reputation for spreading smiles and sunshine wherever I go. Now you do it!

Chapter 12

GET YOURSELF ORGANISED

If your goal was not to make a million, but to climb Mount Everest, your preparation would not be limited to putting on tennis shoes and buying an Air India ticket to the base camp, would it? You would prepare carefully. You would learn all about climbing in general and Everest in particular. You'd get your personal affairs in order; make sure of your financing. Then it would be necessary to spend a few years on smaller peaks, getting yourself into shape mentally and physically. After all that, with tried and tested gear, you'd make the climb and you'd be successful. Mountain climbers tell me that when you make it to the top, the feeling of exhilaration and freedom is unequalled by anything. Maybe that's true. But to me, once you get to the top of a mountain there is nothing to do but come down again. That's why I'd rather put all that effort into becoming very, very rich.

The freedom that means something to me is financial freedom. Attaining wealth is a lot easier and less risky than climbing mountains. Don't get me wrong, this exhilarating financial freedom requires the same planning and preliminary testing as climbing Mount Everest.

Life today is 'Answerland'. Everybody used to try and sell me answers to what I wanted in life: Encounter groups! Primal scream! The spiritual path of yoga and brown bread. To me, working on my inner life was not an answer. I wanted to be financially independent. Only two years after starting my business career, I made it. I didn't have to work another day after my 24th birthday.

I don't have 'the answer', but one thing is certain. This book is not designed to make you feel better between your two ears. This is no head trip. I'm telling you how to get out in the real world and work effectively. If you follow my programme, the rewards will be great. You can make a year's gross salary or more, on one deal! With a lot of effort you might be able to do it once or twice a week. If you can do that for a year or two, outmanoeuvering petty bureaucrats and outwitting the tax man, you will be a millionaire. Within two years! Now, that may not be 'the answer', but being rich is a comfy solution to a lot of problems. Don't let anyone tell you money doesn't buy happiness. I've been poor and miserable and rich and miserable. Rich is better. However you look at it, rich is more happy than poor. What stands in the way of you becoming a millionaire?

Making a few million, getting ahead, achieving independence – whatever you call it – can be done by anyone. Sometimes people create their own mental barriers that make success more difficult to achieve.

Some barriers are more binding. Like being married, for instance. I've found that making money is easier if you are single and can move with opportunities. That goes for men and women. Getting tied down, particularly if your spouse doesn't share your vision, gets in the way. Children can absorb money like a sponge and make it even harder. If you have ever marvelled at those terrific success stories of the penniless immigrants, like Onassis, who made it big in a foreign land without ever knowing the lingo. If you ever wondered what they had going for them, well, they had one big advantage. They were single. Don't be in any rush to get hitched – unless, of course, your spouse is very well endowed, financially I mean.

Now if you've already got a penniless spouse and hungry kids, that doesn't mean you have to give up. Certainly not. The fact is that most tycoons do make it while being married. Some even had their kids early in life. Of course, because there are more married people than single people, it is likely that there will be more married tycoons than single ones.

So if possible, hold off on having those kids until your tycoon career begins to blossom. If you already have children, don't despair. Let them earn their keep as soon as possible. Even a three-year-old can put on postage stamps, seal envelopes, sharpen pencils and help around your office. What's more, they love it. Had your own daddy put you to work when you were three, you wouldn't have to be reading this report now. You'd have had your million and your financial freedom by the time you were 21.

However, if you are planning to tie the knot, here are a few things to look for. Get a spouse who is either very rich or has a career of his or her own. You want a mate who will be busy pursuing his or her own interests while you go about yours.

Second choice is a spouse who leaves you alone during working hours, doesn't give you any opposition and, most of all, one who will not be a consumer and spend all your capital. If you can't marry a partner, next best is the quiet, traditional-type mafia spouse who doesn't get in the way or ask too many questions. The worst partner is a neurotic nut who keeps you

If you want to be rich,
don't get married! Don't have kids!

worrying all the time, can do nothing but spend your money and disparage or interfere with every project you work on. The one-word solution to this type of marriage is divorce! I know this from several personal mistakes. If your wife drives you crazy and causes continual stress in your life, dump her fast. Cut your losses. The same rule applies to any partner, business or social.

In some communities, local prejudices can be a real barrier to financial success. If you have unusual sexual preferences or if your skin colour, religion or politics are considered to be unacceptable in your present community, I have another one-word solution – move! For more material on the subject of mobility, read my other reports *PT 1* and *PT 2*.

Frank The Family Man

Years ago, when I started my first business tracking down missing heirs to estates, most of the people I hired were duds. But a year or so into the business, a man named Frank answered an ad and started working for me. He was intelligent, motivated and hard-working. He made a good working-man's wage before he met me and this rapidly doubled in my employ. I suggested he invest some of this income in property to build up a nest egg, but Frank had nine kids. Even when he doubled his income once again by working for me on a contingent-fee (which he did the following year), orthodontists, music lessons, athletic gear and other family expenses absorbed all his extra income.

Now, I'm sure Frank enjoys his family. He spends all his money and spare time with them. But Frank's timing was off. In my opinion, he should have made his million first and had his nine kids later. A big family may be fun, but it certainly limits your freedom of choice.

Overcoming Hang-ups

Many people create barriers to success with imaginary handicaps. They blame their loser-status in life on irrelevant things. My friend Anna, for instance, felt she was unattractive. Before becoming successful or even trying, she just had to have a nose job. If the nose job did her any good, it was 99 per cent psychological. A big nose won't have any effect one way or the other on your business effectiveness.

One of the world's greatest orators, Winston Churchill, couldn't speak very well when he was a boy. He lisped. Another person with a similar affliction was Demosthenes the Greek, who practised speaking with stones in his mouth until he overcame his handicap. Like Winston Churchill, Demosthenes became one of the greatest orators of his age. My personal acquaintances include a friend from school who had polio. Yet he went on to become a champion golfer. I myself was never a very good student in high school. I barely passed English composition in college, but you're reading my report, aren't you? I doubt if my teacher ever got a word in print, but I have about two dozen good-selling reports to my credit now. The best revenge is success! .

Instead of dwelling on faults or defects, just get on with your plans. Don't cop out. You'll find over and over again that people who had problems far more serious than yours were able to overcome them. If you have something wrong with you, don't use it as an excuse. Act; do something about it. Or do something in spite of it.

Psychologically Incapable Of Success

A friend of mine from high school was named Cory. He was good-looking, talented in sports and music, and was voted 'Most Likely to Succeed'. He had the sort of personality that everyone likes. Women were crazy about him even in high school. I cultivated him because he was everything I was not. He was far more popular and talented. At parties he was the best dancer. He had a smooth line for the ladies and a snappy retort to make everyone laugh.

He was always the colourful one. We started out in the army together. He came out tops on the leadership tests and was soon an officer. I stayed at the lowest level and was never considered a very good soldier. After the army, he moved in with a stunning New York fashion model. Together, they moved out to California, where he built magnificent houseboats. Life magazine even did a story on his architectural creations. Cory never cared about money. He spent it as fast as he made it – one of his endearing qualities, people said.

During all these years, however, I was living a non-flamboyant life. When I started to get rich I tried to do business with my old friend Cory. At one point, he invented a process for making artistic stained-glass windows out of plastic resin. I found a builder who placed a big order with Cory. But Cory failed to deliver. Another time we were in a property deal together. When the time came to sign the contract papers, Cory was off waterskiing. He never showed up. Cory had talent, people liked him, but he never followed through on a deal. Eventually creditors were following. I invited Cory and his lady friend over to my place for an occasional free meal. I knew times were rough for him. Once, a few sterling silver knick-knacks were missing. I found them in a pawn shop and learned that Cory had pledged them. By that time we were in our late 30s. Not kids anymore. Cory was still charming and a good talker. But for reasons I will never understand, Cory seemed intent on putting barriers between himself and financial success. Even from me, his only substantial friend in the business community, Cory cut himself off by stealing a few unimportant trinkets. Last I heard, Cory had an alcohol and drug problem. His life after age 40 was a disaster, plagued by poverty and bad health, which he had brought upon himself through irresponsibility.

Maybe Cory had it too easy. Maybe the girls who aren't so pretty or the guys with crooked buck teeth are the ones who will make it as tycoons. They have to show a world that does not accept them just how good they are. Maybe that's why top capitalists are often members of minority groups or, at least, are seldom selected in school as 'Most Likely to Succeed'. That's my theory anyway.

The Mañana Syndrome

What is the main reason that so many enthusiastic, healthy, capable men and women never make much money? They never start. Or, having prepared the first step of a plan, they piddle away time until the 'long run' arrives. And in the 'long run' we are all dead. Making money is like being an athlete. You have to organise yourself, develop good habits and keep at it. Once you start to become a champion, work even harder! Have you ever known exactly what you had to do, but just couldn't bring yourself to do it? You did something else to waste time, like cleaning up the house, going to a movie, fixing a snack or sleeping. You just didn't feel like working because you weren't properly inspired. So you procrastinated.

Then, first thing you know, other things come up – busy work, social obligations, a TV programme you couldn't miss. The mañana syndrome has hit you. Without something to snap you out of it, it could be terminal. You suddenly realise that there are so many other things to do that you dread even starting the main project.

So you waste time with trivia. You begin to feel 'too tired' to do anything. You wake up feeling guilty. You finally decide that you have to get organised, but first you must buy some vitamin pills and have a few drinks. Finally after piddling away the day getting in the mood, you belatedly start your project. But within a few hours, you find yourself back in the old mañana rut.

Well, you are not alone. We all have the mañana syndrome, this mental and physical paralysis that starts when we are in school and gets worse until we apply the following simple cure. Here's my secret:

*Having a creative accountant and a successful business-
oriented lawyer on your team sure doesn't hurt!*

Remember the Popeye cartoons when you were little? Popeye the Sailor Man always got himself into bad trouble, but one way or another, at the very high point of the story, he'd open a can of spinach. He munched. Then swallowed. And then the musical theme signalling the victory of spinach over the mañana syndrome came on loud and clear. Ra, tah, ra ta ra tah. Ra ta ta ta ra ta TAH. By the last ra ta, Popeye could do anything. His muscles swelled. He bent iron bars. His enemies fell before his mightly onslaught.

Think of the Popeye song whenever you are procrastinating. Have a drink of carrot juice, a candy bar or your own spinach substitute. Hum the theme song. After that, there is no excuse. Go to your list (of what you have to do) and do the first thing on it. Schedule exactly how much time you will need, but if you run over the time, keep at it until you are finished. If you are in the middle of a deal and something goes wrong, keep at it. Don't take no for an answer. Find a way around the problem. Go over it. Go around it. And if none of that works, try barrelling right through it. Persistence is always the difference between success and failure.

When hard work brings home a deal and a good profit, reward yourself! Have a good meal out or treat yourself to whatever turns you on. By psychologically conditioning yourself with small rewards for jobs well done, you will get as much of a charge out of your accomplishments as from the reward. An actor or performer gets more out of giving a good show and the applause than from his pay cheque. So it should be with the tycoon. Pulling off the good deal is the thrill. Increased wealth is a secondary pay off.

So, go to it. Don't procrastinate. Put the TV in the closet. Cancel your subscription to *Playboy*. Stop all reading that tends to make you think like a consumer instead of a producer. Go to it and start. The voice will tell you, "Do it now!" Why wait till mañana?

Now that you have seen some of the barriers people set up to stop themselves from becoming tycoons, how can you organise yourself for success?

Educate Yourself. Read not only the biographies of successful business people, but read all the property and business books you can find. If they give you one good idea, it could be worth plenty. Still, reading is not to replace action. Reading is for sitting on the toilet, getting yourself to sleep, riding on a bus or while waiting for someone. And there is more to read about than just property. Salesmanship, accounting, trade magazines. Any public library in a big city will have plenty of specialised magazines, more than you can dream about. All of them can be the source of the idea or concept that will be your vehicle for success.

Finally, take the most boring course in the world – Accounting. I flunked it, but it was probably the most valuable course I ever took. Sometimes it is given other names, but always take the first basic course. Remember business is in many ways like a game. Accounting is the way you keep score. Without this skill you just don't know where you are. When you move to bigger deals, a deal that looks great and sends goosebumps of ownership pride up your arms, your attempts to understand the financial statements involved may leave you in a state of rigor mortis unless you attend to such basic and necessary preparation. College business and basic law courses are good too, but nothing is as helpful as a strong basic accounting course.

Learn the Jargon. Every profession has its own special vocabulary. Many of the new terms you come across are explained in this report. Learn them. Use them.

Stop Consuming. Ben Franklin, one of the world's richest self-made men of the colonial era, had the right idea. Working in the print shop as a kid, he saw all the other printers apprentices smoke and take several beer breaks a day. Ben drank water. He ran extra errands for extra pay. Within a few years, Ben had his own print shop. Then, with what he had saved by not smoking and drinking, he started his own newspaper. Ben Franklin was big on saving.

Don't waste your time on a theoretical economics course. Like astrology, it is just nonsense. If you put all the economists in the world in one room, you'd have as many worthless opinions as you had economists.

The Five Per Cent Rule

You can discover a whole new world if you apply the five per cent rule. The five per cent rule is something to strive for, not to accomplish all at once. When I told a stewardess girlfriend about it, she said I was absolutely crazy and never wanted to see me again. But I explained to her that it was one of the most important early steps on the trail to tycoondom.

Here it is:

Determine what your gross income is. For example, $2000 per month.

Take five per cent. That would be $100 a month. Plan to spend no more than that on your living expenses and taxes.

That leaves $1,900 to build your empire. Find a way to channel this entire amount into deals or investments that will double, preferably in a month.

That is the goal. Now there are lots of ways to reach that goal. Let's take Sally, my stewardess friend:

Gross Income	$2,000
Income Taxes	$600
Rent	$500
Clothes	$200
Car Payments	$200
Food	$200
Entertainment and Travel	$400
Medical and Dental	$100
Insurance and Miscellaneous	$200
Total Expenses	$2,400
Net Loss	$400

Obviously, with the above budget this girl could never become a tycoon. Her Christmas bonus was the only way she got out of debt once a year. However, within two years of applying the five per cent rule, she owned a thriving basket import business. Sally's tax-free income grew to $140,000 per year. This is how she did it.

If she was going to live on five per cent of her gross income, she decided that the amount she was earning was far too small. She began looking for ways to increase that income. At one of her regular stopovers, Manila, there was a native basket weaver who sold rattan fruit baskets for 35 cents. Sally brought back a gross, duty-free with her $200 allowance. As she was a 'stew', she had no transportation costs. At home, she sold the baskets for $7 each. In only a few months, she was picking up a few hundred extra dollars every week. And that, of course, is where most other stews would have stopped.

Next, Sally introduced the five per cent rule. Instead of squandering the extra profit, she reinvested it in more baskets and other similar handicrafts. To get more capital, she eliminated her rent by (together with her boyfriend) offering to become manager of the apartment building they lived in. Presto, she had generated another $500 a month for her high-profit import business.

One problem, however, remained. Sally liked nice clothes. Fortunately, she soon realised that as manager of an apartment building, an abundance of cast-off clothing from former tenants came her way. (This is the source I had been using for years). Adding a new twist, she began to trade or sell, primarily with other stews, the items that either didn't fit her or that she wasn't crazy about. Soon, she was at the point where she never spent a penny on clothes, but through this combination of cast-offs and trades, she was able to keep herself looking sharp.

There are several ways to eliminate car expenses. The easiest is to just simply sell it and get along without one. It amazes me that people will buy brand-new American wheels when they fully understand that after four or five years, they will only have a rusted hunk-o-junk to show for their investment. You might also want to consider a part-time job which provides you with a company car. At worst, you can shop around for a used car at a good 'all cash' reduced price, assuming that the car will hold its value if you take care of it.

As far as for food, entertainment and travel, Sally didn't have much cutting to do in this department. As her basket business grew, business dinners were paid for by clients and suppliers. When she did pick up the cheque, the dinner was turned into a deductible business-related expense. This helped reduce her income tax. By purchasing a small rental property and gaining overflow depreciation deductions, she succeeded in getting rid of the remainder of her tax burden.

If she keeps up the good work for a few more years, this stew will be a millionaire. Property played only a small part in her story. She owes it all to the five per cent rule, which started her thinking of ways to reduce expenses and invest the saved capital in money-making ventures.

How could the five per cent rule work for you?

Perhaps you could eliminate much food expense by helping out as a busboy, waiter, or hostess during rush hours. The usual pay is a few dollars plus a free meal. If you can't eliminate an expense, the five per cent rule says find an alternate source of income that gives you the same effect as if you had saved. In other words, make profitable use of your spare time.

Be creative! Be inventive! There are hundreds of ways to earn extra money if you put your mind to it. Remember, find a need and fill it.

I once came across this money-making scheme, which has to pull a high rank in ingenuity. This card was shoved in my US post office mailbox:

Dear Fellow Boxholder:

I drag my bones down to the post office each morning to check my box for mail. So while I'm at it, why don't I look through your little window too? If I see that you have some mail, I will call you immediately.

This saves you (literally) dozens and dozens of time-wasting, sometimes fruitless, trips to the post office. So why not join the rest of the folks on my 'call sheet' for a couple of weeks to see if you like it? Give me a call at 345-6789.

Yours in rain, sleet or snow

Mr J Frost   PO Box XYZ   Your Town

Whether Mr Frost had many takers I don't know. But at least he was trying. Later Mr Frost started a franchise operation, a private mail-drop and message service. I hear he is doing very well. Find a need and fill it!

Another way to success is to develop the traits of the successful. Assuming that you haven't quit your job or even made your first property offer, start revamping your image or changing it if necessary. Most important, create a reputation for extreme dependability. If you have an appointment at noon, don't arrive at two minutes past. Arrive early and stand there looking at your second hand. At precisely noon, ring the bell. If you have promised to return a book or a borrowed dollar on Monday morning, get it there at 9am. Be very punctual. Hold up your end of every bargain or transaction. Don't argue or give excuses to anyone. Do what has to be done. Your reputation for being cooperative, dependable, prompt and fanatical at meeting your obligations will be worth more than anything else as you move up in business. It works for Swiss bankers. It will work for you.

Finally, what is the best, most productive thing you can do to get yourself organised as a property tycoon? Eat, dream and live property. If you drive past a vacant lot, think of how you might improve and develop it. What would be its best use? When you see a junky or abandoned structure, figure out how you would remodel it and what would bring in the best rents. Stop your car at property agents and discuss your ideas with their sales people. Get to know them all on a first name basis. Let them know that you are in the market for deals.

Let's Get Organised!

The main difference between a tycoon and the other 99 per cent of the population involves three factors. The first is ambition. I covered ambition, motivation and persistence in the chapter "Think Like a Tycoon". The second element is having a workable, realistic plan. Realistic means not spinning your wheels on projects that cannot produce a good profit within a month or two. A tiny business, like a neighbourhood gift shop or hot dog stand, simply can't ever make it big. You must expend energy only on high-potential projects or educational experiences that will give you a very solid return for the hours and money invested. What's a good return? If you can't anticipate a venture making at least $50,000 profit after taxes in a year or less, don't bother. The third factor is your ability to put this plan into effect.

Your time and money must be organised in such a way that it is spent only on activities that will produce maximum financial reward. With most businesses you will notice immediately a great torrent of required paper work. There are lots of records to keep, mainly for the tax people and other government agencies. If you don't get your paperwork organised at an early stage you will find yourself hopelessly buried in insoluble accounting problems. I know, because it happened to me. Again, it will help you to enrol as soon as possible in a course of basic accounting. Don't take a specialised course. It's better to understand the overall basics first. People who go into a business without any background in accounting have a 90 per cent chance of failure.

Remember, business is like any other game. You need a scorecard to know how you or your team is doing. The scorecard in business is your accounting record. Profits or losses are revealed only by good accounts. Because you may not have taken an accounting course yet, I will give you enough information here to set up a rudimentary accounting system today. However, I still recommend that you take that accounting course at some future time. Remember also that, when you take a serious course with serious people, the new friends and contacts you make can be just as important as the technical knowledge you pick up.

If you hire a certified public accountant to do your tax returns, ask the same accountant or his staff to help you set up a system for keeping books and records. It is essential that you fully understand your own accounts. Then you can also know where you are and what the score is. How much do you owe people? When is it due? How much do your customers or tenants owe you? You must be able to meet all your short-term financial obligations out of the payments due to you from others. The reason businesses fail is insolvency. This is simply an inability to pay bills on time. Often a business that is profitable and healthy can still fail if its obligations can't be met on time. This is why accounting is so important. A big profit that you won't get for three years doesn't pay today's creditors. If you don't pay you will be put into bankruptcy. Kiss your assets goodbye.

A Simple Accounting System

Here is a basic record-keeping system for those who know nothing about accounting.

Let's assume you have just closed escrow on your purchase of a two-unit apartment house at 1234 Anystreet, Yourtown.

The first thing I like to do is to give each of my buildings a name. A good name can add charm to a property. Personally, I like the exotic touch. But you can name your property anything you like. Buy an attractive little plaque and put it up over the front door. For example:

Casa Paradiso Apartments

For information concerning this property:

Phone 333-3333

I don't like to use my home phone, personal name or give my home address on a property, because I don't want anyone just dropping in. Yet, I want anyone who is interested in buying or renting a place I own to have an easy time contacting me. That's why you should have an answering service or phone answering device in service 24 hours a day. You should also get a post office box or use a mail drop service.

From the start, I suggest having a separate bank account for each property or business venture. It makes life easier. At tax time all you have to do is give your accountant the cheque register for Casa Paradiso and let him figure things out from that. I like to have each business or property account at a different bank too. That keeps things well separated.

At the bank, ask for the sort of cheque book where there is a separate book for the record of cheques, deposits and notes. Cheque books where the records are kept on hundreds of stubs are far harder to work with. If you have an assistant, spouse, secretary or other trustworthy person, put them on the signature card for the account in case you are away or physically out of commission. Have your cheque printed:

Casa Paradiso Bldg. Account

Your Name

Your PO Box, Your Town

Your Phone

Your Drivers License Number or appropriate Identity Card information

Naturally, you must keep in mind that for income tax purposes, repairs in general are immediately tax-deductible. They can be used to reduce or offset your taxable income in the year incurred. Capital improvements, in contrast, are not usually deductible and must be charged off over the remaining life of the building or the life of the improvement (whichever is shorter). When in doubt, it is always better to have a 'repair' than a 'capital improvement' because it generates a larger tax benefit. Assuming that the cheque register sample constituted your entire annual income and expense on Casa Paradiso, this is how the summary you would prepare for your accountant should look:

Casa Paradiso – Accounting Summary

Repairs and maintenance

Cheque # 5074	$ 375.00
5075	$ 25.00
5077	$ 52.00

Advertising

Cheque #5076	$ 15.00

Capital Improvements

    New Carport

        Cheque #5078 $1,000.00

Utilities

        Cheque #5079 $ 15.00

Insurance

        Cheque # 5078 $ 275.00

Taxes

        Cheque # 5081 $ 875.00

Cash Flow

Rents	$ 400.00
Washing machine	$ 3.75
*Security deposits	$ 600.00
*Deposit on pending sale	$ 5,000.00

*Not taxable income

I keep all original insurance policies in a bank safety deposit box in case of fire. Photocopies of fire insurance policies are kept in my office file titled "Insurance – Fire and Casualty". Into this I put all fire, earthquake, and other casualty policies. These are filed in alphabetical order by property so that once a month my secretary can review all policies and be sure they are up-to-date and that the value insured is for the approximate replacement cost of the property. A summary of the basic facts on each policy is written on the outside of the file jacket in chart form. From time to time a mortgage lender will want to physically hold an original insurance policy. He has that right. However, to ensure the accuracy of your filing system, you must request, and always have on hand, a photocopy of each policy not in your files. Other insurance is broken down into several categories: namely "Insurance – Motor Vehicles" (policies and correspondence); and "Insurance – Liability" (policies and correspondence).

Billing

As long as you have only one property, keeping expenses and income credited to the proper account is easy. But suppose you have 20. During a busy day you get a notice that your insurance premium on account 2233445566 has not been paid and your policy will lapse in three days. Since it would take hours to find out which building the policy refers to, I use this simple trick. When setting up any insurance or other service relative to a property, I see to it that the address on each bill should not refer to me alone, but should also refer to the property by name. In that way the notice on this particular bill would come addressed to:

Your name

Casa Paradiso

Your PO Box

In my early days, when bills, tax statements, bank statements etc. came merely addressed to me, I had a devil of a time just allocating them to the proper parcel of property. Needless to say, if we are talking about several businesses you are running out of your bedroom, the same reasoning applies. You'd be "Joe's Mail" and "Happy Dates Matchmaking". A distinctive name that tells what you do is better than just doing business under your own name. In most places you don't need anyone's permission to be Joe Smith doing business (or trading) as "Happy Dates, Fruits & Nuts".

Filing System

I suggest you purchase two matching standard letter-sized two-drawer files. Not only will they be a convenient and semi-portable place for your records, but if you purchase a factory-second flush door (before door-knob holes are drilled) as a desktop, you will have acquired an attractive typing table as well. Each property will have about four or five folders, for example:

Casa Paradiso – New Roof. This file might contain your plans, building permits, contractors' bids, a copy of notice of non-responsibility for liens and all else pertaining to this project. When the project is underway, it is kept in an upper drawer. When the new roof is completed, final inspection has been approved and all bills have been paid, it is filed below with the other closed files.

Casa Paradiso – Tenants. This might contain copies of ads, leases and photocopies of tenants' cheques. Why should you copy tenants' cheques? So that if at any stage they don't pay up, you can sue and know in which banks they are still likely to have a chequing account. Your lawyer can lien and attach these accounts.

Casa Paradiso – Financing. This would have a copy of the mortgage note and trust deeds, showing how much was borrowed. It would also have a payment book or other computer print-out showing how much was paid on principal and how much interest is due each month.

Casa Paradiso – Original Purchase and Depreciation Schedules. This would contain a copy of original escrow statements, any side deals with the former owner and a letter from an estate agency setting forth his estimate of the percentage of depreciation applicable to land, building and personal property. It would also contain your bill of sale on the personal property and estimate.

Rents Received. This file would include a list of all properties in the form of a spreadsheet with a place to enter each monthly or weekly rent as it comes in. I set it up so that column one on the left is the property address, column two is security deposits and column three is scheduled rents with January, February, March etc. marked out. Each month I enter the rent received. If there is a special transaction, for example, a tenant got $25 off for painting or whatever, a note is made. If a tenant fails to pay, or is late, I mark a yellow magic marker circle around his name. If he gets too many circles, I might take some action, such as having a little talk with the tenant.

More Record-Keeping Tips

Your record-keeping system should also take into account a few other tips. Some banks offer free current accounts if you have a minimum balance of say $500 in the account. How do you get that first $500? Well, one way is in the form of a security deposit from your tenant. The security deposit from a tenant will usually be one month's rent. (I personally prefer two months, but each to his own). If you put this security deposit in your bank as a minimum deposit, then you should get the free account. If a tenant ever asks you for interest on his deposit, say truthfully that you don't get interest, as the deposit is in a current account. Therefore, he isn't entitled to interest either and get an interest-free loan.

Open a separate account for each property or business that you own as well as for all individual deals that involve more than half a dozen transactions. That way every expense and everything relating to a specific property or business can be assessed easily. If someone else is preparing your account books, this will make it easy for your book-keeper or accountant to figure out what you took in and what was spent on each situation.

If you pay for something in cash you can still maintain the same clarity. Keep a record in the cheque book itself of cash paid out. For example, always note the cash spent, its purpose and to whom it was paid, just as you would if the transaction had been paid by cheque.

When you get a cheque from a new tenant or customer, have that person make it out to 'cash' or 'bearer'. That way a tenant cannot stop payment on a cheque he has already given you. We would all prefer to trust people, but when you've been doing business as long as I have, you'll find out a lot of cheques turn out to be "duds". If they are not bad cheques today, they might be by tomorrow. Never keep cheques lying around. Cash all cheques immediately on the day received. If you are the least bit doubtful or unsure about the signer, take it to the bank it was drawn on immediately and cash it there. That will save a couple of days of waiting. Sometimes cheques go bad unintentionally. Tenants overdraw their account. The excuse may be, "I had to buy my sick mother a present." What should you do? You should have standing orders with your bank to re-deposit all returned cheques for collection. That means any bad cheques will not be returned to you, but will stay at the debtor's bank for up to 10 days or until your tenant deposits enough funds to cover it.

Save Time By Delegating Repetitious Tasks

I find it a real bother to write out the same cheques each month, i.e. the same mortgage payment to the same company month after month. Why not use post-dated cheques? If I buy a property and the seller carries the financing, I will write him 12 post-dated cheques, each dated the first of the month over the next year. Since banks rarely look at dates on cheques, I write in bold letters over the top, "Do not cash before. . . " Thanks to this little added protection, the bank should notice that there is something special about the cheque.

Whenever possible I get post-dated cheques from my tenants too. That way I don't have to chase them for payments. I just tack their cheques to the bulletin board and then pull them off as the payments come due.

A banking service known as 'transmatic' in the US and as 'standing orders' or 'direct debit' in the UK, offers another way to handle things automatically and efficiently. Most banks in most countries offer this sort of bill-paying as a free service to customers, the name just varies slightly. Nonetheless, the service is the same, and it saves mounds of time. Say, for instance, that you are an institutional mortgage holder. You owe Fidelity Savings $500 per month. Occasionally, you just forget to write them a cheque. Even though it's a simple mistake, you still incur a substantial charge and are labelled a 'late payer' on their records. The transmatic plan will automatically withdraw your mortgage payment from the checking or savings account that you designate. Hence, you save not only lots of time, but also potential aggravation.

Knowing Your Colleagues

Next, a very helpful step in any potential tycoon's career – join the local association of small business or property owners. In most cities there are several such clubs or political action groups. Most counties or towns will have more than one association. If you consult a phone book under 'clubs and associations' or ask around, you will find appropriate groups in your area. Join them. These associations probably cost peanuts for dues. Besides the obvious advantage of associating with people of similar economic interests, these associations put out or recommend many useful publications, which are cheap or free. They have special deals with merchants who give members big discounts on office supplies, carpets, drapes, washers and dryers or whatever you need. These associations also take an interest in laws and regulations that are pending both nationally and locally. Their opposition to rent control, for instance, is the only bulwark standing between you as a property owner and the fuzzy-thinking leftists who would like to take all your property away and smother the free-enterprise system.

Therefore, one of your first steps in getting organised is to join your local organisation (like the association of income property owners). If your business is owning single-family homes, perhaps you'll also want to join the local association of home owners. This group would have a name like the 'Forest Park Improvement Association'. You'll always be able to make friends there. When you have problems, it is nice to have experienced old timers to help you out. Nothing is more helpful than personally knowing local public officials. Important politicians will often be your co-members. They want your votes and financial support. There is a spirit of camaraderie in all such associations. Additionally, these groups often sponsor low-cost educational forums, field trips and seminars. Such courses will help you be more effective in buying, selling, managing and trading. Every industry or profession has at least one trade association or group.

To summarise, borrow and read all the books on the business you go into, or on property, from the public library. Acquire paperbacks if you can afford them. All books and lectures should be considered if you feel they will be of value to you. Take all the night courses, weekend seminars and join all the clubs you can find. Take an accounting course. Join your local businessman's clubs and the association of property owners. Your education and contacts are capital, just as valuable (probably more so) than money in the bank!

Time Is Short – You Must Not Waste It!

Here is how to plan your time! First, it's a good idea to list all the things you want to do on a big sheet of paper. Perhaps two sheets. One for short term (six months) another for long-term (up to one year). Then rearrange the list in order of priority, putting a number one next to the things of great importance and so on down the list. Each specific project on the list should be related to your general plans and goals in life. If your main goal is financial independence, one of your first steps is to get an education, both formal and in the real world, before you jump into a deal.

Get some education in property by going to classes or reading books. Most important by far, however, is to get out and look at the deals available in your community. You won't make a penny if all you do is read, think and take classes. You will know when you are ready for your first deal. When you start out, the first thing to do is circle interesting classified ads with magic markers, or clip lots of ads from local newspapers. Organise them and spend some time, perhaps all weekend, looking at deals and properties. Later on, your priorities may change from looking at new deals to digesting the ones you have already looked at. Once you get into owning a few businesses or properties, you'll be making needed administrative decisions, repairs and improvements. You'll make changes in tenants or seek out new sources of revenue as appropriate. You should never get up in the morning without preparing a written plan for what you will accomplish that day and that week. Do not spin your wheels doing things unrelated to your major goals in life. It's too easy to get side-tracked. Remember, you have a goal. Presumably that goal is to achieve financial independence in the shortest possible time. Every minute counts. Thus, you must spend time only on those things relating directly to your goal.

That doesn't mean cutting out all pleasure. You must give yourself some treats now and then. But try to arrange going to the movies, or whatever else turns you on, only as a reward for accomplishing a high-priority activity. In other words, if you have 10 or 15 things in the number one category to accomplish, do not go to a show or take time off until you have done those things. Movies can wait. You can't. Accomplish an important objective, then treat yourself to a night out. Psychologically, it is very helpful to look forward to a reward you promise yourself for closing a deal or doing something you have been putting off.

I have also found it most essential to get a diary or appointment book with a separate big page for every date. That way I can put down in detail what I want to attempt that day. At 7am I have to do one thing, at half past another and at 8am still another, all the way to midnight. Time from now on should be closely scheduled. Your days should be filled up with properties to look at, books to read, people to call upon, etc. Don't get discouraged if you don't accomplish everything you map out to do on a given day. I always seem to schedule twice as much as I can accomplish. Even if I am usually a little bit behind, I would rather have the feeling that I am behind than that I have nothing to do.

People sometimes ask me, "Are you really happy?" Frankly, the only unhappy people I have ever met are those who are bored. These are usually rich people with too much leisure time. Just as often, however, there are working people who get home from work and the only thing they can think of doing is to open a beer and watch television. These days, in our affluent society, even poor folks often have too much leisure time. Either way, maximum unhappiness is waking up one day and wondering, "How come I didn't get anywhere?"

Happiness is having a goal and working towards it.

Many people spend money on shrinks instead of doing something productive to make themselves happy. The shrink gets happy and rich, but does the patient? Not usually.

In business you may have to devote almost every waking hour to your objectives if you are going to be extremely successful. You will have to cut out all time-wasters. Stop seeing people who don't have a direct and positive bearing upon your main activity. Get rid of useless or negative individuals who might lead you in wasteful directions. If you are lucky enough to find a boyfriend or girlfriend who shares your interests, he or she could be a very good influence on you. There's nothing like a lover with similar objectives to help you reach your goals. Every race horse has a pace-setter. Unfortunately in my life, and the lives of most of my friends, it is very difficult, if not impossible, to find the perfect partner. By this I mean someone you like to be with, like to make love with and who also thinks the same way you do about acquiring a great fortune. If you have such a partner, you are in an ideal situation. Chain that person to your wrist! You might even consider marriage! But if you are going to marry, have a property settlement agreement in advance.

Making friends is another aim at property courses. If no courses or clubs exist in your community, why not place an ad in your local newspaper? Put together a group of like-minded entrepreneurs to share experiences and work together on deals. If you are married and have a spouse who is interested in working with you, you might want to join another couple on projects. If your spouse does not share your interest, perhaps you can find another married individual with whom you can work. If you are married, to keep problems at a minimum, your business partner should be either extremely ugly or of the same sex. This assumes you are not gay. If you are, I still say it's enough of a problem to stay on good terms with a business partner. Put a love triangle in your life and it means nothing but trouble. On the whole, short-term romances and property deals don't mix. You are out to make money, not whoopee. Property deals I have made with compatible partners have been more satisfying and more enjoyable than those I have done alone. It is simply more fun to share your high and low moments with someone else.

So where do you find a compatible business partner? Often through ads in the paper. Or you might meet people selling their property or buying yours, at property seminars, property auctions or through groups you join or organise on your own. If you make your desires and interests known, like-minded individuals are guaranteed to come your way.

Stop Consuming

You can no longer be a 'consumer'. You should never spend your time and money on acquiring fashionable clothes, unless of course fashion is your business. Normally clothes will have little impact on your business success and being 'in' will only waste your time and money. There was once a book published called *Dressing for Success*. As if dressing made any difference! A few years ago, a friend and I both used to dress in patchy blue jeans and frayed flannel-checkered shirts. We thought about putting out a parody of this book, in which we would be visiting our banker in raggedy jeans. Then, in the same jeans, dressed like hicks, we would be looking at property and closing deals. In other words, we'd dress the same for every occasion. I am convinced that bankers, sellers and everyone else are more interested in what you have to offer than in the name of your tailor. So don't kill a lot of time worrying about how you look, what kind of car you drive or other status symbols. You'll soon have the only real status symbol – lots of money. Don't get sidetracked. Just stay neat, clean and presentable. Again, put your TV in the closet. They don't call it the 'boob-tube' for nothing! If you just have to watch a particular programme, then schedule it in on your calendar and don't get sucked into wasting more time in front of the TV after your show is over. Watch nothing else but the programmes that directly relate to your goals. TV is a prime time-killer. The same is true to a lesser degree of the radio. Instead of always listening to music, have a cassette player in your car. Then, when you're driving you can slip an educational cassette course into your player and spend the time learning as well as driving.

You might also, while you are driving and learning, try flossing your teeth. You can floss with one hand if you use a plastic holder. I give you this helpful hint because most people lose their teeth by the time they are 50. Not decay. It's the result of gum disease. Nobody wants to do deals with, or make love to, a toothless wonder. Flossing with a little plastic holder will keep the gums healthy and your mouth smelling fresher. It will prevent you from wasting time and money on dental work when you could be out looking for deals.

I didn't bring up flossing your teeth to be funny. In fact, being healthy is a tycoon's biggest concern. If you do not work at maintaining a healthy body, all the money in the world cannot buy you a new one. Luckily, property ownership means that you can get plenty of exercise by working on your properties. Don't be afraid of strenuous physical activity! Others would have to go to an exercise club or whip themselves into a frenzy playing tennis. But as a property owner (or in any business) you get to do all this healthy work, like shingling, stonework, painting and landscaping. Doing some of the manual labour yourself is also a way to save you $50 an hour. Improvements and sweat equal more money in your pocket. I much prefer painting my own building, to playing golf. The paint job may bring me an extra $1,000 per month in rent. That's at least $100,000 in increased net worth. In the meantime, I manage to keep fit.

Look Out For Special Situations

In the next few years, you may want to leave your regular nine to five wage-slave job. But take that action only after accumulating enough wealth and cash flow to live comfortably. As I have said time and time again, one of the most important steps before making your first deal is to use the 'Hill Hundred House Rule'.

Here is what happened to me on a property called Villa Bayview. It was a gorgeous home with a magnificent view of the Singapore skyline and all of Singapore Bay. It was also one of the first deals that I closed outside of the US and proved to me, more than ever, that my methods work anywhere, in any market. The property was worth about $150,000 at the time. I considered it out of my league and figured there was no way I could make money on it. It was a very attractive redwood and glass house. Apart from the pink trim, which screamed to me for a coat of 'Barcelona Brown', there was nothing wrong with the place.

Yet, after I completed my hundred house look, it was still on the market and the price had been reduced to $125,000. I was told it had been vacant for a year or more. I smelled a problem. Inquiring of the neighbours, I heard this disturbing tale. A year earlier, just after she moved in, a beautiful young girl had had her throat slashed in the Bayview, reputedly by a mafia don who had caught her in the arms of another man. This other man had been strung up in the kitchen in a very unpleasant way. It appeared that the hoodlum-cum-murderer had purchased the Bayview for his girlfriend, but after the 'incident' had taken off for parts unknown. The heirs of the girl had been told they owned the property, but they, wanting nothing to do with the situation, merely told a local lawyer to sell the place and just send them a cheque. The lawyer had the property appraised ($150,000) and listed it with a property agent. From time to time offers were made, mostly by people new to the area and who had not heard the murder story. When they heard the grisly tale, they generally backed out of the deal, figuring the house had bad 'kharma'. By the time I returned to the house six months later for a closer inspection, the neighbours had even embellished the tale. The girl, it turned out, had been a belly dancer who often did exotic things like stripping to the nude to cavort outside her house on moonlit nights. According to the neighbours, the ghost of the slain girl was still doing her striptease on the front lawn every time there was a full moon. The story was retold and found its way in to the papers. Nobody in town would buy the haunted property.

My reaction was a little different than most. I figured that if I owned a haunted house with a full moon show of that calibre going on, it would sure beat going to a drive-in. The property had been listed with several agents and all their listings had now expired. Even the local property agents didn't want to be bothered showing what they had come to regard as an unsaleable property. I asked more questions and ordered a title report; this shows how much money is owed and if any lawsuits affect the property. I learned from the title report that a private loan on the property amounting to $75,000 was in default by several months. It appeared that the people who originally owned the property would get it back in a foreclosure for $75,000. This sum was less than half what it was worth. The owner of the mortgage turned out to be a widow living about 200 miles away in Malaysia.

I drove down to see her. The information I got might have upset most people, but for me it represented an unusual opportunity. She told me she would under no circumstances take back the property even if she had the legal right to do so. In a foreclosure, if no-one bids the amount of the mortgage, the mortgage holder gets the property. If the mortgage holder does not want the property, a person who comes to the sale and bids three cents (or anything) gets it. I told her that if she didn't bid for the property it was likely to go for a song and that I would personally bid $10,000.

I asked her why she didn't just take over the property and rent it out for the $1,000 per month it should rent for. She broke into hysterical tears. When she regained a measure of composure, this is what she told me:

"My husband committed suicide in the bathroom of that house four years ago. Two weeks after we moved in, he shot himself in the mouth with a shotgun. It wasn't pretty. The house was then vacant for a long time. Two weeks after Mr Moravia and his beautiful young wife bought the Bayview from us, well, two weeks later you know what happened. I don't want to go near the place."

I gulped. But thought to myself, "What the heck!" So I offered the lady a deal whereby I would take over her mortgage and tax payments of $600 per month. She agreed that I should bid the full amount of the mortgage at the foreclosure and if I did this she would extend the loan for five years. Assuming there were no other bidders at the sale, I would have made a no-money-down deal.

Feeling I wanted to be sure of my ownership, I placed a long-distance call to the heirs of the dead girl. They were resigned to the fact that the house would be taken from them in a foreclosure and had no interest in doing anything about it. To be sure that there would be no surprises with an outside bidder going against me at the sale, I offered the heirs $300 for a 'quit claim' deed. They accepted at once, since that was $300 more than they had expected to get. I became the owner and holder of legal title.

With the permission of the lady who held the loan on the property, I called off the foreclosure sale and moved into the house. I never even thought about the two-week jinx until 15 days after I moved in. I got a lot of calls from the mortgage lady and neighbours asking if I was OK. I was, of course. As a matter of fact in the two years I lived in the house I never had an unhappy moment.

The view was great. I watched big ocean liners pass and freighters from exotic lands unloading their cargoes. The house itself was laid out as two apartments. The smaller unit downstairs was rented by me to another bachelor who was in the wholesale fine wine business. I got $375 a month, plus $50 in wine for the lower unit. My cash outlay every month for loan and taxes was $600.

$600

375 Rent for lower unit

$225 Net outlay

The place I was occupying had to be worth at least $600 a month rent. It had three bedrooms, two big bathrooms and a super-modern kitchen, etc. In fact it was a little too big for me, though with all that wine to drink each month I kept it pretty full with parties three times a week. In due course I painted it, put in some rosewood panelling, expanded the size of the living room and took in a girl roommate. She paid me $275 per month, which more than covered utilities and kept snacks in the refrigerator. She was good company too, though to keep the relationship business-like I made another rule which I have always followed – never sleep with your tenants. As a result, we stayed very good friends. When she was depressed or down she could rely on me for a shoulder to cry on. But most of the time our relationship was quite formal and correct. It worked out well, for over a year. And I did have a bit of fun with several of her girlfriends.

The net result of my first deal, including the roommate's contribution, was that I got a free place to live in, all the good wine that my friends and I could drink, utilities paid for, free food, usually cooked by my girl roommate and plenty of good company. Not only that, when I went to see my accountant at income tax time, he told me I had a slight tax loss or write-off from the depreciation I was allowed on the property.

In two years, the property I bought for $75,000 with nothing down was sold for $275,000. By trading up, I came out with $200,000 cash, tax free. Part of that $200,000 was due to the devaluation of paper money, or inflation. But don't forget, the property was worth $150,000 when I bought it, so as soon as the ink had dried on my purchase contract, I was (even then) $75,000 richer. Without any inflation or increase in the general price of property, I made $75,000 just as soon as I had changed the image of the house from a deserted, deadly, haunted place to a swinging bachelor pad of fun and parties. As it turned out, I had bought at the start of a property boom. But even without a boom this deal would have been a winner.

That's why you must get yourself organised and look at one hundred deals. I'm sure you will find several of your own winners.

The Tycoon's Credo

A Tycoon is:

1. **Organised**

   I will schedule a written programme of my activities and objectives and stick to it the entire day.

2. **Dedicated**

   I will do at least one thing I should have done, but have been putting off.

3. **Confident**

   I will feel as good as possible and achieve a sense of well-being by meditating 15 minutes every day. I will exercise or jog another 15 minutes.

4. **Appreciative**

   I will tell my family, friends and business associates "I like you" and mean it. I will be generous with praise and compliments.

5. **Optimistic**

   I will not dwell on past failures but will think positively about the present and the future.

6. **Educated**

   I will read something to improve my mind each day and will keep away from nonproductive and time-consuming people and activities.

7. **Thrifty**

   I will not be a consumer or a taxpayer any more than is absolutely necessary.

8. **Sociable**

   I will be charming and agreeable to everyone and speak badly of no-one.

9. **Alert**

   I will be open to new ideas, experiences and people who might teach me something new. I will not let myself fall into a rut or routine.

10. **Dependable**

    I will meet all my business, social and moral obligations punctually, honestly, and honourably.

Chapter 13

NEGOTIATING TIPS AND PLOYS

You have probably heard people say, "Never take no for an answer". This, of course, is easier said than done, but not that much easier. Sometimes you can get the answer you want, that is the yes answer, by merely asking the question right. When you are on the prowl for property and spot an owner diligently working in his yard, you could say to him in a negative way, "You probably don't want to sell your property right now, do you?" What a silly way to ask the question; you've already given him a suggestion of the answer. The only logical response is, "Yes, that's right, I don't want to sell my property." Why not think like a tycoon and ask the question in a positive way?

You could do it much more effectively this way: "If I can show you how to trade up for a much better property tax-free without taking a penny out of your pocket or bringing in an agent and his outrageous fee. Would you be interested?" Almost every homeowner and would-be seller will immediately become interested. His ears will perk up, and he will be eager to know what you have in mind. Furthermore, if you can show this fellow how to trade up, he will probably be willing to sell and move himself up to a bigger and better property, meaning you've got yourself a deal.

Another way of posing a proposition positively is to approach a potential seller and say something like, "If I can show you how to get much more rent money than you are getting now, would you be interested in listening to me?" Now, how many potential sellers would refuse to listen to your proposition, even if they are considering the sale of their property? You have thus created the opportunity to talk to him about instalment sales. You may even be able to convince him that by selling his property to you and acquiring a different, larger property, he would receive a larger rental income and thus enhance his own financial position. If an owner asks you to help him outline and implement a plan through which he would generate a better income, he will feel psychologically committed to deal with you throughout the deal. On the other hand, if the first response to your original (negatively phrased) question is "no", any attempt to further explain your plans is likely to be met only with a wall of resistance.

When you are trying to get someone to interact with you, to work effectively with you or to make a deal with you, remember that people are generally not interested in your needs. It's up to you to show them what you can do for them, where you can do it, when you can do it and how you can do it. How can they profit by dealing with you? What are the benefits to them? What are the risks they may want to avoid? How can they protect themselves against loss? The tycoon anticipates needs, fears and all questions before beginning negotiations.

It is true that you should seldom take "no" for an answer in a business relationship. But to get a "yes" you must structure your proposition so that the person you are dealing with has no choice but, in his best interest, to accept your offer. In other words, like the Godfather said, "Make 'em an offer they can't refuse".

The same approach can be used outside of property. Suppose you're looking for a job and the employer says, "I don't need you. My overhead is already too high. I can't afford another employee." Your answer should be, "That's true, I agree with you. I see your point, but I will work for you for free for two weeks. If in two weeks, I haven't made you far more than the salary I'll ask for, then you don't have to use me. Now, how can you refuse an offer like that? I'll work for you and make you profits of more than $1,000 a week and you don't have to pay me anything. And if I do work out for you, all I ask is that you pay me half of what extra money I make you." When you make your offers to people in such a way, it is difficult for them to refuse to deal with you. You'll find that if you really can increase someone's income, you will always experience success.

If the person with whom you want to make a deal has some objections to your proposition, treat those objections (even if they are stupid or irrational) with respect. Never argue. Always agree with what they have to say, then add, but... and take it from there.

Another point is, after you have an agreement that gives you what you want, don't jabber beyond the sale. Sometimes, once the person on the other side has done what you wanted, if you keep talking, they may have a change of heart. All you should do in a property deal, once the person has agreed to sell, is to sign and have the seller sign an informal written contract. To keep an inexperienced person calm, don't use the formidable 'C' word 'CONTRACT'. Instead, your contracts should be innocuously titled "memorandum". Remember, in property all contracts are meaningless unless they are in writing. After signing the 'memorandum' and closing the deal, you should say something to encourage the seller that he did the right thing.

One of my favourite remarks is, "Boy, Mr Seller, I certainly didn't intend to come up to your price of $100,000. I didn't think I'd have to go over $85,000. You sure know how to drive a hard bargain." In this way the seller's opinion that he got the best of you will be confirmed. Give him that satisfaction!

Obviously, if you were to say at the closing, "I was prepared to got to $110,000 on your deal. I'm sure glad you sold it to me for $100,000," you would, by your uncalled-for remark, cause him to renege or speak ill of you for decades.

Regardless of the contract you may have with someone, remember a contract is only as good as the people who make it. If either side to the contract wants to get out of it, they can always do so. Once they do, all you have left is a costly and frustrating lawsuit. Never get into a lawsuit. Keep negotiating, never lose your cool or give up, no matter how unreasonable that idiot you are dealing with can be. A bad settlement is better than a good case against someone.

Sometimes it is wise to use testimonials which praise your good character and reliability. Rather than giving a reference to be used later, I find it very effective in negotiations to say to the doubting Thomas opposite me, "Look here Thomas, if you are worried about me keeping up my side of the deal, Mr Jones at the First National Bank has dealt with me successfully many times. I'm sure he will give me a good reference. I'd be happy to step out of the room while you call banker Jones for a reference on me".

That way, if you can supply the name of a person who is respected in the community, you may be able to close a deal that would otherwise have been impossible because the seller in question thinks you are some sort of flake. Developing good references and using the name of someone well-respected in the community, like the local banker, is particularly useful for younger tycoons, who, at the age of 20 to 26, may not be taken seriously by older sellers of substantial property. Don't appear too wealthy, bright, slick or money-hungry. Being sincere, understanding, helpful and interested in the other person's problems are your best negotiating tactics.

Chapter 14

THE MAGIC QUESTION

Once you have made a bit of money, in spite of valiant attempts to keep a low profile, word of your prosperity will leak out. Then a steady stream of investors, promoters and conmen of all shapes, colours and sizes will convincingly offer to triple your money. The deals touted will be wonderfully entertaining, but don't part with a penny unless you want to lose it! Listen to their stories. Make them wine and dine you. But remember, there are more than the two choices most people make when approached by a pie-in-the-sky salesman. Obviously, you could say a firm "No thank you and goodbye." Or, you might be a fool, take the deal offered and lose your shirt. Here's a third alternative that has made me a little richer, several times, not to mention the psychological rewards! There is nothing quite as satisfying as out-conning a confidence man. When a hot-shot salesperson departs from my home leaving his money behind, a warm glow radiates from me for days! Here's how you can make money out of these fast-talking conartists.

Ask the magic question, "If this deal is so good, why don't you keep it all for yourself?"

The answer will always be, "I would if I could, but I just don't have the money".

Here is where you turn the tables. You say, "Instead of investing in your deal, Mr Conniver, I'll lend you money in return for half the profits you just promised me. That way you, Mr Conniver, can multiply my borrowed money and keep half the gains for yourself without putting up a cent. You will take the risk of course, but as you've told me, it's a sure thing. All I want is some security pledged plus your personal note and a postdated cheque due six months from now." You should casually throw out some bait with the comment, "If and when this deal works out, my rich friends and I will probably invest lots more money on similar deals".

Why should you offer to make a loan to every promoter? Why must you always ask for security?

Most promoters and inventors will be personally broke and totally worthless to you. They will (if you let them) take your hard-earned cash. Usually you will never see any of it again. Sometimes the magic question will give you the opportunity to create a profit for yourself. If the conniver in our example has any assets at all, and really believes in his scheme, then one time out of a hundred you will both make a profit. But whatever happens, even if his deal goes sour, you'll come out smiling.

First, find out if the conartist has control of any significant assets. Car? House? Listed stocks? Perhaps his wife owns an expensive piece of jewellery. Maybe he has a fine oriental carpet or a minor work of art. Anything of verified or genuine value will serve your purposes. My favourite security is a deed or trust on property. A home is good if a conniver's 'equity' over his mortgage, or the net value involved, is at least triple the amount of money he wants from you.

Second, after establishing that old super-salesman has an object worth $15,000, you can offer to lend or rather 'invest' one-third of that value, say $5,000.

You might properly comment that the contracts I am about to present are the strangest loan package you have ever seen. It may look more like you are about to buy a car at a bargain price and will get a 50 per cent interest in a risky venture thrown in purely as a gift. Actually, that is exactly what you are about to do. The contracts will allow you to buy a car, diamond, house or whatever at a bargain price. Conniver will probably lose the car to you while losing his shirt on the deal he is trying to sell you. In 95 per cent of all cases, he will not be able to raise the cash to exercise his option, and you will end up with his property at a bargain price. As a result of this type of deal, I personally have ended up with many goodies.

Once I got a nice sports car at a bargain price from an operator who was going to triple 'our' money in three months. His scheme was to open a chain of massage parlours in Alaska to service the boys working on the Alaska Pipe Line. For one reason or another, as I predicted, it didn't work out. In a different deal I got a $50,000 house for $3,000 cash when I bought it from a self-proclaimed wheeler-dealer for $3,000 over his mortgage of $30,000. What went wrong?

In the first case, I was told that Alaska had the best cops money could buy. Unfortunately for my partner, they didn't stay bought and unexpectedly shut down his rub-down emporiums. In the second situation, the big profit was supposed to be made by buying silver coins at near their face value from a 'secret source' and reselling immediately at their collector value or triple the cost. But instead of buying silver coins, the wheeler dealer (without informing me of his alternate plan) bought a plane load of Columbian marijuana. The dope was hijacked away from him in Mexico. (What else should one expect!) In this case, however, the dealer 'saved' enough cocaine to offer me two pounds of nose candy in lieu of the $3,000 needed to repurchase his house. Terrific! I politely refused his offer, as I suggest you do in any deal involving illegal substances. Not that I have any great moral feelings against cocaine. I personally think it should be legal to drink Draino or anything else your heart desires, but life is just too short for me to traffic in anything illegal unless my very survival depends on it. In the end, whatever went wrong, I ended up all right because I had the title to and possession of something I bought at a bargain price. If the seller's big scheme had made money, we'd have both profited. Since it didn't, he took the loss and I came out smelling like a rose.

To sum up this magic question bit, if and when some person comes to you with a 'red ribbon' deal where all you have to do is hand over your money to get a fabulous, absolutely safe, super-return in a short time, remember, 99 times out of a hundred, you will lose every penny that you put up. The loss can result from incompetence, dishonesty or often, an ill-advised, illegal venture. The person trying to sell you a deal often does not own the proverbial pot to pee in, but sometimes he does have assets. In these cases there is often an opportunity for you to make a risk-free profit. It will work out well for you in the comparatively few instances where:

The promoter believes in the project.

He or she has assets.

When a conman with assets wants to get you involved and is wiling to give you a handsome phoney profit on your first venture with the belief that he will be able to sucker you in more heavily without security on the next deal.

Don't be a sucker. The sting (loss) will come at a time when you are holding no security. Grab the first profit and run!

To repeat, even if you make out like a bandit on your first deal, do not assume that you can have a repeat performance without the same security agreement.

Can you trust anyone?

I used to say you can't trust anyone except a major Swiss banker. Then some years ago a Swiss banker, manager of Swiss Bank Corporation's Chiasso (Switzerland) branch, was found to have diverted almost one billion dollars into personal and disastrous speculations. He went to the pokey. Today I have no exceptions. Not even Swiss bankers. Don't trust anyone!

How To Avoid Lending Money

If someone approaches you with a request to borrow money, always assume that one or more of the following will happen:

1. The person pushing the deal is involved in something illegal and will soon be in jail.

2. Within 10 minutes of getting your money, your new partner or debtor will:
   a) Be abandoned by a lover. He'll decide life isn't worth living and will split the scene (with your cash) for Brazil. Or perhaps he'll go to an even more celestial region by jumping from the top of a skyscraper.

   b) His mother, father, sister, brother, spouse, and children will simultaneously be afflicted by terminal leukaemia, or another fatal disease, and meeting their medical bills will become far more important than returning your money.

   c) He will turn into a certified lunatic or have an accident that will make him an incoherent vegetable.

   d) He will be murdered or fatally injured.

   e) A person that he trusted with the investment will turn out to be a thief and will disappear not only with your money, but with you partner's or debtor's alleged life savings, those of his widowed mother and so on.

   f) The business deal that was so highly touted in the initial meeting just "didn't work out."

After hearing those stories in at least 50 deals, I vowed never again to invest in a red ribbon deal or lend out money without being physically in possession of the security for the loan.

A basic rule to remember in dealing with other people is, if anything can possibly go wrong, it will! Assume that all of the above (and more) will really happen in every deal, loan or investment. Protect yourself in advance. With a little bit of luck, you'll do a lot better than I did, particularly if you meet an investor.

The most dangerous person you'll ever meet in your business career is not a robber, murderer or even the infamous tax man. The most dangerous person you'll have the misfortune to encounter will be an inventor. Once an inventor has you believing in his new product or process, your entire fortune and all your prospects will go down the tubes. The time demanded of you to promote the invention and attract further investors will become an endless treadmill. Your money will go into a bottomless pit!

I want to repress all memories of the time I became involved with the inventor of a solar panel. The small-scale prototype was convincing. It produced usable heat and energy in arctic climates with only a few hours of sunlight per week. Once installed, fuel and operating costs were almost nil. Because of tax credits and a financing package available to the buyer, any user of these panels would actually make money from day one. Nothing could possibly go wrong. Wealthy Arabs (he said) had already been after the patents for $3 million, but the inventor didn't want them shelving his project in order to sell the world more of their oil. That was his story anyway.

It seemed like the opportunity of a lifetime. The inventor's projections showed that my $10,000 investment would return a million a year. At least! Of course once production began, there were a few "minor bugs" to be worked out. Three more $10,000 contributions were required, each one to "turn the corner". To my sorrow, the corner never was turned and probably never will be turned. I kissed my $40,000 goodbye.

What went wrong? In my case, the invention in large size just never worked nearly as well as the doll-house-sized prototype. But with your inventor friend, it might be anything. Go over my points on "How To Avoid Lending Money" on the previous page. These are only a few of the things that can go wrong.

Dealing with a product that works is tough enough, but backing an unproven item – a new invention – will give you what I got from my solar panel a lot of useless hot air.

DuPont or IBM can afford research and development. They can afford a dead loss on 99 out of a hundred ideas because of the one product that makes it big. You are not in that league. Don't be a pioneer!

A sound rule to follow is that if someone wants your money (inventor or otherwise) ask the magic question. If you can be placed in a 100 per cent secured position, run like hell in the opposite direction!

The sad truth is that most inventions, like most movies, most oil wells, most property syndicates, most new products, and most commodity options never make the novice investor a penny.

The only 'sure thing' in an investment is probably in your back yard. Or your neighbour's back yard. Something that you think up, promote and control 100 per cent. Now let's move from the exotic to the mundane. I'll show you how to maintain your property empire by dealing with the every day basics and the people who will most directly help you make money – your tenants.

Chapter 15

MANAGING PROPERTY AND PROBLEM TENANTS

Once you become a landlord, your major challenge will be getting, and keeping, good tenants. You'll note I said "challenge" and not "problem", because, as in every aspect of your career, mental attitude is extremely significant. If you can meet the challenge of picking good tenants, you will preside over a smooth-running operation. Rents will be mailed on time. There will be a cordial tenant relationship, low turnover and a minimal vacancy factor.

When you buy your first rental property, existing tenants normally come with the building as part of the package. As soon as you take over management, adjust rents to market levels and evict undesirables immediately. Tenants expect it when ownership changes. If you procrastinate before introducing your new policies, tenants will be more apt to argue, get a lawyer or show resentment by destroying your property.

What is an undesirable tenant? If you are already a landlord, I don't have to tell you. If you are a novice, you'll discover that problem tenants come in two major categories:

A. Irresponsible deadbeats.

B. Inconsiderate slobs.

Often these qualities will be found combined in one disgusting individual. When you inspect each apartment in a building you are about to purchase, the slobs will be easy to recognise. A slight mess doesn't worry me, but if I were to describe the sort of visual and nasal experience you can expect every now and then, sometimes even in middle-class buildings, I might scare you out of being a landlord altogether. But suffice it to say, that you'll definitely recognise a slob's style of living when you see it. You want to evict them at once, if not sooner.

The second category is the deadbeat – someone who won't pay their rent when due. They can't be detected by sight or smell, but during negotiations most sellers will be glad to give you a thumbnail sketch of their tenants. Some will be described as prompt payers, others late payers. No-payers are the ones to get rid of. If your seller doesn't tell the truth, you'll know the deadbeats on the next rent-due date. You want to reform the slow-payers with a rent discount arrangement. Deadbeats are deadbeats are deadbeats.

Generally, tenants you want to get rid of will leave without court proceedings if you give them proper notice. It's better to bribe a deadbeat to leave by giving him a cash offer, than to go to court.

The kind of tenant you don't want.

Once your bad tenants are gone, you will begin to show the unit to new prospects. Don't ever show an apartment inhabited by a problem tenant until he is out and the place is cleaned, fumigated and repainted. If you show a pig-sty to a prospect, everyone except other slobs will be turned off. However, you may be able to develop a rapport with another tenant in an identical well-maintained apartment and show that one as your model apartment or show flat. Obviously, a day of vacancy represents an irretrievable loss. Still, it's better to have a vacancy than to rent to a loser. A bad tenant could be so annoying to his neighbours that you could lose all your good tenants. And if you get a deadbeat, slob or fuzzy-thinking leftist as your tenant, it will give you grey hair. Not only will he let the property run down and refuse to pay rent, but he will have legal-aid lawyers wear you out with frivolous legal proceedings that take up inordinate amounts of time, money and energy. You could lose even the building if Mr Deadbeat's rent was needed to meet your mortgage liabilities.

All of these problems can be avoided by careful tenant selection. Follow these suggestions and you will seldom, if ever, have tenant problems or problem tenants.

Advertise appropriately in places likely to reach the market you seek. If you want gay (male or female) tenants (who are usually pretty good), there are newspapers and publications read solely by that market. Local neighbourhood papers are much cheaper and often more effective than the large metropolitan dailies. Your ad should be attractive and designed to weed out undesirables before they apply. Here's one of mine:

Romantic Cabin in the Woods

$400/mo. Fireplace, Deck, 2 Bdrms, 2 Baths. Adults. No dogs. Tenants must be employed w/goodreferences. Call 332-2345 from 6pm to 10pm

When the prospect calls, you should interview further to ascertain desirability. If you detect a hostile attitude towards landlords or the slightest tendency towards litigation, it's best to suggest that they seek other accommodation. It is hard to reject a potentially bad tenant, but you must keep out problem tenants in order to have a successful property

Don't make the mistake of accepting sex or dope in lieu of rent.
Never get sexually or illegally involved with your tenants.

management programme. Set up two specific times per week for all prospects to come at once to look at your property. There are several reasons for having your prospects all come at once. The first is that at least half of your phone prospects will not show up for the appointment. Thus, rather than wasting time going to and from the rental unit, if you set up a generally convenient time such as noon on Sunday for everyone, even if five out of 10 are 'no-shows', you will not have made five useless trips.

Psychologically, if there are several prospects at the same place, you create an atmosphere of competition for the rental. Hopefully at least one desirable prospect will feel it necessary to make a speedy decision rather than say, "I will think about it and call you back." If any prospect is interested in the property, have them fill out a rental application form. Reading over their application carefully will help you weed out undesirables. Check the references! Call not only the present landlord of the prospect, but also the predecessor landlord. The reason is that the present landlord may be so anxious to get rid of a loser that he will give him a wonderful send-off, even though he is the worst deadbeat or slob imaginable. The prior landlord, on the other hand, has nothing to lose by telling the truth about your applicant. Always call the named employer and the bank of the prospect to ascertain his general level of responsibility and to verify the fact that he is employed and does have a bank account.

WRONG!　　　　RIGHT!

Be reasonable! Be rational!

If you, as a landlord, pay a surprise visit to the tenant at his own home, you can quickly determine whether his style of living is civilised and acceptable. You also discover, rather quickly only by visiting, if the tenant has a large collection of mangy dogs, smelly cats or disreputable friends camping in the living room. When a tenant who looks good has completed a rental application, I always ask if it's okay for me to accompany him back to his home. A quick look determines whether he is suitable or not. That takes care of selecting qualified tenants. Next we'll cover money.

Never agree to 'hold' a rental unit for a prospect without a substantial deposit, upfront. A substantial deposit to me is at least one month's rent, but preferably six weeks' rent, my standard security deposit. Normally this sum will be paid in the form of a cheque. Until that cheque has cleared, the prospect should not get keys to the unit nor should other prospects be turned away. The law is such that once you give a tenant possession of property, even if he gives you a bum cheque, you will have the problem of evicting him. During that period you take a dead loss, two to six months, plus you spend a bundle on attorney's fees.

When you have obtained the proper deposit and have checked out your tenant thoroughly, there is still one step more. Go through the apartment with the prospect. Fill out an inventory and condition check list. I have found that most arguments with tenants occur in connection with the refund of their security deposit. The tenant often moves out leaving unclean areas, broken windows or other damage. The invariable argument is, "It was that way when I moved in". With a condition and inventory check list, signed by the tenant, you can refer to that "move-in" dated document and quickly ascertain if the tenant is correct. You have a description of the property at 'move in time' in black and white. Reference to this document makes it possible to deduct the cost of any damage or clean-up from the security deposit without further discussion.

Now for those who end up with a problem tenant in spite of all precautions. Money is the problem 95 per cent of the time. But sometimes you get a tenant who is breaking his rental agreement by doing something undesirable, like dealing heroin or keeping 12 puppies that are pooping on your new wall-to-wall carpeting. You want to get rid of a bad tenant? You want him out as quickly as possible? First, consider 'self-help'. Did you know that it's financially very risky to forcibly lockout or throw a tenant out without a court order? Nor can you go to the apartment, unscrew the doors or remove the windows. You can't shut off utilities. You can't harass the tenant. You can't pop in at any time you feel like it and you can't bother him unreasonably for the rent. You can't do any of that without risking being sued yourself for very substantial damages. So, stay away from that sort of illegal self-help. But there is something you can do before going to court. You can visit your tenant and appeal to his sense of fair play. You'd be surprised how often this works. Tell him that things aren't working out and you would like him to move. Ask him how much time he needs. In many cases, a very reasonable approach works. The tenant agrees to move in a few days. You'd be surprised what you get just by asking politely.

Sometimes the tenant will tell you he doesn't have the money to move. If he's already behind in rent, maybe you'd be able to make a deal something like this. You say to him, "Look, I will pay for your moving. You just be out of here by 10 o'clock tomorrow morning and this $100 bill is yours. The place is to be left clean. You get moving money after I put a new lock on the door". That $100 bribe may be your best bet, rather than waiting the lengthy period it could take you to get a tenant evicted legally. During that time, you'd lose more than $500 in rent, not to mention time and aggravation. So, the first thing to do when you have a problem tenant is to talk to him – be reasonable, be rational. Appeal to whatever it is that you can appeal to in that particular tenant. Try to talk him out. Also, keep your cool. It's only money. Don't get all emotional. Leave if an argument develops. Sometimes you can find a new place for your tenant by making a few phone calls yourself.

Now, let's assume that Plan 1 – talking – doesn't work. When you go to talk, you should have with you the basic form that starts eviction proceedings. You need to serve a notice on a tenant before you can file a lawsuit.

Now, let's assume just for the moment, that your tenant isn't behind in rent but is breaking his rental agreement in some other way. Then you write in the body of the notice what the tenant is doing that bothers you, like having a dog in violation of the lease.

You can't kick anyone out in most countries these days, solely because of race, creed, religious preference or national origin. Nor can you discriminate against potential new tenants for those reasons.

You can't do something that is called a 'retaliatory eviction'. For instance, a tenant has complained to the building department that you don't supply enough heat or that there are rats. You cannot get a tenant out through court proceedings simply because he has made an official complaint against you. He has a legal right to complain to the building or the health departments. You cannot evict him for this reason. Even if he has consistently lied, just to get you in hot water with the bureau-rats.

But, suppose that you want to get rid of a trouble maker – a bad egg – who is organising a rent strike, calling up the authorities with unjustified complaints every day, and so on. In the US, simply give him 30 days notice to move. Assume this tenant has made a complaint to the building department, but you really want him out on general principles. For your day in court, you'd better keep in mind only the other reasons that you want him out (like he has a dog, he's too noisy or there have been tenant complaints against him). In a 30-day notice you are not obliged to tell a tenant what it is that bothers you. In court, or in your conversations, don't even mention that he made a complaint. If it is so much as mentioned, the judge may well accept his retaliation eviction defence. You don't need a reason to ask a tenant to move if he doesn't have a lease. But if the court finds you have an improper reason for asking a tenant to move, that tenant can stay just about forever – with no rent increases.

In the UK, you should always let on an assured shorthold agreement, obtainable from a stationers, which allows for letting on a fixed term (minimum 6 months), with two months notice, on either side.

Chapter 16

PARTNERSHIPS CAN MAKE YOU RICH

For some of us, the immediate problem is making enough money so that we can someday be in the enviable position of working out how to keep it from the tax man. In earlier chapters, all I did was talk about ways to make your fortune. You remember that the best way to get rich was to identify a common need or problem? Then you, as an opportunist, can create an appropriate product or service. All the great fortunes made in the past 10,000 years were amassed by people who could find a need and fill it.

There are two types of individuals who commonly go into tax shelter partnerships! Doctors, lawyers, accountants, plumbers and others who are sick and tired of paying huge taxes, but who simply have no time to spend looking for suitable investments and the 'Young Hungry Hustler'" who finds the deals and sets up the paperwork. The people in the first group are tickled pink to have someone else do all the work and in return for up to half the profits. Many medical doctors, airline pilots and highly-paid professionals have all had experiences with investment groups and tax-shelter syndicators and found them almost always to be abysmal. Over a four-year period, my own surveys (of approximately 3,000 investors) indicated that more than 97 per cent of all 'tax-shelter' investments are pure garbage. They never return the original investment (much less any profit) to the guy who puts in the money. This is because most of the people in the tax-shelter business are flakes, phonies and promoters who know little about investments and even less about the tax code. The world needs honest, knowledgeable originators of tax-shelter investments.

On the other hand, the typical Young Hungry Hustler is usually a recent college graduate who does not yet earn enough to worry about his own taxes. He has to have motivation, time, intelligence – but little or no money. It is possible for the Hustler (you perhaps) to make no-money-down deals when starting in business. But no-money-down deals are usually available only on relatively small problematic businesses or properties. The Hustler has to pass up the multi-million-dollar deals even if a small amount of cash is required.

Then the inevitable happens. A more creative Hustler announces that he would like silent investor partners in on deals of this type. This is the standard arrangement. Hustler will find the deal, do all the negotiations, manage the property and eventually refinance or resell it. The investors do nothing but look over the deal and the paperwork at the beginning. They put up all the money, hold title to the property (if desired) and take all the tax benefits. When it comes to sell or trade up, profits are split 50/50. The investor first gets his capital back and a minimum of 10 per cent annual return on his money before Hustler gets anything.

As it turns out, this sort of arrangement can prove to be wonderful for both parties. The Hustler doesn't get paid unless he produces, and the investor gets a minimum return. In some booming property markets, for years investors will average about 50 per cent or more per annum returns on their money. And the Hustlers? Well, they get an infinite return on no investment at all. Of course they earn it. They seek out good deals and make them work out.

The difference between these private deals and the standard property syndication is immense. The investment that is packaged by a major investment house is normally the garbage of the property market. It may be a good property, but the price is double or triple what experienced property people would pay. Further, most property syndicators are not compensated 'on the come' – or on the contingent fee principle. Typically, little or none of the investor's money finds its way into a syndicated deal. Most of it goes for commissions and advertising. The syndicator is paid 'upfront'. His profit is already made once the investors are found and the deal is closed. Obviously, there is no incentive to give investors a particularly good deal. Thus, they get garbage!

In what I am going to call the 'mini' or 'private partnership' there is a close relationship between the investor and the active partner. Usually there are just two of them in the deal; the active partner and the silent or passive investor. With proper buy-out agreements, if the active partner does not perform, the investor can kick him out of the deal and owe him little or nothing.

To accomplish their objectives, many of my early disciples drew up a partnership agreement that was fair to both parties. Let me emphasise that the basic agreement on the next page is for use by beginners on small deals.

Now you may be just an average plumber making $275,000 per year, in which case you can use this agreement as a model form for a deal with your son-in-law. Or, if you are not as wealthy as a plumber but think you can put deals together, here is an outline you can use to give your investor a fair shake. This partnership agreement, with minor variations, can be used for almost all property or business deals, mineral exploration or even leasing ventures. It is exempt from all forms of legislation and regulation, both local and national, because it is a private agreement strictly between a small, closed group of partners. Unless you have a disagreement that can't be resolved (and the partnership agreement is shown to an arbitrator or judge), you and your partner(s) are the only people who ever have to see it.

My suggested agreement is only meant to be a guide. Obviously, it must be modified to suit the needs of the venture, local laws and the desires of you and your partner.

Most people of substantial wealth have this choice: 1) Pay taxes to a thieving, rapacious government or 2) Give pre-tax 'soft dollars' to thieving, rapacious promoters of garbage tax shelters.

This agreement may give them a third alternative.

Partnership Agreement

Date: January 1, 2001

This agreement is between Irving Investor and Tom Tycoon, hereafter known as "I" and "T".

[Note: Under the laws of most states and the US federal government, up to 10 investors may be involved with a deal before it is considered a "public offering". Also, it may not be shown to over 25 potential investors. Check the rules for your country, state and jurisdiction. This form is intended for use by no more than a pair (2) of Active Investors and a pair (2) of Passive Investors.]

The above named partners have agreed to acquire a 20 unit apartment building to be owned and operated by them as the T & I Partnership. The business address of the partnership shall be Apartment 1, 123 Amen Drive, Salt Lake City, the residence of Tom Tycoon, who, as part of this agreement, shall receive said apartment rent-free and shall manage said apartment building without further compensation from the partnership, except as here provided.

This agreement shall be effective as of this date which is the date title and possession of the said apartment building passes to the T & I Partnership. *[Note: If Tom Tycoon is not a "proven quantity" it is suggested that title to any property acquired be kept in the name of the investor(s) who put up the money.]*

This partnership shall continue for a period of three years unless dissolved by mutual agreement or as otherwise provided herein. 32 months from this date the property will be put up for sale by listing it with *Peter Property Broker* at a price to be set by him.

The parties to this agreement agree to contribute to the business as follows: I will contribute all cash needed to acquire the property. Thereafter, in the event of any negative cash flow (ie losses), repairs or other contingencies requiring funds, both partners agree to contribute equally. T will contribute no initial cash, as his contribution to the partnership involves locating the investment property and negotiating for its acquisition and financing. By this agreement T undertakes to supervise all physical repair work needed to improve the property, to manage and collect rents and, to the best of his ability, take over all problems of running this partnership on a day-to-day basis, including the obtaining of a suitable tax-free exchange property or sale within the next three years.

For their respective contributions, any cash flow or other proceeds are to be used in the following order:

1. Return in full the original contribution of $25,000 made by I.

2. Return to I any additional contributions plus a minimum annual return of 10 per cent per annum on any cash invested.

3. Return to T any cash invested in the deal plus a return of 10 per cent per annum on any outstanding investment.

4. Any balance is to be shared between the parties on an equal basis.

5. In the event of losses from any cause, they shall be shared equally.

In the event that either party refuses, or is unwilling, to put up his agreed share of needed funds to cover losses or operating expenses, the other partner may do so and for all such funds advanced, upon dissolution of the partnership, get a triple return (i.e. 30 per cent per annum) on such advances.

Books and records of all expenses and receipts shall be kept by T on the Safeguard Account SystemTM for property by T. (This, or any other standard software accounting package, is better than most 'home-made' book-keeping systems). All books and records shall be available for inspection by I or his designated agent during normal business hours.

All funds of the partnership shall be deposited daily at the Desert National Bank of Salt Lake City in a joint account. Withdrawals of over $500 shall require the signatures of both parties. A third person shall be designated by both parties as an alternate second signatory in the event of illness, death or unavailability of either partner.

DISSENTING REMEDY

In the event that either party wishes to dissolve the relationship, he may offer to buy out the other at a certain price set by him. Thereafter, the other partner shall have 10 days to either accept the offer or pay the other partner the price previously offered by him. Provided, however, that if T is making the buy-out offer, it must be for at least the amount of I's investment plus 20 plus per cent per annum return of all funds advanced. In the event a third-party buyer has materialised and either party does not wish to sell, the partner who wishes to hold hereby agrees to buy out the other party within 10 days for whatever his share of the proposed sale would have been. The partner selling agrees to convey his interest immediately to the holding partner.

DEATH OR ABANDONMENT

In the event T dies or is absent from the project for more than five continuous days, or does not properly cope with the day-to-day business, I shall automatically acquire a 100 per cent interest in said project with no further obligation or debt to T or his estate.

In the event I dies, T may a) complete the project as planned and pay I's share to I's heirs, or, at T's sole option, b) T may buy out the interest of I's estate for the amount invested by I plus 12 per cent per annum return.

COVENANT NOT TO SUE

T covenants not to sue I at any time during the life of this agreement, and T expressly agrees that his maximum damages in the event of a lawsuit shall be the amount of his actual investment returned to him. The parties shall submit all disputes to third party arbitration as set forth in this agreement.

OTHER ACTIVITIES OF PARTNERS

It is agreed that I is not expected to put in any time or effort running the partnership property. I is not restricted in any way by this agreement from making other investments.

T agrees to devote all his spare time to the project and not, undertake the management of any other businesses or property ventures without the express written permission of I. In the event I gives such permission for T to engage in other spare-time entrepreneurial activities, it is agreed that I shall have no interest in profits from other ventures. In the event that 123 Amen Drive is fully occupied and is being properly managed, I agrees to give his permission for T to work on other projects.

DEPRECIATION AND TAX BENEFITS

Since I is putting up all the cash, it is agreed that for all income tax purposes he shall get 100 per cent of the write-offs and tax benefits, including any tax credits or depreciation allowances generated by this property. *[Note: a tax lawyer should carefully conform, especially this paragraph, to the requirements of the ever-changing tax codes.]*

INSURANCE

It is agreed that T will, prior to the closing hereof, insure the property with a comprehensive fire policy in the face amount of $500,000; and procure liability insurance in the amount of $1,000,000 with a waiver of the business risk exclusion. Title to the property shall not be acquired until such insurance coverage is obtained, with a binder in writing.

ARBITRATION

In the event the partners cannot agree, both parties shall submit any dispute to Albert Arbitrator. The partners agree that Albert's decision shall bind them as a final judgement in a court of law.

MISCELLANEOUS

The parties agree not to endorse any note nor become surety for any person(s) without the written consent of the other. It is further agreed that any contracts or obligations undertaken by either partner in respect of business other than the 123 Amen Drive property shall in no way bind or obligate the other partner.

In the event that there are more than three vacancies in the property for more than three consecutive months or delinquent rents in three units or more during this time period, T agrees to either contribute to the partnership an amount equal to said rents, in cash, or to remove himself from the premises, quit-claim the property to I and renounce any further interest in the entire venture to I. *[Note: This paragraph was included to indicate a type of minimum performance standard to be set by I for T to live up to. In the event that T does not do his job, I will, for all practical purposes, be able to fire T and terminate T's interest in the property. A quit-claim deed should be executed and delivered to I at the time of the agreement to implement this.]*

On Date: 1/1/2001, the parties have signed this agreement.

Irving Investor   *Tom Tycoon*

[Note: In the US always use a public notary to acknowledge partnership agreements or any contracts involving property.]

In my own personal business dealings, I seldom took in partners because I just didn't want to be bothered by a bunch of idiots who would always be telling me how to run a business I understood far better than they did. But to my surprise, I was left alone when I laid the law down to a few selected investor partners and said, "If you want in on my deals, you will read your semi-annual statements and keep out of my hair". This tactic worked effectively to keep out the "Nervous Nellies". My agreement (in contrast to the sample provided) was a lot tougher to the investor, simply because I knew I could and would average about 100 per cent return per year for the investor – but only if I made the decisions and wasn't second-guessed or harassed by them.

You personally can make pots and pots of money as a syndicator or general partner in deals. The reason is simple. Suppose you find a million-dollar property that you hope to upgrade and sell in a year for $1.3 million. If it takes $100,000 down to make the deal, you can get an outside investor to put up the whole $100,000. A year later you sell. The investor gets a 100 per cent return, and you have $100,000 to play with or trade up into another profitable building. Putting together only one big deal a year can make you a multi-millionaire without a penny of your own money at risk. The investors will love you because you will do all the work and produce better profits than they can on their own. You will soon be able to take all the good deals that come along because you have developed a following of eager moneyed investors. Eventually, you may have dozens of different groups of investors. If you don't take all your profits out in cash, but trade up to bigger and better deals, your own personal wealth can build up tax free. You can live on tax-free refinancing proceeds, as I did, for many years. And that's how you can make millions! The same principles apply to taking over property or any other business. Now go out and do it!

Chapter 17

INFLATION CAN MAKE YOU RICH

Throughout this report you have heard much talk about that magic "I" word, inflation. As you have probably also surmised, I have a bit of a different outlook than most. You won't hear me glooming and dooming as inflation creeps back up. Of course, this word most love to hate is the fable enemy of television economists and the favourite peeve of politicians. (They have to have something to talk about). For me, inflation is simply there. I learned long ago that, rather than struggling to make the world fit a certain preconception, it is much better to accept things as they are and get on with making some very serious money.

The double-digit inflation figures of the 70s and 80s have made a very rich man. You can make inflation work for you. Don't worry that it's temporarily bouncing in the low end of the single-digit numbers in most Western countries. As explained earlier, inflation will probably soar again before the end of the 90s. In a nutshell, the politicians simply can't resist running those printing presses just a little longer each year. Despite all of the pretty pictures that those PhD economists draw, at the end of the day, this is the only reason for inflation. More paper dollars against the same amount of gold in Fort Knox, or more paper pounds (with the Queen's smiling face) against the same amount of silver equals, inflation.

You have probably noticed that government programmes only get bigger, never smaller. (Just like taxes are only raised, never lowered.) This increased spending succeeds in accomplishing little else except increasing the national debt. Luckily, the politician has one last trick up his sleeve to cut back his exorbitant borrowing – inflation. Furthermore the greedy politician can benefit from it.

Every time I read in the papers that the cost of living has increased again, I am delighted. It makes my day! Every day inflation creeps up even the smallest amount, I get richer. You can do the same, if you think like a tycoon. I have included this chapter as a guide, so that when inflation returns to ridiculous amounts, you will know how to make it work for you. Let's take an example:

Pretend that it's Monday. Pretend that on Tuesday, all salaries, wages and prices will double by government order. If McDonald's hamburgers were $1 on Monday, they will be $2 on Tuesday. If houses were $75,000 today, they will be $150,000. And, of course, if your savings account was $10,000, it will still be $10,000 tomorrow, but money will only buy half as much in the way of goods and services. The national debt will be the same in dollars, but it will have been effectively cut in half, meaning the politician has saved his precious power structure from collapse.

How about taxes? Income taxes, after a heavy dose of inflation, will take an increasing bite out of your earnings. Huge capital gains are artificially created so the government can take a big chunk of your non-existent 'profits' when you sell. If you are not already in the highest tax bracket, inflation will put you there. Every wage earner will soon be in the same maximum tax bracket with the super-rich. The old 'soak the rich' income tax has become 'soak the middle class'. Creating inflation in just one of several sneaky ways a government reneges on its debts and increases its tax revenues.

Back to our example, if you knew that inflation and taxes would devour your savings and 90 per cent of your visible or unsheltered income in 24 hours, you'd do something! If you knew that the price of everything was going to double tomorrow, you'd do something about it! Then you'd be acting like a tycoon.

Tomorrow will be here very soon! Again, don't let the temporary dip in the rate of inflation fool you. Tomorrow may take a few years to arrive, but till then, prices will continue to increase, sometimes at an increasing rate. Higher percentages of your income will be taken in taxes and used to fund various unproductive schemes of government. Irresponsible politicians will continue to discover that inflating the money supply by printing more and more money is the least politically objectionable way of raising taxes and government revenue. And the most stupid people will actually believe that just because they are earning more dollars, lira, pounds or francs, they are richer. But it is really only the ownership of productive assets that can make one richer. Few people realise this. Taxes will be raised, public spending will increase and public and private credit will be expanded. Worthless paper money will continue to be printed. This is inflation. Before you can get rich, you must take fairly obvious steps to protect yourself against debauched paper currency and government schemes to tax you into oblivion.

And as you protect yourself, you will take advantage of inflation and put it to work for you. Stop and think! Try to think like a tycoon. What can you do to profit from a doubling of all prices in the next 24 hours? How can you profit from higher taxes? Do not read on until you have spent at least 10 minutes writing. Make a list of what you can do to reduce the government's ability to squeeze taxes out of you. List at least five ways to increase your real wealth if you could be sure that inflation was going to make the price of all things double 24 hours from now.

What To Do?

You'd go into debt or use the option techniques explained elsewhere in this book to acquire productive or valuable, non-depreciating things, wouldn't you? Be very specific in listing a number of businesses or investments that should do well under the pressures of increasing inflation. Get your hooks into as many assets or deals as you can handle. Then cut your overheads and expenses to the bone.

If you know that your taxes will go up drastically, learning how to reduce taxes should also be in your first line of defence against inflation.

Let's talk about reducing taxes:

Who is always raped the worst by taxes? The worker! The wage-slave can't afford lawyers and accountants. Unlike an executive or business owner, he has little opportunity to create imaginative deductions or arrange for tax-free distributions or expense-account money to himself.

Remember who is hurt the worst by inflation. It's the same unlucky people! If you ever hope to be rich, you must first stop working.

1. The wage-slave, whose income usually rises less rapidly than inflation, pays a greater portion of his earnings in taxes each year even though his 'real' spending power may be dropping.

2. During periods of high or even moderate inflation, the 'saver', or someone who keeps his money in money – bonds or savings accounts, for instance – is even more damaged. Investors lose earning power even faster than wage-slaves. To break even with a bond, bank account or any monetary instrument, the effects of inflation must first be countered. Notice that as inflation has fallen, so have interest rates. Does it feel impossible to make any money out of a bank account? It is, as, always has been!

The answer for you becomes as simple as pie:

* Don't be a wage-slave!

* Don't keep your money in a bank or its equivalent*! Invest in high income-producing property deals or other businesses that will produce a very high return on your investment of time, energy and money!

Given a time frame of two years instead of 24 hours, you should begin a programme of acquiring things or saleable skills. What exactly should you do with your time and money?

You'd be a lot better off than a wage-slave if you could make your spending money from tax-sheltered property or small businesses that you personally own and operate. During times of inflation, service or cash businesses do very well. Night clubs, hotels, bars, restaurants and entertainment enterprises also do well. Sporting events, religion, gambling, escapist books, cosmetics and self-improvement products also prove to be continually popular. And, of course, there are the professions. As taxes become more and more oppressive, lawyers and accountants increasingly become a survival necessity. Perhaps a night course in para-legal or book-keeping would enable you to do paid consulting or part-time work. Your customers might come from classified ads or notices posted in your own neighbourhood.

If your income comes from cash (dealing in services, stamps or coins, for instance) it becomes harder for tax authorities to nail you if some of that cash does not get properly reported. Of course, I always advocate using only legal methods to avoid taxes. Tax evasion is illegal and unnecessary. But with taxes in some countries hitting 80 per cent and more, survival may someday depend on how much you can hide from the tax collector. If you can barter and do business 'off the books', you can get many of the things you need tax free.

If you are going to beat the system and act like a tycoon, the first step is to make yourself knowledgeable about taxes and thus less tax vulnerable. You must put yourself in a position to generate untaxed benefits or tax-sheltered cash. Virtually any small business, profession, part-time trade or income property investment is a preferred way to beat the wage-slave high-tax trap. Offshore corporations or trusts can be useful as well. Scope International can recommend an appropriate consultant if you are interested in exploring this route.

For those who must remain at least part-time wage-slaves, only one major 'loophole' exists – property. Owners of income property can do their accounting in such a way that taxable income from any outside job or investment can be sheltered or wiped out 'on paper' so that no taxes are due. This report is mainly about using property to escape taxes and acquire wealth only because that is what your author did for many years. Eventually I sold out and moved myself and my assets to another country where there are no taxes. But what happened then is the subject of my other reports on PT, passports and tax havens. You have to have assets before you can start to think about expatriating them 'offshore' to safer places.

Obviously, in times of inflation and confiscatory taxes on unearned income, those who lend money (owners of savings accounts, mortgages, bondholders, etc.) get a swift kick in the pants. Borrowers who have bought income-earning properties or businesses sit on top of the world! One can borrow (without any risk of loss) the entire cost of a building. After making a no-money-down deal, the tycoon will make money two ways. First, well-selected property will go up in value when measured against paper money due solely to the effect of low inflation. Second, the property will, of course, also increase in real value, meaning nominal currency value, because it was purchased at well below market price and has been given value-enhancing improvements like a coat of paint, good tenants and appropriate financing. Borrowed mortgage money can be paid off with ever-increasing rents. When every other price doubles, rents (if not artificially regulated) will double too. The property or business owner's income increases each year by at least the amount of inflation. Tenants who pay $200 per month for a small office will be paying increased rates in three years. But loan payments, with a property negotiated fixed-payment loan, will remain relatively constant.

Suppose that in year one you were to buy $1,000,000 worth of property with $1,000,000 in borrowed money. Suppose also that you have done all of your homework and arranged it so that this income property breaks even, meaning that the rents received are enough to cover expenses and loan payments during year one. What would happen in year two if inflation was operating at 10 per cent? Your financial picture would look like this:

Value of building	$ 1,100,000
Loan due (original cost)	$ 1,000,000
Equity, or net worth	$ 100,000

Naturally, paper money in year two would be worth only 90 per cent of what it was worth in year one. However, the $100,000 increase in your net worth in year two would still be worth a real solid $90,000 in terms of buying power in year one. Or, to put it another way, $100,000 in year two will still buy you $90,000 worth of goodies at year one prices.

Before being boggled by the thought of owning a million dollars worth of property, remember that a very ordinary run-down house in a coastal city of California or suburban London can be worth $250,000. Thus, a million dollars worth of property is about four very unimpressive little homes. Obtaining this much property in the course of a year is about as difficult as falling off a log. Getting your properties for no-money-down and making them pay for themselves without any negative cash flow is harder – but it is possible – if you know how.

Tycoons know how to do it. So will you if you have read this report carefully and have the ambition to follow its plan.

Much of my best material on how to achieve wealth is in this report. Read it carefully. Do half of what I tell you here, and you'll be a millionaire in two years!

Chapter 18

EXTRA HINTS AND TIPS FOR PROPERTY TYCOONS

B usiness men and women are more often born than self-made. In other words, the best way to become a successful entrepreneur or business person is to have a father or mother who is a successful entrepreneur or business person. Nothing beats being brought up in an atmosphere of moneymaking. It helps one learn the real value of money and appreciate what it takes to get ahead. Kids of self-employed people observe early on that there is no such thing as a free lunch.

Of course, this is not a steadfast rule. Despair not, if your hippie parents didn't paint exactly the perfect entrepreneurial picture. The good news is that, whether you have a business background or not, by following the advice in this report and having had the good sense to read this far in the first place, you will gain the proper outlook and attitude to turn yourself into a millionaire.

I recall an old friend of mine who always marvelled at the way I made money out of property, indeed out of anything I did. He watched me and tagged along as I made deals. I tried to teach him everything I knew, but he still couldn't make it. He expected deals and money to come to him by magic or some divine right and thought it unfair when they didn't. As you should know by now, you have to get up and create deals by filling the needs of sellers and buyers before your competition does. Making money requires energy. Never put off until tomorrow what you can do today. Continually think of new ideas and new angles.

There are many ways to make money. I specialised in property, but the same principles apply in every entrepreneurial endeavour. Once you know the market (how to fill needs) you can make your fortune in no time at all. Indeed, you could put me in virtually any town or city in any country in the world and very quickly I would be able to root out the opportunities. How? Well, here are a few ideas to set your mind thinking. I have tried all these myself and can tell you they work. If there were more hours in the day, more days in the week and more weeks in the year, I could get more deals done. The market is always there. Opportunities to profit are just waiting for you like the bugs beneath a stone. They are not visible to the average Joe out for a Sunday stroll, but for those willing to stoop down and turn over the rocks in their path, there is an unlimited supply. You too are limited only by the amount of effort which you are prepared to put in.

Playing In The Garden

One of my best ways of finding deals is to obtain a copy of a large-scale map of a town or an area. Look at it carefully, look at the houses, look at the gardens, look at what land is undeveloped. In suburban areas, look for houses on corner sites with big yards fronting down a side road. You will often be able to subdivide off what was a rear garden and build one or more houses. If the depth of the site is insufficient to meet local zoning requirements, you may need to buy part of the back garden from the house next door as well.

If you offer a sufficiently attractive deal, you will be met with success and smiles in about half of the cases you approach. Indeed, you might even be able to go right down the road adding garden after garden, so ending up with a sizeable area of land on which a good-sized development may be sited.

Another trick is to look for houses on corner sites which are on the market. You can buy the house and chop the rear garden off for development, leaving just sufficient garden space for amenity or a garage. Once you have acquired this site, you can approach the neighbour to buy his garden. As you have the prime piece of land with road access, it is probably worth 70 per cent of the developed site value. The rule of thumb is to pay up to 20 to 30 per cent of the total site value to the owner of the adjoining house if it is required as a building site. If it isn't required, you should be able to pay less.

Also, look for single family houses anywhere with large gardens. Often the house can be pulled down and the entire site redeveloped at a higher density. Land is normally worth vastly more with multiple unit or commercial building permission than without, the ratio varying according to area. It may be possible to leave the existing house on the site and convert it into professional offices, stores or apartments. The more apartments that can be obtained from a house, the higher the value of the whole. Small 'bedsits' or studio apartments, for instance, are now fetching far more rent per square foot than one-bedroom apartments. One-bedroom apartments earn more per square foot than two bedrooms and so on. You may, by law, have to be able to provide off-street parking. However, with any large house, particularly if it is in poor condition, it is almost certain that you will be able to make money by converting it into as many units as possible.

Mixed-Use Properties

Also, look out for mixed-use properties. This means that part of the property is commercial and the rest is residential. It is common for stores to be let short-term while the remainder of the property is leased. You should be able to motivate the occupiers to deal with you in their own best interests. For example, suppose you were to buy a mixed-use site, say a large old building with a shop on the ground floor, two apartments above and a rear yard let for caravan storage.

You could deal with the various occupiers in a number of creative ways. You could sell the flats upstairs to their tenants as long-leasehold condominiums. If the existing tenants are not interested in such an arrangement, they could be paid a sum to vacate, meaning you could then sell long-leasehold interests in their apartments to a third party.

The shop downstairs will probably be leased. The tenant may be interested in buying a long lease in the property rather than just paying a rack rent which is revised and increased every three years or so. By arranging this sort of scenario, you would receive a lump of cash, up front. This could then be transformed into start-up capital on other properties.

How about the man who rents the yard at the rear? See what permissions can be obtained on the site if it appears to be under-used. No doubt 10 parking spaces will bring in more than one stored caravan or sailboat. Then again, you could simply sell the freehold to one of the neighbours or tenants. You might also consider redeveloping the site yourself with a new building. In general, as a mixed-use property becomes more complex and tenanted, it increases in profitability and decreases in cost.

For whatever reason, you may be unable to follow through with one or all of these plans, perhaps because the individuals involved are being completely unreasonable. If, after trying your hardest, you still meet with nothing but resistance, sell the entire or remaining property and move on to something new.

The Man With A Plan

Look out for property, especially that listed on the open market, that only has planning permission for developments that fail to make full use of the site. For example, you may find a piece of land advertised that only has planning permission for a single house. The tycoon will immediately wonder if he or she can fit two houses on the site, or perhaps even a block of four apartments or a shop with two apartments above it.

When you are just starting work with this sort of deal, you should probably make enquiries with local planners before diving in. However, once you have gained more experience, you will be able to follow your instincts, buy the site and then draw up the plans. If the use that you envision is similar to that of existing developments in the area, you will usually obtain the permission you want. I have personally followed this little strategy countless times, always to great advantage.

Many lazy property men buy sites with existing permission for houses, factories or whatever and then simply develop it. They hire architects to design the building and engage builders to put it up. Then they sell or let. Once let, the buildings are sold off to institutions as investments.

New first-class buildings let to good commercial tenants would probably be able to obtain capitalizations of five per cent, so realising the maximum value of the site. Why should an insurance company or pension fund buy a property from you yielding five per cent on their investment when they can get 15 per cent from a trouble-free bank deposit? Purchasers of prime properties are most interested in the combined effect of the actual increase in the value of the property, largely due to inflation, and the future and inevitable increase of rents received. (The same two things you as a budding tycoon are interested in). These institutions, like you, are not interested in the bottom line at the time of purchase, as long as the property is generating even a small cash flow. Thus, even a lazy property developer can often sell a finished and rented property at double or triple his costs.

There are more multi-millionaires who made their pile out of property than out of all other fields of business combined.

Making Money Out Of Rent Control

Yes, that's right, I said rent control. You can put together a few sweet deals by buying rent-controlled tenanted properties and then simply paying the tenants to vacate. The newly created 'vacant possession' property can then be sold on the open market for probably more than double what you paid. A good rule of thumb is that tenanted property will sell for only about 50 to 70 per cent of its vacant possession value.

For example, suppose you find a rent-controlled house that would have a vacant possession value of $100,000. You would probably be able to easily buy such a property from a landlord for, say $50,000. In most cases, the existing landlord will be happy just to get rid of the property and its eager tenant. You could then offer the tenant up to 50 per cent of the difference between the price you paid and the vacant possession value, in this example up to $25,000. For most working stiffs or retired people, that will be enough cash for them to buy a home or apartment in a cheaper area.

In some places this little procedure is illegal; in some not. In any case, check out the local laws in your area before proceeding. Most tenants, who don't have too much in the way of assets, when offered $10,000 to $20,000, or even $25,000 cash, will be only too pleased to take the money and vacate. You may also want to consider simply finding the tenant alternative accommodation. Perhaps you could even tempt him with a one way ticket to Tasmania or some other bargain paradise of his dreams.

Look Out For The Unusual

Once you have established a track record of success with practical, value-enhancing ideas, buy any site that you come across that nobody else wants and that is going cheap. Even if you can only get permission initially for a parking lot or something very simple, buy it! It's always good to have income property to use as a stepping stone. It always looks good on a loan application and can always be traded.

I recall a long strip of land adjoining a housing estate which nobody wanted. Nobody could think of anything to do with it. I bought the site for $1,000. At the time, it represented only a maintenance liability for its existing owner. The council had refused it as a gift because they didn't want the trouble or expense of cutting the grass or pulling the weeds.

I went on to obtain planning permission for eight blocks of two garages, hence bringing the value of the site up to $15,000 without laying a brick. I then went back and obtained planning permission for eight bungalows on the site. In the end, I sold the land with these plans to a developer for $225,000. The lazy developer built the project on borrowed money with a few twists of his own creative imagination and walked away with another $100,000 profit. Not bad, considering that three years earlier this site couldn't even be given away.

Industrial Sites And Factories

With the decline of heavy industry throughout the Western world, many large plants and warehouses are redundant. As a lot of them have been on the market for a long time, you can often pick them up for a song. They can then be converted into small units to be let as combined dwelling and work-space for emerging small businesses, or to artisans, tradespeople and artists. Units can be as small as 500 square feet or custom-tailored as large as the occupiers require. These smaller spaces can bring in 10 times as much rent as the entire factory would if rented to a single occupier, particularly if you have short leases or flexible terms. To keep your investment low, you can rent space 'as is' and let the tenants put in the expensive improvements.

Make it easy for small businessmen without much capital or experience to set up. Remember the phrase "easy in and easy out". Tenants will pay you higher rents for part of your old building if they can rent it month to month, particularly if there isn't much else available at such a low price or with such flexible terms. Most landlords insist upon long leases. You'll do better to rent by the week or the month.

Suppose you have some spare land. Consider building new industrial, commercial, residential or combined-use units on it. See what permission can be obtained. If the location is reasonably convenient and you can rent below going market rates, you'll easily find new tenants with small classified ads. If the site is already an industrial one, you should have no problem erecting new industrial buildings or even demolishing a redundant or badly situated building and redeveloping the site. You could also sell off part of the site with or without plans and permits for redevelopment, while retaining the old redundant buildings yourself for future councils, collieries, steel works and other industrial operations. Many are now surplus to requirements. Many years ago, particularly in Europe, factory owners would build houses for their workers, mainly because no other accommodation was available. With changing times, people have moved away from these worker estates. Thus, these properties were sold off, normally in large lots, some vacant and some tenanted.

One site of almost 100 houses in a coal mining town in Derbyshire, England was sold off a few years ago at auction for approximately £4,000 per house; about half were empty and half were let. Most were in appalling condition. What did the buyer do? He offered the tenants their houses for sale at approximately £10,000 each. However, as the tenants were not of the property owning kind, he found few takers. He then offered them £2,000 each to vacate, but again few complied. So the developer let the occupiers pay their peppercorn rents and remain in the houses while he did as little maintenance as was legally possible. Meanwhile, he did cosmetic renovation (i.e. painting) and was able to sell off all the vacant houses at £10,000 to £15,000 each. They went like hot cakes. Why? The next cheapest houses in that area cost at least £30,000.

Within six months, the developer had pulled all of his initial investment out of the deal. He went on to acquire his stock of 50 tenanted houses free. Over the years, as the tenants died or vacated, he sold the houses off. As they were now on a predominantly private estate, values rose fast. What a pension he had secured for his old age!

Roll With The Ups And Downs

England appears to be slowly pulling its way out of recession. To more hardened tycoons, this comes as no surprise. Property markets typically go through a period of major boom for a dozen or more years, during which prices triple or more, followed by a few years of bust. The bust, this time it's called the recession, usually involves price declines of one-third to one-half.

The most recent boom came to a close with the 80s. Like all other booms, during this one, every amateur or would-be speculator was sucked into property. They thought they were clever and hurriedly joined the crowd that merely bought anything and would then wait anxiously for it to appreciate. These amateurs lack initiative and know-how. They don't understand how to raise rents, subdivide or otherwise maximise their investment. Of course, they invariably end up in a financial mess. The good news for you, a budding tycoon, is that they can also generally be bought out cheaply.

Even when we have finally seen the last of recession, there will be a number of badly decorated rental units that remain vacant for in excess of six months. These people will still be forced to sell cheaply. Distress property, as mentioned, is another area to look out for. Sales are forced when unexpected repairs (frozen pipes or a leaky roof) put your competition out of business. Advertisements in newspapers, public auctions, mortgage foreclosure notices and bankruptcies are all sources for this sort of deal. See the chapter "Buying Distress Property" for more information.

Ex-Council Apartments

In many Western countries, large tower blocks of low-rent apartments were built by councils for rent. Now, 20 years later, no-one wants to live in some of these high rise apartments. They are badly maintained, and nobody cares for them. Often tenants have moved out. Sometimes these 'public housing' apartments are sold for a peppercorn to anybody who will take them. If your tycoon senses are working, you should sense some golden opportunities to buy, refurbish and sell.

Why would anyone want to buy an apartment from you which nobody currently wants to live in, much less own? Answer – everyone wants to own his own little part of this planet. Once the squatters and bums have been removed, you may even find your best customers are some of the council tenants who moved out! Once apartments are cleaned, painted and owned privately, newly formed 'home owners' will develop a sense of pride of possession. All of a sudden, they are 'men of property'. Most will now look after their apartments and take an active interest in maintaining their surroundings. The class of person who is an owner is of an entirely different mentality than a 'charity tenant'. You will often find that your new owners will be grateful single people who find it very difficult to buy any sort of accommodation at a cheap price with a low down payment.

Don't Expect A Fan Club

Almost everyone who owns his own house regards himself as a property developer. But remember, only a few people do it year in and year out. The amateurs keep abreast of property prices in the local paper. They constantly have a rough, although often inflated, idea of what their property is worth. In times of boom, they pat themselves on the back as the value of their little freehold home rises over the years. In times of bust, they feel the same confidence simply to stay in positive equity. Their house is normally their major asset, so the higher its value inches, the more clever they think they are. The reality is that these homeowners, even if they have a rental unit or two, are only retail buyers of houses. They are merely benefiting (or suffering) from the prevailing conditions of the market.

It is amongst these people that you will encounter the type that wears sandals, votes 'green' and hates all property developers. In fact, nobody loves a property tycoon, so get used to it now. The granola-eating-vegetarian-instigators will protest everything you want to do. To become a successful property developer, you will need to be able to accept being despised and looked down on. My advice – develop a skin with the thickness of a rhino and prepare yourself mentally for insults, brickbats, picketing and all the jealousy which will surely come in your direction. Quietly and decisively, proceed with your plans. Try to make peace with the self-appointed protectors of the environment by meeting with them privately and kowtowing to their demands. Often the sandalistas can be pacified with fairly minor concessions, meaning inexpensive. It is better to have them on your side than as pickets causing trouble.

Moral of the story, if you find anybody who loves a property tycoon, please let me know.

What To Read

The biographies of successful tycoons can be both inspirational and educational. You will find that most millionaires have very little in the way of formal education. How to make money is not taught in any university.

A notable property magnate, Sir Nigel Broakes, former Chairman of The British Trafalgar House Group, maintains that one can become a multi-millionaire starting from scratch, without ever going outside the square mile of the City of London. He personally concentrated his attention on this famous bit of land, coming to know every street and every building. This variation of the 'Hill Hundred House Rule' showed him which sites were under-utilised. He went on to acquire these buildings with the help of investors. He then tore them down and re-built much larger structures with higher rent rolls. Like all successful property developers, he knew how to utilise the full value of the site. 'The City' (downtown London), like Wall Street was, is and probably always will be considered one of the highest rent districts the world.

In addition to reading all of the biographies that you can get your hands on, you should subscribe to auction catalogues, property journals and any trade magazines where property is advertised. Marvellous opportunities for dealers will be found in page after page of advertisements. Public notices or legal notices are also potential gold mines.

Now, all that's left is for you to go out and do it. Why not start today? You have a fear of the unknown, perhaps. The only cure is to look at say 50 run-down, small properties. Then, once you know the market, you'll be hooked. It sure beats being a nine-to-five wage slave. The possibilities are limited only by your imagination and creative powers.

Chapter 19

NEW DIRECTIONS

Now that I've explained the basics of how to make a million in three years, I know that a substantial portion of my readers (hopefully you among them) will have the stamina to achieve financial independence in the near future. What will you do then? From my life and from your own observation of the rich, you can see that merely being well-off doesn't ensure happiness. But as Mae West said, "I've been poor and miserable and I've been rich and miserable. Rich is better." Not that I'm particularly miserable. Things are going rather well lately.

I learned that once you've obtained financial independence, you can do whatever you want. You can move out of undesirable situations to a climate, or among people, you find more enjoyable. The world is wide open. You can write, teach or politic. And if you are rich, people will listen to you a bit more attentively. You might go back to page one of this report and start doing all those things that I told you were a waste of time to do before you get rich, like getting high, buying a terrific car, going round the world. You can be promiscuous, or even get drunk until you tire of it. But you will have freedom in a world that permits very very few people to be free. You can do as you will with all the days of your life.

You've read through my report now. Perhaps you wonder how I spend my personal time and my freedom. I've avoided the trap of being tied down by business ventures and properties. I hired a bright associate to handle administrative details. When being indirectly responsible became burdensome, I simply sold out, moved abroad and began to live on the interest from my interest. I'm free to come and go as I please. I zip off to fun places in

Europe, America, Africa or Asia several months every year. I explore new investment opportunities or look after old ones. Every deal I make now has to involve people I enjoy working with. Every new venture has to have a minimum of aggravation and maximum of fun for me.

Originally, I thought I'd like to buy a part of a resort in some friendly tax-haven country, like the Caymen Islands, perhaps Hong Kong or Thailand. But then I realised that ownership involves hassle. Today if it flies, sails, rolls or if I can sleep in it, with it or near it, I rent it. I try to keep a low profile. Maximum profit is no longer my primary goal. A pleasant climate, meeting attractive, intelligent people, good food, a government that doesn't hassle me – that's all I ask for. My new philosophy is contained in my reports *PT1* and *PT2*. Don't read them till your net worth is at least $250,000, at which point you can retire and enjoy life. I no longer seek out any social relationships or business ventures that require administration, care or feeding. Why?

Animals have been eating other animals since the beginning of time. Civilised westerners now consume each other with due process of law. The 'poor' majority steals from a productive and harder-working minority. Learning and teaching ways to preserve the products of one's own enterprising – our hard-earned money – has been my most recent project. If you're ambitious and hard-working, you will have the same problem. How can you keep what you've worked for from a cynical, rapacious government? How can you avoid lawsuits, alimony, palimony, tax collectors and even criminal charges placed by ambitious prosecutors. Increasingly, journalistic and political careers are based upon bashing the rich.

As you see, these days I am getting my kicks by solving my problem (and yours), having fun and making money doing it. By the way, there is never an end to problems no matter how much money you have. Having 'do-it-yourself' projects, preferably projects that will also help other people and filling needs makes me truly happy. I generally go to bed each night fully satisfied. I'm no longer looking for any guru to give me a life plan. Nor do I want to be your guru or leader. Life is a do-it-yourself project. I wrote this report and all my other reports to help you be self-sufficient, busy and productive – adding a bit each day to the collective wealth of the world and the comfort, pleasure, and freedom of everyone in it.

After all, when you come right down to it, freedom is what this report, as well as all of my other reports are really about. I don't mean the sort of freedom that the politicians talk about and throw around. I mean real freedom. If my description of my idle days and carefree existence on the previous page made you cringe even slightly with envy, you know what I mean. But don't envy me, get out there and do it for yourself. Life's problems never go away; not unless you face them head on and then formulate and implement a plan to take care of them.

To tackle the so-called human condition and arrive at an enjoyable and comfortable lifestyle, you have to face the music. You have to prepare and act. Don't just sit back waiting for things to happen, because then other people will make your decisions for you and then who knows where you'll end up.

Don't Ever Allow Yourself To Become Human Garbage

The picture was there on the front page of the tabloid newspaper. I had seen it before. The caption read, "Suffering Refugee." There was a tear-stained, dirty face. He was holding a dead infant. He would likely be dead in another week. "I can't understand how this happened to us. Two months ago I had a business employing 30 people. My sister was a doctor. My brother was a university professor. Now we are starving refugees camped on a mountain, with nothing. We have no hope unless we get aid from strangers or the United Nations. My grand-child just died of exposure and starvation. Nothing in life prepared me for this. Look at us now!"

For the newspaper, the dramatic photo was a way to sell papers. For the do-gooders, it was yet another 'cause'. But for me it was a warning:

Expect and prepare for the worst sort of treatment from your own government! Governments have killed more innocent people prematurely than any disease, including cancer, heart disease and AIDS. Don't allow yourself to become human garbage! For every victim who has money before the crisis, there is an opportunity to acquire a second (foreign) passport. There is an opportunity to put some assets aside in a different name and a foreign safe-haven. One can almost always see the handwriting on the wall and predict possible war, famine, revolution or ever more natural calamities. With a second passport and with funds on deposit abroad, the guy in the picture could be watching the suffering in his homeland from a hotel on the placid shores of Lake Geneva. He would not be an unwilling personal participant in unfortunate tragedy. Major disasters, lawsuits, criminal charges or personal crises engulf the vast majority of the world's middle class population at one time or another.

If one is desperately poor and can barely survive day-to-day, then perhaps there is not much that can be done by way of preparation. But for my readers – professionals, people wealthy enough to prepare a nest abroad – there is no excuse for inaction. To put one's trust in that unholy band of self-serving cynical bureaucrats and politicians we call 'government' is to simply guarantee that you will eventually be raped, disposed of jailed or sent out to be murdered in a war.

To achieve control over your own destiny, arrange for the travel documents you need to extricate yourself from any conceivable domestic problem. Do it well in advance! Have the necessary tickets, cash or gold coins necessary to buy your way out of any dangerous local situation. Have some funds or property abroad to be able to survive and recoup your fortunes in the event of temporary or longer term exile.

The fact of the matter is that very few nations, very few families have escaped wars and devastation for more than a generation or two. Even Sark, that utopia in the Channel Islands, was captured by the Nazis in the Second World War. Many harmless and insular citizens died in German concentration camps. In neutral Switzerland, during World War Two, many Swiss residents were handed over to the Nazis to be murdered. Others died in Swiss-run slave labour camps. Three times in American history and dozens of times in English history, loyal supporters of government were forced into exile or murdered by opposing forces. Events like these are omitted in history texts designed to encourage absolute faith in 'the present form of government'. The secret truth is told only in my tycoon, passport and PT series and other reports from Scope International.

Don't lull yourself into any sense of false security. Even the most successful financier of our age, Michael Milkin, an American with a net worth of two billion dollars was forced to plead guilty to technical crimes, like 'stock parking' that few knew existed. He is likely to spend most of his remaining life in jail. With a little less trust in 'justice', he could be living on an interest income of over one million dollars a day in the pleasure domes of Europe. This is the path that was followed by his more intelligent colleague, Mark Rich! The difference? Rich is a PT, and international man. Milkin, like the man in the picture, became human garbage because of the jealousy and ambitions of a bureaucrat, yet another victim of government. If only he had not been ignorant of his options, he would now be living life to the full.

I am not painting this picture to scare you or to push you into a sense of hysteria. I only want you to be aware of your options, to be aware that there is an alternative to becoming yet another thankless victim of the system. First, follow the plan I have outlined in this report and become a tycoon, i.e. independently wealthy. But on the way up, learn from my mistakes and listen to my advice. You should have a *PT*-type plan to set aside enough for your escape. Have the necessary paperwork in place to prove that you are a 'foreign' person with 'foreign' assets. Hopefully, it will never be necessary for you to move A+A (Ass plus Assets) abroad and out of a dangerous jurisdiction. Yet, only if you are ready, willing and able to move, with an alternative identity and nationality, can you be reasonably certain that you won't share the fate of Milkin, or the man in the newspaper picture! You will never become human garbage, dependent on the charity of strangers or the United Nations. We all know the value received from depending on such good intentions zero.

How To Live Tax-Free (And Stress-Free) For The Rest Of Your Life

This chapter is not intended to discourage you from setting out on your path to independence. Again, I am merely portraying the world as it really is – no fairy tales here. You may consider much of this material to be nothing more than an advertisement for my other reports, but the plain fact is that, although money is the only sure path to true freedom, once it has been acquired in any serious amount, it creates a new series of needs and dangers. You need not make the same mistakes that I have. Learn from me as you already have (if you've read this far) about the process of formulating deals, buying property and acquiring wealth.

How I coped, survived and came out sane and solvent is the subject of several other reports that could be helpful to you. I regard *PT 1* and *PT 2* as my best reports. They form the keystone that ties the whole puzzle of life together. This report, now in your hands, is all about how to make money. My other reports are on how to enjoy it, invest it and keep it from the many predators and villains who will want to steal it from you. As I have talked much about those two elusive letters, PT, throughout this report, let me explain the concept behind them in greater detail. That way, when you start piling up your own personal fortune, you'll already have a rough idea of the best direction in which to move.

Do you want to escape the control over your life and property now held by modern Big Brother government? My PT concept could have been called Individual Sovereignty, because PTs look after themselves. We don't want or need authorities dominating every aspect of our existence from cradle to grave. The PT concept is one way to break free.

In a nutshell, a PT merely arranges his or her 'paperwork' in such a way that all governments consider him a tourist, a person who is just 'passing through'. The advantage is that, by being thought of by government officials as a person who is merely 'Parked Temporarily', a PT is not subject to taxes, military service, lawsuits or persecution for partaking in innocent but forbidden pursuits or pleasures. Unlike most citizens or subjects, the PT will not be persecuted for his beliefs or lack of them.

PT stands for many things. A PT can be a 'Prior Taxpayer', 'Perpetual Tourist' or "Permanent Traveller" if he or she wants to be. The individual who is a PT can stay in one place most of the time, or all of the time! PT is a concept, a way of life, a way of perceiving the universe and your place in it. One can be a full-time, dedicated PT or a part-time PT. Some budding tycoons may not want to break out at once, or never become a PT at all. They may just want to be aware of the possibilities and be prepared to cash in their chips and modify their lifestyle in the event of a crisis. Knowledge will make you a sort of PT, a 'Possibility Thinker' who is 'Prepared Thoroughly' for the future.

The PT concept is elegant, simple, and requires no accountants, attorneys, offshore corporations or other complex arrangements. Since the income of most PTs is immediately doubled and most frustrations of life with Big Brother are instantly eliminated, the logical question is only, can you afford not to become a PT?

Unlimited, untaxed wealth and the power to dispose of it as you please is one of the major benefits of becoming a PT. PTs can work and be paid in full (without withholding tax or deductions) and then spend their earnings on whatever gives us pleasure. Until you become a PT, the range of opportunities denied you is inconceivable. We don't miss the things we're unaware of. PT, the report, will raise your consciousness as to the nature of freedom and the ways to rid yourself of all limitations. The constitutions of most nations give lip-service to the absolute freedom to travel, but in practice every government severely limits travel with passport, visa and other requirements.

By imposing restrictions on foreigners, most nations invite tit-for-tat reciprocal measures. Personal finances, currency controls, domestic situations and job requirements make the freedom to go anywhere at any time just a dream for most people. The PT, once properly equipped, operates above and outside of normal constraints, gaining mobility and a full slate of human rights. The value of these rights cannot even be perceived by people who have never experienced them.

You don't need to found a new country or displace someone to make yourself a sovereign. The PT need not dominate other people. He or she must only be willing to break out of a parochial way of thinking. The PT must be superior only in that small area located between the ears. We speak of the potential PT now in terms of wealth, talent, intelligence and creativity. Who is this PT in the upper miniscule of the population? It might well be you!

The PT's Five Flags
People of intelligence and wealth owe it to themselves and their descendants to have five 'flags'. No-one with common sense should give all their assets or allegiance to just one flag.

Why? Because no country or government has ever survived more than a few generations without totally annihilating itself or its own middle and upper classes. Even in that 'last bastion of capitalism', the US, people of property were thrice forced to flee the country. In 1780, one third of the population (the entire middle and ruling class), was forced to move to Canada. These were the Tories who supported England in the Revolution. In 1870, it happened again. All large land owners (who supported the Confederacy in the Civil War) were forced to migrate to Mexico, Europe or South America. In the post 1917 period, prohibition, confiscatory taxes, compulsory military service, the proliferation of hungry contingent-fee lawyers, socialist judges and suffocating government regulations once again caused wealthy Americans (and Europeans) to seek new flags. Five million of the wealthiest and most productive Americans live abroad. A similar proportion of the best Swedes, French, Germans and British have discovered that gaining freedom involves moving away from their native country. 85 per cent of all liquid private wealth is already anonymously registered 'offshore'. Can you afford to have only one flag? Not if your net worth is over $250,000'

What are the 'five flags' of the PT?

Flag 1. BUSINESS BASE. These are places where you make your money. They must be different from where you legally reside; your personal fiscal domicile.

Flag 2. PASSPORT AND CITIZENSHIP. These should be from a country unconcerned about offshore citizens or what they do outside its borders.

Flag 3. DOMICILE. This should be a tax haven with good communications. A place where wealthy, productive people can be creative, live, relax, prosper and enjoy themselves, preferably with bank secrecy and no threat of war, confiscation of property, lawsuits or revolution.

Flag 4. ASSET REPOSITORY. This should be a place from which assets, securities and business affairs can be managed anonymously.

Flag 5. PLAYGROUNDS. These are places where you would actually physically spend your time. We look for quality of life. For no nukes, beautiful countryside and good fishing: New Zealand. For the most interesting sex life imaginable: Thailand, Costa Rica or the Philippines. Superb climate: California. Gourmet delights: French Riviera. Stimulating cities: Paris, London or San Francisco. To buy the best things for the cheapest prices: Singapore, Hong Kong or Denmark (for cars).

In Parting

Once you've made it financially, usually you'll become a much better person. You can be generous with your time and money in a way that was not possible before. Self-indulgence in illegal, immoral or fattening pleasures isn't as much of a thrill as it once was. It's there for the taking. The Free Enterprise System, if left alone, can still produce the best products, the best people and the best society that this world has ever known.

Hopefully you have enjoyed this report and will drop me a note letting me know how you feel about it. How can I improve it for later editions? In any event, I hope this report will help you get where you want to be!